The Dynamics of the
Social Worker-Client Relationship

The Dynamics of the Social Worker-Client Relationship

JOSEPH WALSH, PHD, LCSW

OXFORD
UNIVERSITY PRESS

Oxford University Press is a department of the University of Oxford. It furthers the University's objective of excellence in research, scholarship, and education by publishing worldwide. Oxford is a registered trade mark of Oxford University Press in the UK and certain other countries.

Published in the United States of America by Oxford University Press
198 Madison Avenue, New York, NY 10016, United States of America.

© Oxford University Press 2021

All rights reserved. No part of this publication may be reproduced, stored in a retrieval system, or transmitted, in any form or by any means, without the prior permission in writing of Oxford University Press, or as expressly permitted by law, by license, or under terms agreed with the appropriate reproduction rights organization. Inquiries concerning reproduction outside the scope of the above should be sent to the Rights Department, Oxford University Press, at the address above.

You must not circulate this work in any other form
and you must impose this same condition on any acquirer.

Library of Congress Cataloging-in-Publication Data
Names: Joseph, Walsh, author.
Title: The dynamics of the social worker-client relationship /
Walsh Joseph, PhD, LCSW, Professor Emeritus, School of Social Work,
Virginia Commonwealth University, Richmond, Virginia.
Description: New York : Oxford University Press, 2021. |
Includes bibliographical references and index.
Identifiers: LCCN 2020047009 (print) | LCCN 2020047010 (ebook) |
ISBN 9780197517956 (paperback) | ISBN 9780197517970 (epub)
Subjects: LCSH: Social workers. | Social service. | Interpersonal relations. | Counselor and client.
Classification: LCC HV41.J67 2021 (print) | LCC HV41 (ebook) | DDC 361.3—dc23
LC record available at https://lccn.loc.gov/2020047009
LC ebook record available at https://lccn.loc.gov/2020047010

DOI: 10.1093/oso/9780197517956.001.0001

1 3 5 7 9 8 6 4 2

Printed by Marquis, Canada

Contents

Introduction	1
1. Definitions and Theoretical Perspectives	5
2. Relationship Boundaries	26
3. The Use of Self	48
4. The Working Alliance and Cross-Cultural Competence	67
5. Relationship Ruptures	86
6. Relationship Endings: Terminations and Transfers	106
7. Relationships with Children and Adolescents	128
8. Clients Toward Whom a Social Worker Feels Attraction	149
9. Managing Negative Feelings About Clients	170
10. Relationship Development with Psychotic Clients	190
11. Physical Contact in Relationships	211
12. Using Humor in Practice Relationships	231
13. The Worker/Client Relationship in Technology-Assisted Interventions	252
References	273
Index	291

Introduction

In the past few decades, in social work and other helping professions, there has been a significant movement toward establishing evidence-based practice (EBP) interventions for persons who experience a variety of mental, emotional, and behavioral problems. EBP interventions are those that have been empirically tested and found to be effective with persons who receive certain mental health diagnoses (O'Neill, 2015). As a result, some practice models are recommended in the literature for use with persons who experience certain problems. As one example, exposure therapy is a recommended intervention for persons who experience any of the phobias (Sizemore, 2012).

While the focus on using scientific methods to develop EBP interventions has been helpful for professionals in making choices about client interventions, it tends to distract attention from the *process* of how interventions are delivered; that is, the *person* of the professional and the nature of the relationship between the practitioner and client. Evidence-based treatments, especially manualized ones, assume that it is only specific practitioner behaviors that account for an intervention's success, but the fact that no two people with the same diagnosis may be alike in any other significant ways demands that a social worker's interpersonal approach be flexible to ensure successful client engagement. In fact, several approaches to relationship development, including the working alliance and common factors models, are supported by research. (Both of those models, and others, are described in this book.) For these reasons there should be a greater teaching emphasis on the importance of client engagement and the social worker's "use of self" in relationship development, along with an understanding of interpersonal dynamics from the perspectives of both the social worker and client.

The position of this book is that the effectiveness of all types of direct social work practice often depends significantly on the nature of the relationship between the social worker and client. This is not a controversial point, but there is disagreement among professionals about the extent of the relationship's influence. While the impact of the relationship may be more or less significant depending on the client, the presenting problem, and the nature of the service, its influence may at times be more considerable than the intervention itself. The following chapters describe and examine in depth the many forms that social worker/client relationships can take in the context of various theories, interventions, and situations common to social work practice. Included are major theoretical perspectives about the relationship, but there is a greater focus on the variety of practice situations and kinds of clients that social workers face. Case vignettes, provided mostly by graduate students but also by practicing professionals, are included in every chapter (except Chapter 1) to illustrate the various dynamics of the relationship, the mistakes that can occur, and how challenges can be resolved. Through these illustrations the processes of relationship development and sustainment, and the complex interpersonal dynamics that can arise depending on how the social worker and client experience each other, are analyzed.

The driving vision behind this book is that students in professional social work programs who aspire to careers in direct practice need, and will benefit from, an engaging, broadly focused, practical volume about the challenges of relationship development with client systems (including individuals, families, and groups). Many excellent social work textbooks about direct practice devote one or several chapters to the topic of the worker/client relationship, but it is rare for a book to be dedicated solely to the topic. The single focus of this book allows for a detailed consideration of a broad spectrum of the types of clients social workers may encounter during their careers. The approach is to present research-based information on one challenging theme in each chapter and through the case illustrations describe how students have encountered and dealt with the challenge. Chapter topics have been selected based on themes in the literature as well as the shared experiences of the author and the students he has known over the years. Students who read the book will come away with advanced knowledge about relationship issues and feel more confident in their abilities to respond to related challenges that may arise in their work. They will also understand how the quality of the relationship determines how well specific intervention techniques will be received.

The presentation of material in the book follows a clear structure. The first four chapters consist of an introduction to the topic followed by reviews of some major theoretical perspectives on the social worker/

client relationship and then considerations of the concept of boundaries, the social worker's personal characteristics that may facilitate client engagement, and empirical work on the concept of the working alliance and common factors models. These are followed by nine chapters that deal with specific relationship issues. Several case vignettes are included in each chapter to serve as illustrations and topics for discussion. They are all structured as follows:

1. The client's presenting problem and relevant background
2. The history of the practitioner's relationship with the client
3. A specific relationship encounter, positive or negative, that was significant to the practitioner's work with the client, or to his or her course learning
4. The major relationship issues that emerged in the encounter
5. How the student's personal and professional selves influenced the outcome of the encounter, for better or worse
6. What the student might do differently (if anything) in this encounter if he or she had the opportunity.

The featured students are placed in, and write about, a wide variety of social service agencies. They write about their experiences in medical hospitals (working with clients of all ages who experience a range of illnesses), outpatient medical clinics, substance abuse treatment agencies (for adolescents and adults), psychiatric hospitals and residence centers, child care agencies (working with children who have experienced trauma), public schools (primary, middle, and high), hospice and palliative care agencies, Veterans Affairs hospitals, foster care and adoption agencies, domestic violence shelters, general mental health counseling centers, juvenile justice agencies, and agencies that serve persons experiencing developmental disabilities, homelessness, and severe mental illness.

The intended audience for the book is social work students at the fourth-year baccalaureate and graduate levels who are preparing to become direct service providers with diverse client populations. Practicing social workers might also find the material to be helpful for their professional development. The topic of the relationship is of universal interest to members of the social work profession but, as noted earlier, is typically dealt with in book chapters rather than full volumes. The courses for which the book is appropriate include any that focus on direct practice.

About the Author

Joseph Walsh, PhD, LCSW is a professor emeritus in the School of Social Work at Virginia Commonwealth University, where he spent 25 years as a full-time faculty member teaching, writing, and providing community service in areas related to direct social work practice. He taught undergraduate and graduate courses in social work practice, human behavior, assessing and diagnosing mental disorders, practice theories, community practice, research, and other topics. Throughout his career Dr. Walsh had a reputation with students as one of the few primary School of Social Work faculty who identified above all else as a clinical social worker, and he saw clients on a part-time basis during those years. Prior to his appointment at VCU Dr. Walsh worked as a psychiatric hospital technician (for 5 years) and a community mental health agency social worker (for 14 years). Since his 2018 retirement he has continued to engage in part-time direct practice and teaches part time at the School of Social Work. Dr. Walsh has written 10 other books on a variety of topics related to social work practice.

1
Definitions and Theoretical Perspectives

One of the most exciting facets of the social work profession is its breadth. Practitioners can work at direct and indirect (public welfare, community organization, policy practice, and administrative) levels with a variety of client populations in the fields of child and family welfare, older adult services, medical and health care, mental health, schools, substance use, interpersonal violence, criminal justice, trauma, and crisis intervention. To be effective in any of these types of practice, social workers must of course be able to engage with their clients and constituents using effective interpersonal skills. The purpose of this book is to help social work students and practitioners become more aware of their relational strengths and limitations so that they can learn to develop and maintain professional relationships that will facilitate positive interventions.

This chapter includes a definition of the social worker/client relationship and its significance to client goal achievement, followed by descriptions of how various (but not all) prominent practice theories conceptualize the appropriate nature of that relationship. Case vignettes from social work students are included in all of the subsequent chapters to illustrate how those theories can serve as a guide for relationship-development strategies.

Defining "Relationship"

A *relationship* can be defined as a binding association between individuals where one (or each) has some influence on the feelings, thoughts, or actions of the other (Farlex, 2019). This is a general definition that can apply to any relationship, those that are close as well as those that are more distant. A *social worker/client relationship* is one that includes a dynamic interaction of beliefs, emotions, and behaviors between the parties with the purpose of the social worker's helping the client to achieve specified goals

(Goldstein, Miehls, & Ringel, 2009; Ruch, Turney, & Ward, 2018). This definition, which is narrower than the previous one, includes several important implications for the social worker (and client) who work together, as follows:

> *The relationship is formal, but it may or may not be intense.* The two parties observe certain overt and implied rules and boundaries but may or may not develop a strong emotional connection.
>
> *It is focused on meeting the needs of one person more so than the other.* This reflects a one-directionality of purpose, with the social worker being intent on helping the client achieve certain desired ends, but not the other way around. Some of the social worker's needs are met in an *indirect* way, however; for example, as he or she experiences a sense of gratification and life purpose in the process of helping others.
>
> *There is a reciprocal, mutual influencing quality during their interactions.* This may seem contradictory to the first characteristic, but the actions of each person always influence the other, in ways great or small. At times the social worker's emotional involvement and investment in the client's processes can be intense.

Relationship-based practice (in which outcomes are considered to be dependent in part on the quality of the relationship) assumes that every client is unique even when displaying similar problems, personality characteristics, and diagnoses. Human behavior is more complex than can ever be fully comprehended, unconscious processes affect behavior, and the nature of the social worker/client relationship is associated with the earlier relational experiences of each party in ways that they may not readily understand (Berzoff, 2016). The social worker's decisions about intervention should thus be based on a client's problem presentation, unique personhood, and goals, not solely on a DSM diagnosis. Similar interventions are not necessarily used with clients who fall into similar problem categories.

While the quality of the social worker/client relationship always has some bearing on the processes and outcomes of an intervention, the extent of this influence will vary depending on the personalities of the parties, the presenting problem, and the impact of external forces on the relationship, including agency policies. (These may dictate, for example, the length or type of intervention that may be used.) The relationship may be rather insignificant to the outcome (limited to facilitating the client's engagement in the intervention process), moderately relevant (when, for example, a client learns about aspects of his or her interpersonal style that are detrimental to his or her well-being, and then makes corrections), or possibly the main factor related to the client's achievement of goals, as in situations where the client's primary problems are related to relationship dysfunction. The potential relevance of the relationship on the intervention process can only be ascertained as the social worker assesses the quality of that relationship over time and determines how it might best be developed to promote the client's goal attainment. Social workers will, of course, have difficulties at times developing or maintaining constructive relationships with some clients due to their own biases, needs, and preferences.

The Relationship as a Common Factor

There is a great emphasis in today's practice world on the empirical demonstrability of positive outcomes (Brown, 2019). Insurance companies want to know that the kinds of intervention they are paying for will be effective in helping clients achieve goals, preferably in the least amount of time necessary. Clients want to know that the money and effort they are expending are worth their time and energy. Practitioners, too, want to know that the profession to which they have devoted their careers is of value to their society. The significance of the therapeutic relationship in helping clients to achieve their goals is widely acknowledged, but there is debate regarding its degree of importance. Some practitioners believe that the relationship is necessary and sometimes sufficient for client change, while others assert that therapeutic technique is just as important, or more so. What does the research say?

Jerome Frank (1961) was among the first to explore the possibility of common factors underlying the practices of a variety of types of professional helpers. He undertook a worldwide study of the determinants of positive outcomes for persons who seek the assistance of helping persons and concluded that the following features were common to all of them:

- The client enters into an emotionally charged relationship with a provider who is perceived to be competent and caring.
- The provider has confidence in whatever theories and techniques he or she utilizes.

- Interventions are based on a rationale that is understandable to the client and require the active participation of the provider and client, both of whom believe them to be a valid means of improving functioning.
- The client is provided with opportunities for learning and success experiences.

The first of these features speaks directly to the significance of the relationship.

Much qualitative and quantitative research has been done since then on the topic of common factors, especially in this era of evidence-based practice (EBP), which asserts that one's practice activities should be based on knowledge drawn from rigorous research studies (Drisko & Grady, 2012). EBP favors some types of research evidence over others; for example, double-blind experimental studies are considered to be more persuasive than other types of experimental studies, followed by quasi-experimental studies, on down to "expert opinion" at the lower end of the spectrum. EBP research has produced a great deal of support for certain types of intervention as being effective with certain types of clients and diagnoses, as well as for the existence of common factors that appear to underlie the effectiveness of any intervention strategy.

Literature reviews and meta-analyses (in which the results of several studies are combined to produce a quantifiable "overall" result) have become prominent means of attempting to generalize results across many studies (Littell, Corcoran, & Pillai, 2008). A decade ago, Miller, Duncan, and Hubble (2005) concluded from a literature review that the two elements of the therapeutic alliance and the practitioner's ongoing attention to the client's attitude about the intervention account for positive outcomes more than anything else. They went so far as to estimate the degrees to which certain factors account for outcomes, as follows: the client's characteristics (nature of problems, degree of motivation, and level of participation) account for 40% of the clinical outcome, the quality of the therapeutic alliance accounts for 30%, the practitioner's guiding theory or model accounts for 15%, and the remaining 15% is a placebo effect. Most researchers do not weigh factors so specifically, but there has been a consistent finding in the research that common factors do exist.

Three recent studies serve to illustrate this point. One research project that involved a literature review and meta-analysis, and which divided interventions into the two general categories of cognitive-behavioral (with a focus on cognition) and interpersonal/psychodynamic (with a focus on affect), identified two prominent common factors: the quality of the worker/client relationship and having the client confront the source of his or her problems (Brown, 2015). In a meta-analytic review, Wampold (2015) concluded that to be effective an intervention must begin with a positive therapeutic relationship (for client engagement) and then proceed through three pathways: the development of a "real" relationship" (a personal relationship as reflected in the degree to which each person is honest and open with the other), the creation of client expectations for positive change (both pathways were said to require the practitioner's ability to show empathy and maintain an observable sense of interest in the client), and the enactment of health-promoting behaviors. A third study began with a comprehensive literature review that provided 22 putative common factors, followed by an "expert survey" in which a convenience sample of 68 psychotherapists rated the importance of each of those factors (Tschacher, Junghan, & Pfammater, 2014). The experts concluded that the three most important common factors were client engagement, the client's experience of emotions during the intervention while facing problem issues, and the ongoing therapeutic alliance. In each of these three studies it is clear that the relationship was deemed to be significant.

Obstacles to Relationship-Based Practice

Not all social workers prioritize the clinical relationship to the extent discussed in this book, but even when they do so it is recognized that there may be external constraints on their efforts (Stadnick et al., 2018; Schwartz et al., 2016). First, high demands for service in agencies with limited staff resources may create situations in which social workers must manage high caseloads, and in so doing utilize interventions that preclude extended attention to the relationship. Further, due to the perceived limited growth potential for clients with some long-term disorders (such as schizophrenia and bipolar disorder), some agencies conceptualize social workers and other program professionals as "case managers" rather than practitioners. It is expected that these persons will manage large caseloads of clients and spend little time with some of them as they focus their efforts on immediate issues related to clients' material needs such as housing and income supports. A related obstacle in some agencies is the requirement that professionals develop technical competence with prescribed models of intervention that de-emphasize depth, professional discretion, and creativity.

In addition to these obstacles it is sometimes said that an emphasis on technique over relationship represents a desire of some social workers and other professionals to erect a firm boundary to protect themselves from the anxiety and uncertainties that are unavoidable aspects of direct practice (Hingley-Jones & Ruch, 2016). Adherence to a medical model of practice, for example, helps to create an artificial emotional distance between a practitioner and client. It is the position of this book, however, that mental disorders are not like physical disorders, and a social worker is never treating a limited aspect (symptom) of a client. Rather, an intervention affects the entire person.

Now that we have presented definitions and some discussion about the nature of the professional relationship, it is important to see how the appropriate nature of that relationship is conceptualized in some popular theoretical perspectives.

Theoretical Perspectives on the Social Worker/Client Relationship

The social work profession has come a long way in developing its values regarding relationships with clients. In its earliest, pre-professional years, social workers were volunteers from Charity Organization Societies who identified themselves as *friendly visitors* (Lubove, 1965). Their "clients," who were predominantly poor people living in impoverished areas of large cities, were considered to be morally deficient and in need of knowledge relevant for self-improvement and modeling from a moral visitor who could instill appropriate values in them. A prominent saying of the new volunteers was "not alms, but a friend," even though these visitors were not friends in the reciprocal sense of the term. Fortunately, this maternalistic position soon gave way as practice became professionalized at the turn of the century. Over the years the social work profession has developed a variety of theoretical perspectives to help focus its work, all of which articulate what should be the appropriate nature of the worker/client relationship.

A practice theory can be understood as a coherent set of ideas about human nature, including concepts of health, illness, normalcy, and deviance, which provide verifiable or established explanations for behavior and rationales for intervention (Frank & Frank, 1993). It incorporates unique perspectives on assessment and intervention with individuals, families, and groups. Theories are neither true nor false in an objective sense but are useful as means of organizing one's work with clients (Forte, 2014). The value of utilizing any theory is that it provides the social worker with a framework to predict and explain client behavior, generalize among clients and problem areas, bring order to intervention activities, and identify knowledge gaps that should be addressed. Still, there is potential harm in rigid adherence to any particular practice theory. Because all theories necessarily simplify human behavior (focusing on a limited number of variables from a seemingly infinite number that can possibly affect a client's life), they are reductionistic. Adherence to a theory may create self-fulfilling prophecies (the practitioner will tend to see what he or she is looking for) and blind the practitioner to alternative understandings of behavior.

How does a social worker choose a theory to use in practice? One's choice may be influenced by a variety of rational and irrational factors, including the theory's research support, a belief that it produces positive results (perhaps, in the context of agency demands, with the least expenditure of time and money), its provision of useful intervention techniques, and its consistency with the practitioner's values, knowledge, skills, and worldview (Turner, 2011). Some social workers cannot, if asked, articulate their theory bases. These practitioners may be effective (what was once a deliberative process may have become automatic) or they may reject the primacy of theory with a focus on transtheoretical EBP models. Still, many social workers adopt one or a few primary theoretical bases that they use to organize their approaches to practice, and all of them include assumptions about the appropriate nature of the worker/client relationship. A sample is presented here.

Person-Centered Theory

Developed in the mid-20th century, person-centered theory asserts the primacy of the worker/client relationship as much or more so than any other theory discussed here (Rogers, 1986). Its articulation of the appropriate nature of the worker/client relationship is considered by many to be the most enduring contribution of the theory. Throughout their interactions, the social worker focuses on respecting, nurturing, and fostering the fragmented aspects of the client's notion of self while modeling an integrated sense of wholeness by providing the following three conditions:

Empathy. The practitioner does his or her best to understand the problem situation from the client's perspective at both cognitive and emotional levels and to accurately reflect that understanding to the client. The social worker accepts the client's formulation of the problem and in so doing affirms the validity of his or her experiences. The phenomenon of empathy has become better understood in the past 30 years with the discovery of mirror neurons in the central nervous system (Decety, Meidenbauer, & Cowell, 2018; Ekman & Krasner, 2017). These neurons, believed to be present from birth, allow the infant to emotionally replicate what it perceives in the environment. This process is adaptive in its advancement of social integration. Mirror neurons are activated when observing emotional behavior in others, and they produce affective empathy in the observer—a sense of what the other person is feeling. Cognitive empathy, or the ability to understand the perspective of the other, emerges several years later. As neuroscientists become better able to locate the sources of mirror neurons they may come to understand why some people experience empathy in greater or lesser degrees than others, and how it might become better developed.

Unconditional positive regard. The social worker values the person of the client and his or her situation without reservation. This stance runs counter to the client's expectations of most significant others in his or her life to provide "conditions of worth," or qualified acceptance. The social worker always sees the client as striving toward self-actualization, or growth, and holds no expectations that the client should meet the arbitrary standards of other people on that journey.

Congruence/genuineness/authenticity. The social worker demonstrates congruence when he or she presents to the client as a "real" person (vs. a detached professional) who has the confidence to engage in a productive helping process. The social worker is consistent and honest in communicating his or her feelings, thoughts, and behaviors. These qualities demand that the social worker has a high degree of self-awareness and does not hide behind a mask of professionalism. If any of these elements is missing, the client may come to doubt or distrust the practitioner's alleged positive feelings.

Person-centered theory is unique in its position that the relationship, characterized by these three conditions, represents the entirety of the intervention. The theories that follow hold that the relationship is important but not the sole factor to rely on in helping clients.

Psychodynamic Theories

The psychodynamic theories, although sometimes criticized for being overly abstract and nonempirical, give extraordinary attention to the nature of the worker/client relationship, and for that reason they receive more attention here than the other theories. Relationship development requires the skills of empathy and authenticity (both described earlier), but the psychodynamic theories go beyond these to include strategies for the social worker's ongoing management of the positive and negative aspects of the relationship, with attention to the mutual impact of unconscious feelings (Goldstein et al., 2009). That is, unconscious feelings can influence the social worker's capacity to understand a client's problems and the nature of their relationship. To maintain a controlled level of emotional involvement with the client the practitioner must be alert to transference and countertransference issues, which call attention to subtle aspects of any relationship.

Transference was initially defined as a client's unconscious projection of feelings, thoughts, and wishes onto the practitioner, who comes to represent a significant person from the client's past (Levy & Scala, 2012). The concept has since expanded to include all reactions that a client has to the social worker. These reactions may be based on patterns of interaction with similar types of people in the client's past or on the actual characteristics of the practitioner. *Countertransference* was initially defined as a practitioner's unconscious reactions to the client's projections, but the concept has also broadened to refer to the effects of the practitioner's conscious and unconscious needs and wishes on his or her understanding of the client (Walsh, 2011). It also refers to the conscious attitudes and tendencies that the worker has about types of clients (such as being drawn to working with children or having an aversion to older adults).

Transference and countertransference are not exotic ideas; they exist in every relationship. People experience others not only in terms of an objective reality but also in terms of how they wish them to be, or fear that they might be. These reactions should be considered in every practice encounter regarding how they influence the social worker's perception of the client, and vice versa. The social worker's awareness of his or her emotional reactions facilitates the intervention process as it helps to better understand the rationales behind the decisions he or she is making.

Object Relations Theory

Object relations, a prominent type of psychodynamic theory, holds that all people share a drive toward relationships, and the development of an emotional self is based on the internalization of relational experiences with primary caregivers (Flanagan, 2016). Relationship patterns tend to become fixed over time, and a client's interpersonal problems may be related to a rigid replaying of old relationship dynamics with new people. Further, clients with primary interpersonal problems will tend to act out these patterns with their social workers. For example, the angry man who is oppositional with authority figures will act the same way, sooner or later, toward his social worker. The social worker's understanding of this process is facilitative toward client goal achievement because the practitioner can point out and discuss problematic dynamics with the client in a safe and accepting environment. This can be challenging for both parties, requiring clear structuring, limit setting, and occasional confrontation (Høglend et al., 2011). The social worker may struggle at times to provide an accepting, "holding" environment for the client.

An example of this challenge is seen in many clients' use of the coping/defense mechanism of projective identification (Waska, 2007). A client, when unconsciously experiencing an unacceptable emotion (such as despair or anger), may project that feeling onto the social worker and behave in a way that provokes the social worker to consciously experience and express that same emotion. The client then consciously identifies with the social worker's expressed feeling, finally getting across his or her message. A survivor of childhood sexual abuse, for example, may feel hopeless about her chances to ever have relationships in which she will not be victimized. If the client is not verbally articulate or is highly repressed, she may behave in ways that make the social worker feel helpless to assist her. She may speak with a quivering voice, express ambivalence, avoid eye contact, become tearful, ask to leave the session, and in other ways exude a sense of despair. If the social worker acknowledges his or her own resulting feeling of helplessness, the client may be able to recognize that she feels the same way and as a result become more self-aware.

Attachment Theory

Attachment theory serves to make the nature of social workers' and clients' unconscious feelings toward each other more explicit. It holds that all children seek close proximity to their primary caregivers and develop attachment styles in response to the behaviors of those persons that persist through life. Theorists initially conceptualized three infant attachment styles (*securely, anxious-ambivalently*, and *avoidantly* attached; Ainsworth, Blehar, & Waters, 1978) and a fourth was added later (the *disorganized* type; Carlson, 1998). Assessing a client's attachment style can help the social worker understand how that person will approach the professional relationship and how the social worker can respond in a manner that promotes the client's autonomy.

Parents of *securely* attached infants are sensitive and accepting. Securely attached children and adults are not preoccupied with their security needs and are thus free to direct their energies toward non–attachment-related activities in the environment. Insecure infants, however, must direct some of their attention to maintaining their attachments to inconsistent, unavailable, or rejecting parents in ways that may predict their relationships with others, including their social workers.

Anxious-ambivalently attached infants become distraught when their caregivers leave, and upon the caregiver's return they continue to be distressed even as they want to be comforted. These children come to employ hyperactivation strategies to maintain attachments. Their caregivers, while not overtly rejecting, are often unpredictable in their responses to the child due to their own anxieties about caregiving. Fearing potential abandonment, the children become hypervigilant for threat cues and signs of rejection. As adults these people may become "people pleasers," feeling that they must satisfy the needs of others rather than their own to earn another's care.

Avoidantly attached infants seem to be relatively undisturbed both when their caregivers leave and when they return. These children want to maintain proximity to their caregivers, but their attachment style enables them to maintain a sense of proximity to parents who otherwise may reject them. Avoidant children suppress expressions of distress, and rather than risk further rejection they may give up the task of seeking emotional closeness.

The *disorganized* attachment style is characterized by chaotic and conflicted behaviors. These children exhibit simultaneous approach and avoidance behaviors, seeming incapable of applying any consistent strategy to bond with caregivers. Their behaviors reflect their best attempts at gaining some sense of security from caregivers who are nonetheless perceived as frightening. The caregivers are either hostile or fearful and are unable to hide their apprehension from the children. In either case, the child's anxiety and distress are not diminished. It is usually difficult to develop good working relationships with clients who have a disorganized style as this features inconsistent and disruptive responses.

Although children with disorganized attachment typically do not attain a sense of being cared for, the avoidant and anxious-ambivalent children can experience some success in fulfilling their needs for care. Social workers will thus be able to form productive relationships with most clients, but as noted earlier, an awareness of their styles may be helpful in predicting possible relationship challenges and providing guidance about how to respond to them.

Relational Theory

Direct social work practice can be described in simple terms as an encounter between two persons, one of whom (the client) is seeking assistance and the other (the professional) provides assistance. This account is sometimes referred to as the "one-person" perspective on intervention, because while two people are involved the focus is on the thoughts, feelings, and behaviors of one of them, the client (Magid & Shane, 2017). It is possible, however, to conceive of direct practice as a "two-person" process, meaning that its quality and outcomes depend on how the parties affect *each other*. From this perspective it is assumed that the social worker and client significantly influence each other's understandings of themselves and their relationship (Storolow, 2013). The possibility of practitioner objectivity is a myth (Katz, 2010).

Relational therapy, an offshoot of object relations theories (Borden, 2000; Segal, 2013), encourages the social worker's authentic manner of engaging with clients. He or she should be willing to express and explore a range of thoughts and feelings with a client for the purpose of facilitating a mutual connection (Freedberg, 2009). We will describe six relationship principles based on this theory. Some of these have already been introduced, and others will be more fully developed in subsequent chapters, but they all come together in this practice approach.

1. *Mutuality*. This refers to the social worker's acceptance of the fact that during intervention each person influences the other in ways that are not always evident to themselves. In some cases, helping the client to participate in a mutual relationship itself is the primary impetus for the

client's growth. Social work literature reflects different views regarding the degree to which workers should keep their personal selves out of the intervention process (see Chapter 3 and Davidson, 2005), but in relational theory, the more energy the worker expends on keeping parts of the self out of the process, the more rigid, and less genuine, he or she will be with the client. The worker/client relationship will risk becoming organized into dominant and subordinate roles.

2. *Congruence* (or genuineness, or authenticity). The social worker strives to be comfortable enough with himself or herself to talk openly with the client about their similarities and differences and how those may affect their work together. The social worker continuously evaluates the relational context regarding issues of diversity such as age, race, culture, and gender (Frey, 2013). Through open dialogue about these issues the parties become aware of the internal and external factors affecting their relationship and come to better understand each other.

3. *Optimal empathic attunement.* Through empathy, described earlier, the social worker communicates understanding and acceptance of a client, which stimulates the healing process. While all theories support the importance of empathy, there are differences among them in how the practitioner is expected to manage his or her emotional responses. Optimal empathic attunement, sometimes called emotional dwelling, encourages the social worker to accept that openness to a client's pain will produce strong reactions in himself or herself and that these are key to getting inside the client's world (Goldstein et al., 2009). The practitioner must be willing to sit with the client's pain while also experiencing sadness and other emotions for the benefit of the client.

4. *Spontaneity.* Social workers generally behave deliberately with their clients, perhaps reacting spontaneously (that is, without evident forethought) in limited ways such as laughing at an amusing story or touching the shoulder of a client who is crying. Interventions should certainly always be thoughtful and systematic, but acting at times on "gut feelings" may be helpful to clients. Instinct may in fact represent wisdom, the product of the social worker's past professional experiences in which he or she learned subliminally that certain responses are therapeutic (Trevithick, 2014). A social worker cannot be sure that spontaneous acts will be constructive, but having a willingness to take such risks is a part of the process. If the social worker's risk-taking turns out to be counterproductive (for example, if providing a hug to a trauma

survivor is experienced as a threat), he or she can process the situation with the client in the spirit of caring.

5. *Attention to transferences.* Common signs of positive and negative practitioner transference include either dreading or eagerly anticipating a client; differential promptness in responding to client needs; thinking excessively about a client during non-work hours; having trouble understanding a client's problems, being bored with a client, feeling angry with a client, or being unduly impressed with a client; feeling defensive or hurt by a client's criticisms; and feeling uncomfortable discussing certain topics with a client (Shaeffer, 2014). Clients bring their own unique set of reactions to the practice relationship. Relational theory holds that these reactions are triggered during the client and social worker's "first impressions" of each other, but they evolve in response to the dynamics of the relationship. The social worker, in addition to monitoring transferences, should be willing at times to discuss them with the client as a way of furthering their understandings of each other, especially when they seem to be creating problems in the relationship.

6. *Self-disclosure.* Self-disclosure is the social worker's sharing of personal information with a client (Siebold, 2011). It may involve a sharing of thoughts or feelings about what is going on in the session between the two parties or feelings and facts about the social worker's past or present that are similar to what the client is experiencing or has experienced. Self-disclosure should always be provided with the intention of helping the client rather than meeting a need of the social worker. Disclosure of personal information is risky because it may negatively affect the client's view of the social worker as a competent professional or make the client think that he or she needs to take care of the social worker. A major assumption of relational therapy is that some clients are likely to be helped by the social worker's relatively high degree of personal sharing. It depends on the client's needs and is perhaps best utilized by social workers with long-term clients who have interpersonal problems. Self-disclosure can help those clients understand their effects on others, feel understood, become more willing to risk sharing personal information with others, feel less shame and aloneness, explore their experiences more deeply, feel validated, and explore the meaning of their patterns of relating. A social worker should not engage in self-disclosure with any clients, however, until their relationship is established as trustworthy.

7. *Clear boundaries.* This topic is the focus of the next chapter, but one of the criticisms of relational theory is that boundaries may become too fluid between the social worker and client, and despite the best of intentions the practitioner may do harm by crossing them. Paradoxically, in relational interventions the social worker may need to be even more vigilant in setting or negotiating boundaries with clients, given that there is a higher likelihood of self-disclosure. Boundaries may be more permeable than in other practice perspectives, but they nonetheless are clearly established and observed.

The next theory calls on the social worker to promote a relationship that encourages a client's deep reflection into issues of identity and to be prepared to do the same.

Narrative Theory

The major premise of narrative theory is that all people are engaged in an ongoing process of constructing a life story, or *personal narrative,* that determines their understanding of themselves (self-concept) and their position in the world (Freeman, 2011; Madigan, 2019; White, 2007). Rather than focusing on universal developmental milestones the social worker accepts that it is the words people use, and the stories they learn to tell about themselves and others, that create their psychological and social realities. These life narratives are co-constructed with the narratives of significant other people in one's family, community, and culture.

According to narrative theory, all personal experience is fundamentally ambiguous, and people must organize their lives into stories to give them coherence and meaning. Problems related to client's internalized stories are, at least in part, byproducts of cultural practices that are oppressive to the development of functional life narratives. As people develop dominant storylines their new experiences are filtered in or out, depending on whether they are consistent with the ongoing life narrative. Narrative interventions may not be well suited for client problems related to basic needs such as food, shelter, safety, and physical health, but they are suitable for issues related to self-concept, interpersonal relationships, and personal growth.

Many problems in living that people experience are related to life narratives that exclude possibilities for creative future action. Through a process of refocusing, social workers help clients to construct new life narratives, or stories, that portray them in a different light. Clients are helped to formulate alternative past and future stories and devise new outcomes for themselves. The goals of narrative therapy are thus not so much to solve problems as to awaken clients from a problematic pattern of living, free them from accepting externally imposed constraints, help them author new stories of dignity and competence, and recruit supportive others in their environment who can serve as supportive audiences to the client's new life story.

Relationship development in narrative therapy features an informal conversational style and a relinquishing of the "expert" role (Richert, 2003). The social worker adopts an "archaeological" position, studying the details of the client's history to understand the building blocks of his or her life stories (beliefs, assumptions, and values). The social worker demystifies the practice relationship by inviting clients to ask questions and make comments about the intervention as it unfolds. In this way, the client is given a shared responsibility for shaping the counseling conversation. Three categories of the social worker's presentation in the relationship are acting as a validating audience as the client tells his or her life story; helping the client to accept the possibility of a new, equally valid storyline; and acting as a co-constructor of a new storyline, often pointing out exceptions to negative themes in the client's presenting narrative to demonstrate that there is more to the client's story than may be assumed. The process is relatively unstructured and, ideally, the social worker does not consider its duration in advance.

The following two theories take a more formal perspective on the worker/client relationship than has been described so far.

Behavior Theory
Behavior therapy promotes client goal achievement through the social worker's adjustment of behavioral reinforcements and punishments in the client's environments (Farmer & Chapman, 2016). It is a highly structured form of intervention that does not attend directly to clients' internal processes. For intervention to be successful, however, the social worker must be perceived as competent, caring, and trustworthy, because he or she will be encouraging the client to engage in corrective behaviors that may feel uncomfortable or threatening. Further, the behavior of both parties in the practice relationship is subject to the same conditioning principles that are utilized in the intervention (Wodarski & Bagarozzi, 1979). The client will be attracted to the social worker if their interactions result in less anxiety and the practitioner is perceived as having the ability to secure rewards (positive outcomes) for the client.

The practitioner's empathic understanding will facilitate these conditions. The social worker should be careful not to use punishing behaviors with a client, at least initially, as these tend to be alienating and result in a diminishing of the social worker's perceived reinforcing potential. The social worker should also be collaborative with the client in devising interventions because the client needs to have a strong investment in change strategies. Over time, the client will evaluate the relationship based on its rewards and costs relative to alternative behaviors (such as different intervention approaches, a different social worker, or no intervention at all) and the perceived likelihood of future rewards and costs. For these reasons the social worker must be engaging and empathic, although otherwise there is no need to explore the nature of the relationship in the subtle ways described earlier. Regular discussions about how the client is reacting to the intervention can help to sustain his or her sense of reward for participation.

Cognitive Theory

Cognitive theory assumes that one's thoughts are usually the primary determinant of feelings and behaviors, and interventions are focused on enhancing the rationality of a client's thinking patterns, the degree to which conclusions about the self and the world are based on external evidence, and the linear connections among a person's thoughts, feelings, and behaviors (Walsh, 2015a). In cognitive intervention the social worker serves as an *educator* in situations where clients experience cognitive deficits (lacking knowledge or understanding) and as an "objective" voice of reason (to the extent that this is possible) when the client experiences cognitive distortions (misinterpretations of external events) or seeks help in devising new rational problem-solving practices. The practitioner is a collaborator and beyond this may serve as a model of rational thinking and problem solving or as a coach, leading the client thorough a process of guided reasoning toward solutions. The social worker must demonstrate empathy with the client's problem situation, in part because confrontation is frequently used as a part of the intervention. The worker/client relationship tends to be formal, however.

It is the responsibility of the social worker to establish and maintain the structure that is inherent to cognitive interventions (Beck, 2011). This begins in the first session as the social worker sets an agenda, provides a mood check, specifies the client's presenting problem, sets goals, educates the client about the cognitive model, elicits the client's expectations for the intervention, educates the client about the nature of his or her problem, sets up homework assignments, provides a session summary, and elicits the client's feedback about the session. Subsequent sessions include brief updates and checks on the client's mood, the social worker's linking of issues between the previous and current session, setting an agenda, reviewing homework, discussing items on the agenda, setting up new homework tasks, providing a final session summary, and eliciting the client's feedback about the session. The practitioner is clearly the leader in these processes and the relationship is one-sided, with the social worker not expected to subsequently engage in self-disclosure.

Crisis Theory

A crisis can be defined as the perception or experience of an event (genuine harm, the threat of harm, or a challenge) as an intolerable difficulty (James & Gilliland, 2017). Most traumatic experiences would be considered crises. These are aberrations from a person's typical stress experience, and he or she cannot manage the event with usual coping methods. The experience of crisis is often said to occur in three stages:

1. A highly stressful event occurs that creates a sharp and sudden increase in the person's level of anxiety.
2. The person tries but fails to cope with the stress, which increases his or her anxiety to a point of feeling overwhelmed. At this point the person is highly receptive to accepting help because he or she cannot help herself.
3. The crisis resolves, either negatively (with an unhealthy coping solution) or positively (with successful management of the crisis and perhaps an enhanced sense of personal competence).

Crisis theory is arguably more of a human behavior than a practice theory, but when a person is in crisis he or she enters into a unique relationship with the social worker. The social worker must be highly active and connect quickly with the overwhelmed client through demonstrations of acceptance, empathy, and verbal reassurance. He or she must convey a sense of optimism and hope to the client, as well as his or her competence to help resolve the crisis. The social worker usually takes charge in helping the client focus and make initial decisions about safety. Clearly, stage two of a crisis is one in which the social worker must act with authority. The practitioner must also elicit and encourage the client's expression of painful feelings toward the goal of helping the client ventilate as a step toward gaining mastery of those emotions and becoming able to focus on immediate challenges. This is a primarily one-sided relationship because the client is temporarily overwhelmed, although once the crisis begins to subside the relationship can become more collaborative. There will be many examples provided in this book of social workers' intervening with clients in crisis.

Family practice theories also suggest different perspectives on the worker/client relationship, as shown in the following examples.

Two Family Systems Theories
There are many family practice theories, but only two are presented here to illustrate how differently the working relationship can be conceptualized.

Family emotional systems theory, developed by Murray Bowen (1978), is not psychodynamic, but several of its major concepts, including differentiation of self, subsystems, triangulation, emotional cutoff, and emotional reactivity, reflect its assumption that all families are uniquely complex in the subtle patterns of interaction that members unconsciously develop over time to maintain an equilibrium. The theory holds that the social work practitioner must be careful not to get unwittingly "sucked into" the family system in such a way as to lose objectivity or take sides. This is best achieved by maintaining emotional distance and acting as a coach. That is, the social worker remains on the sidelines of family interaction and maintains a calm demeanor while asking questions and making suggestions that the family members can discuss and enact with each other. The social worker strives to be the focus of the family's attention, to free them from tendencies to react negatively to one another, and to set a productive tone for their exchanges. He or she serves as a model for rational thinking and interaction. This relative detachment precludes client/worker mutuality but preserves the integrity of the intervention.

Structural family theory includes very different prescriptions for the social worker. This theory assumes that an appropriately organized family will function productively for all its members, and the role of the practitioner is to actively restructure a family toward that end (Minuchin, Lee, & Simon, 2006). The social worker utilizes such concepts as executive authority, family power, family hierarchy, rules, roles, triangles, and boundaries to develop prescriptions for family change. The social worker is highly directive of in-session tasks (enactments) that are intended to illustrate problem areas and suggest solutions. From the first meeting, the social worker participates in family enactments, often by joining with (supporting) a member or subsystem to ensure that all perspectives are clearly shared. Minuchin did not share Bowen's concern about the difficulty of maintain objectivity with a family, and thus the social worker is encouraged to be verbal, personable, and collaborative. The social worker attempts to develop positive relationships with each member and in so doing is more likely to use self-disclosure and observe fluid boundaries.

Environmental Influences on the Relationship

Most social workers understand the importance of client engagement and relationship development, and the ways they approach the relationship will be guided by their theoretical orientations. Many examples of the theories described here appear throughout the book as they influence the decisions social workers make about how to interact with their clients. Still, practitioners can benefit from an awareness of the broader environmental factors that influence how they behave and how clients will respond to them. Two researchers have proposed a list of factors illustrating how the social worker/client relationship fits with other elements in and around the practice situation, summarized as follows (Cameron & Keenan, 2010; Cameron, 2014):

> *The social worker's personal factors*—personal values, knowledge, and skills
> *The worker's social network factors*—agency policies, procedures, other administrative and professional supports, family, and friends whose influence can assist (or inhibit) the social worker as he or she tries to meet the needs of clients
> *The client's personal factors*—level of distress, expectation of change, motivation to get help, and a view of the social worker as credible
> *The client's social network factors* —family, friends, work peers, neighbors, and outside organizations that can help or inhibit the client's functioning and support his or her change efforts.

These factors should always be a part of the social worker's assessment. The ways in which relationship quality can be monitored will be addressed in the remaining chapters of this book.

Summary

The social worker/client relationship is always important to the client's ability to achieve goals, but the appropriate nature of that relationship can be conceptualized differently depending on client factors, the presenting issue, agency factors, the values of the profession, and the theoretical perspective of the practitioner. The values of the social work profession are such that practitioners tend to be open to a more egalitarian relationship than is evident in many other related professions. In this chapter the nature of the social worker/client relationship has been described and explored from the perspectives of a variety of direct practice theories. A common factors model of practice was presented to demonstrate how the relationship is influenced by the social worker's and client's environmental factors as well. Theories also influence practitioners' beliefs about appropriate boundaries with clients, an important component of those relationships that is the topic of the next chapter.

2
Relationship Boundaries

Jeffrey is a clinical social worker in private practice. He sees clients on the hour for psychotherapy, greeting them with a smile and brief handshake in a waiting room shared with 10 other providers, after which he leads them to his formally decorated office. Wearing a sport coat and tie, he always sits in a stuffed chair and invites his clients to sit across a small coffee table on a couch. He waits for his clients to begin the conversation and then engages with them, saying relatively little while asking them to elaborate on problem-related themes. At 50 minutes past the hour Jeffrey announces that the session is over and schedules their follow-up visit.

Vicki is also a social worker, a case manager at a public mental health center where she manages a caseload of 30 clients with severe mental disorders. She checks her email and messages each morning before deciding which clients need her immediate attention. After that first hour she is usually in her car, driving comfortably in jeans to and from clients' homes where she delivers medication, provides supportive counseling, helps them solve pressing problems, takes them for short social outings, or escorts them to various appointments with other service providers. Vicki's meetings with clients range from 15 minutes to several hours in length. She and her clients usually listen to the radio while in her car and they talk informally about what they have seen on TV, what's in the news, and their recent activities. Sometimes they have lunch together, which is reimbursed by the agency.

Both of these social workers observe worker/client boundaries, but the ways in which they construct those boundaries are quite different, based on their job descriptions, their clients' needs, and their own preferences. The concept of boundaries and how they are managed is important to all types of social work and will be featured in discussions of the practice relationship in this book. In Chapter 1 it was noted that the various theories of social work practice include different assumptions about appropriate worker/client boundaries. Because this concept is ubiquitous it will be helpful to closely examine it in this chapter. In keeping with the theme of social workers attending to their personal and professional selves, both personal and professional boundaries and how they interact to influence relationships with clients will be considered.

Personal Boundaries

Boundaries can be understood as the assumed, and generally unspoken, rules that people internalize about the physical and emotional limits of their relationships with other people and groups (Bruhn, Levine, & Levine, 2002). They protect one's privacy and reflect one's individuality. Through boundaries people organize their social worlds and communicate their positions within them. People differentially construct boundaries to facilitate their desires to be close to, or separate from, others, and they open and close them to control the flow of their interactions.

Personal boundaries emerge as early as six months of age, when infants first develop a sense of separateness from their primary caregivers (Walsh, 2015a, 2015b). Boundaries continue to develop through life, although they tend to become more patterned over time. The nature of one's personal boundaries is determined by past influences (traditions rooted in family, gender, culture, religion, and other environmental forces), their successes and failures with relationships (what practices have been helpful or harmful in getting their needs met), and areas of vulnerability (those situations in which they tend to become negatively entangled). It is considered healthy to be relatively flexible in boundary setting, as one can then adapt to changing situations, including those in one's professional relationships.

Boundaries exist along a continuum from rigid to flexible to entangled (Davidson, 2005). People with *rigid* boundaries tend to be uncomfortable with ambiguity, value predictability, and behave in ways that are controlling and guarded. Those who maintain *flexible* boundaries tend to be adaptable, arbitrative, and open. People with *entangled* or *fluid* boundaries, which are undesirable, are tolerant of ambiguity but tend to be impulsive and ambivalent about others, have a high external locus of control, and need to be liked. Regarding *social* boundaries, people may be included with, or excluded from, other groups based on, for example, their gender, race, ethnicity, class, position in a hierarchy, and cultural traditions. Natural boundaries tend to exist between members of successive generations, gangs, students at different schools (think about "school spirit"), and subgroups of families (such as children vs. parents).

Boundaries often refer to limits, but they also have implications for bridging and access. All people experience natural tensions to remain apart from and to join with others, and this tension underscores the importance of flexibility, permeability, and balance in boundaries. People decide whom to *let in* as well as whom to *keep out*. In most relationships that persist, boundaries change over time. As one gets to know another person, one may test boundaries with them, perhaps by gradually sharing personal confidences, to learn more about who they are and how one wants to interact with them. If a person attempts to cross a boundary about which another person is not comfortable, for example by initiating physical contact with a potential romantic partner, that other person may choose to withdraw and perhaps erect tighter boundaries in response. If the other person is welcoming of the adjustment, the relationship may deepen.

There is an important difference between *crossing* and *violating* a boundary. Crossing a boundary refers to an action intended to increase emotional or physical closeness. It may or may not achieve its desired aim, but it would not be considered inappropriate by the recipient in its intent. An example would be inviting a relatively new work acquaintance to a social outing. A violation, on the other hand, refers to an action toward greater emotional or physical intimacy that would be considered inappropriate by the other person. An example would be asking that new acquaintance about intimate details of his personal life shortly after being introduced. Some writers consider boundary crossing to be inappropriate as well, at least in professional relationships, but it will be argued here that it need not be considered as such (Reamer, 2014).

Professional Boundaries

The definition of professional boundaries is the same as the one already presented but refers to interactions with clients. A person's professional boundaries will (or should be) different than those with friends because the nature of those relationships is inherently different. The way in which social workers organize their boundaries will include some commonalities based on the professional code of ethics but also include differences depending on one's theoretical perspective, job description, and agency practices. It can be useful to think about professional boundaries with regard to the following five aspects of social worker/client interactions (Herlihy & Corey, 2015):

Contact time. How much time is appropriate to spend in the company of the client? Will this vary depending on whether that time is spent face to face, on the phone, online, or otherwise? On the time of day, day of the week, or time of the year? On the purpose of the contact?

Types of information to be shared. What is the appropriate range of topics to discuss with the client? Will it be limited to aspects of the presenting problem? What about social topics, politics, religion, and sex? How much depth can the client be expected to provide about these topics?

Physical closeness when together. What are the social worker's expectations about personal space when in the client's company? How closely will the social worker sit with him or her? Can the client touch the practitioner? What range of nonverbal communications is appropriate?

Territoriality. To which of the social worker's environmental spaces does the client have access? Is he or she restricted from others? Can they meet at the client's home? Will interactions be limited to the office? What about community settings? Which ones?

Emotional space. To what extent is the social worker willing to share his or her feelings about sensitive topics with the client? Are there limits to the topics about which the worker will share feelings?

The Importance of Clear Professional Boundaries

Clear boundaries, however they are established, are important to both the client and social worker (Grant & Mandell, 2016). For clients, they provide a relationship in which the person feels affirmed and respected in a safe, predictable environment. In such a secure environment the client is more likely to feel comfortable sharing appropriate personal information. Clear boundaries also provide clients with a sense of individuality when they have a voice in establishing the scope and limits of the relationship and a basis from which to determine whether and when to attempt to adjust boundaries with the social worker toward greater closeness. A client will loosen a boundary when he or she perceives some benefit to doing so and trusts the integrity of the social worker. Finally, for some clients with a disorganized sense of self, such as those with psychosis, the external structure produced by clear, consistent boundaries helps to promote the development of a clear internal structure (Lavarenne, Segal, & Sigman, 2013).

Clear boundaries are also important for social workers. They provide role clarity regarding the range and limits of the worker's activities (which helps to prevents burnout based on overextension), a basis from which to make decisions about how and when to cross physical or psychological boundaries, and physical safety when territorial boundaries are maintained.

A social worker's boundary awareness is important because, despite the profession's attention to egalitarianism, a power differential almost always exists between the worker and client. Social workers control certain material and emotional resources desired by the client, so the client must be reasonably compliant with the worker's agency-enforced procedures to receive those resources. The lack of equal power in the relationship may compromise the client's ability to defend himself or herself regarding privacy issues, such as objecting to a social worker's offer of home visits or his or her expectation that certain personal information must be shared. The client will not necessarily articulate negative reactions to ambiguous boundaries, however, because he or she has less power and perhaps is unclear about what appropriate professional boundaries should be.

Some social workers, it must be acknowledged, object to what is sometimes called a "patriarchal" model of professional boundaries in which the professional assumes responsibility for monitoring boundaries and enforces distance from the client (Dietz & Thompson, 2004). An alternative model of the relationship is one characterized by mutuality, which assumes that both parties are partners who jointly develop relationship guidelines. This protects against the possibility of professional abuse of power by transferring control of the relationship to the social worker/client dyad. When boundary setting includes client input, those persons are more motivated to participate in the helping process.

A challenge in professional boundary development is that it is sometimes unclear what specific boundaries are appropriate in a given situation (Shevellar & Barringham, 2016). This is partly because direct social work practice assumes different forms depending on the client population, the presenting problem, and the setting where services are being delivered. Appropriate boundaries may be different if the client's issues pertain to mental health, physical disability, child and adolescent acting-out behavior, refugee and immigration status, medical concerns, aging, and hospice practice, to name a few. Further, interventions may be delivered in the practitioner's agency but also in the client's home, coffee shops, restaurants, clubhouses, hospital rooms, churches, libraries, athletic fields, and other community settings. Given the uniqueness of all people it is not always easy for a social worker to establish appropriate boundaries even in relatively predictable office settings.

There is certainly a consensus among social workers that some boundaries should *always* be observed, such as avoiding romantic entanglements, engaging in sexual behavior, and pursuing friendships, but there are many gray areas as well. Most authors avoid settling for a bulleted guidance list of "dos" and "don'ts" for social workers, as these can never adequately consider all circumstances in which boundaries are constructed. One author who focuses on professional development argues that the best way to help social workers avoid boundary violations is to provide them with regular opportunities for real and hypothetical case reflections so that they may develop better professional judgment (Clapton, 2013).

Social workers of course differ in how they assess their boundary behaviors and manage dilemmas that may arise (Trimberger & Bugenhagen, 2015). Some practitioners seek to rely on previously formulated rules about correct and incorrect behavior, which might be available as agency policies, state statutes, and professional codes of ethics. Others rely on their prior learning about boundaries in such social institutions as the family, school, church, and other organizations with which they have had extensive involvement. Other social workers are skeptical of the degree to which they should rely on the judgments of others and work toward developing their own sets of rules about professional boundaries. These persons presumably seek input from a variety of outside sources but in the end take responsibility for their own judgment. There are benefits and limitations to all these positions.

Part of the challenge in boundary establishment with clients is that one's personal feelings can come into play, as demonstrated in the following vignette presented by a 24-year-old White female social work student named Robyn.

The Boyfriend

> *"Meghan was a 15-year-old White female, adopted at age two, although her adoptive parents divorced a few years ago. Meghan's adoptive mother was a registered nurse and her adoptive father was absent from her life. According to her adoptive mother, Meghan was severely neglected during the first few years of her life by her birth parents. She had an attachment disorder and her*

current problems included consistently getting into trouble at school, not following her adoptive parents' rules at home, and getting involved with a string of boyfriends, most of whom were poor influences. Meghan had received therapeutic case management services from social workers at my agency for 10 years.

"I worked with Meghan for seven months, helping her to develop positive coping, anger management, and social skills. I thought we had a good relationship. We worked steadily toward her goals and she seemed able to confide honestly in me. Prior to the following problem encounter I would normally schedule Meghan's visits around lunchtime or dinnertime and we would go to a park near her home to eat. The agency expected that most client meetings would occur in the community because it was a more comfortable, less intimidating environment for the adolescents.

"One day I picked Meghan up at her grandmother's house and we went to McDonald's to get lunch. During the ride Meghan seemed angry and complained that her mother didn't like her current 18-year-old boyfriend. I tried to calm Meghan down by letting her play music of her choice in my car. After Meghan and I got our food we went to the park to eat and have our session. I noticed that Meghan kept checking her phone, and I asked why. Her tone became snappy and she replied she was texting her boyfriend. I reminded Meghan that she could not contact her boyfriend because this was our time to talk. I should mention that, against my better judgment, I didn't strictly enforce a 'no phone use' rule with Meghan and the other girls because I didn't want to come off as rigid. But my comment about the boyfriend made her furious and she walked about 30 feet away from me. I texted my supervisor to tell him what was going on because I had a feeling Meghan's anger might escalate.

"I approached Meghan and tried talking to her but she stormed off to wander through the park. Ten minutes later her boyfriend showed up and Meghan went to talk to him. I approached him, too, and said that he was not allowed to be present during our visits. He told me to mind my own business, and then Meghan threatened to beat me up. She got inches away from my face and yelled at me regarding her 'right' to see her boyfriend. I held my hands behind my back to show Meghan I was not going to fight her and I reminded her again that this was our therapy time. She backed off, and in her frustration she knelt down and started punching the ground. I went to my car and locked myself inside to be safe, in accordance with agency policy. Meghan tried to get into the car, but I told her I was not going to let her in until she calmed down.

I called my supervisor and he advised me to call both the police and Meghan's mother, which I did. Her boyfriend left the scene, and after the police and her mother arrived, Meghan eventually left with her mother, but only after a loud argument.

"The major relationship issue with this interaction was my lax attention to boundaries. I think now that letting Meghan use her cellphone during our visits was a big mistake. I initially let Meghan use her phone because our visits were long, and I thought it would be okay if she looked at her phone a few times. I should have been firmer. My personal style is relatively laid back and I need to be more aware that some clients, especially adolescents, might take advantage of that. I knew that Meghan did not react well to authority figures, and although I was one, I wanted her to feel comfortable with me. I thought that because she had experienced so much neglect in her life, she needed someone who was warm and understanding, but I think I came off to her as a pushover. Until this encounter I was not holding her accountable for some things. Maybe I just felt bad about her upbringing.

"If I had the chance to conduct this session again, I would not let Meghan use her phone. She probably thought that if I allowed the phone issue to slide then I could let other things slide, too, like her boyfriend showing up. After this incident I told Meghan that her phone was forbidden during the rest of our visits and that we would limit our meetings to the agency office for the next month. I wanted to show Meghan that her behavior was unacceptable and I was not going to just sweep it under the rug, even though we did process and resolve the boyfriend issue during the next session."

Robyn worked in a program where interventions took place in the client's natural environments. It would be important for her to observe boundaries about territoriality (who could be present) and the types of interaction to be shared (only issues pertaining to her program, and not the phone) in this kind of situation as a means of maintaining control over what transpired during their lengthy interactions, not to mention her own safety. While Robyn seems to have done good work overall, she made a mistake in letting Meghan cross one boundary—being able to talk to friends during their visits and inviting a boyfriend to come by. Robyn knew at the time that this was probably a mistake but she felt sorry for her client and wanted to be liked by her. She also admitted that she had a hard time being firm with limits due to her personality style. Robyn became aware after this episode that she had to work against her tendency to be a "soft touch."

Warning Signs of a Social Worker's Possible Boundary Violations

In the previous example it was the client who tested the limits of her boundaries with the social work intern. However, often the social worker is the source of ambiguity, and social workers should accept that it is normal to experience confusion about boundaries at times. The many indicators of *possible* boundary violations by social workers that may emerge in the course of their practice will be discussed here (Cooper, 2012; Sinason, 2017). None of these is necessarily a transgression—whether it is so depends on the context, as will be considered later.

> *Exceptional behavior*, such as doing too much for a client, protecting too much, identifying too much, having extended meetings—or the opposite (doing too little, being emotionally distant, minimizing contacts). Such behavior may indicate more or less motivation to work with a client for reasons that should be analyzed.
>
> *Experiencing strong positive or negative feelings about a client*. This is a normal human process that happens at times to all social workers and should not be denied (as it tends to be). It is an indication that the social worker needs to understand the reasons for those feelings and how they affect service delivery. This issue is explored in detail in Chapter 9.

The next vignette illustrates these two warning signs of possible boundary problems. It was written by Gwendolyn, a 44-year-old divorced White woman with no children, whose strong emotional reactions to a client's health scare prompted her to engage in a level of self-disclosure and advice giving that may have constituted an inappropriate breach of professional boundaries.

The Health Scare

> *"Helena was a 22-year-old White heterosexual female, active-duty military and stationed at a nearby fort. She had a diagnosis of PTSD and her treatment at our medical center focused on helping her to better understand her diagnosis, begin to process some of her trauma, and help her build healthy coping skills. She had been at our mental health outpatient program for two weeks at*

the time of this encounter. Helena reported close relationships with her family members and boyfriend, although none of them lived nearby. She lived on the base while her boyfriend lived an hour away. Her parents and siblings lived a thousand miles away, as did her many aunts, uncles, and grandparents.

"I met Helena when I did her intake assessment, at which time she informed me of physical symptoms that raised a red flag for me and for which I encouraged her to follow up with a medical doctor. Our interactions after that were primarily in the psychodynamic therapy group I co-facilitated that focused on coping skills development, defense mechanisms, and self-understanding, but I saw her occasionally on an individual basis. Helena was engaged in her groups and was always open, honest, and willing to do the hard work needed to make progress. She and I had a good rapport both inside and outside of group. Helena had a way about her that was reminiscent of members of my own family. This, together with the fact that her age and need for care brought out motherly feelings from me, made me conscious of the potential for loose boundaries on my part regarding contact time, types of information to be shared, and emotional space.

"After a few weeks, Helena shared that her doctor had ordered a biopsy, and one week later she told me that she had been diagnosed with ovarian cancer. I was immediately flooded with a variety of strong emotions, including fear, anger (at the injustice of it), and a desire to protect her. It was important to me that she knew I cared for her and wanted to support her moving forward. I told her these things this while I worked to keep my emotions in check. I wanted to ask her questions about her current medical care and her plans moving forward, but first I asked her what, if anything, she needed. She responded that she did not think she needed anything, and that she was scheduled to have the tumor removed at the naval hospital, the closest military hospital that could do the surgery. She was happy that she would be able to keep both ovaries as she hoped to have children someday. I validated her feelings but wondered, given the extent and severity of her symptoms, if the naval hospital and not removing the ovary were the best options. I expressed to her that it must feel scary to have to deal with all this right now, especially since she was far away from her family. She said that it was indeed overwhelming but that her mother planned to fly out for the surgery. She said that she really missed her family.

"Here is where I may have violated boundaries. During this conversation I decided to disclose to Helena that I had friends and family members, including my mother, who had had ovarian cancer, and that I knew of some additional resources that others had found to be helpful. I said I would be happy to share

them with her if she was interested. Helena responded that she would welcome such information, so I wrote it down for her, including the name and phone number of a highly respected gynecologic oncologist in the area. I desperately wanted her to seek a second opinion as I did not trust that she was getting the best care. I pointed to the doctor's name and said, 'One thing I and others have found to be very helpful is to seek out second and even third opinions when it comes to diagnosis and treatment options.' I added that she should not feel any pressure to use the doctor whose name I had written down. I also told her that the type of treatment one takes initially can often dictate what type of treatment one is able or unable to receive later, if the need arises. Helena expressed gratitude for the suggestions. I told her to not hesitate to let me know if she had any questions.

"In this encounter my emotional reactions significantly affected my behavior. As discussed above, I knew before this health crisis that my feelings for Helena were strong. While they were not difficult to contain initially, they became a significant intervening factor when the issue of her diagnosis arose. Worth considering in this encounter were whether I was promoting in her a sense of self-sufficiency or dependency, whether I was crossing interprofessional boundaries in regard to her medical care (my role did not include participation in medical consultations), and whether I was hearing her wishes for herself or pushing my own wishes upon her. Here was this young woman who was away from her family, already struggling with so much, and now dealing with a frightening diagnosis. I wanted to wrap her in a hug, carry her home, and be the mother that I felt she needed. I wanted to take on any battle that needed to be fought, with the doctors, her medical insurance, or the Navy to make sure she was seen by the best doctors and treated at the best facilities. I was flooded with both compassion and fear. I had lost people close to me with this disease.

"I knew I couldn't take Helena home with me or become a surrogate mother. Likewise, I knew I couldn't push her to see particular doctors or connect with certain supports. Still, my professional self felt that it was appropriate to offer these names and resources if she requested as much. I put heavy emphasis on the importance of second opinions. I still wonder, though, what degree of restraint on my part would have been more appropriate. At the time, it felt appropriate to disclose the fact that I had family members and friends who had had this disease. It felt like a way to foster our connection during this difficult time, normalize a part of her experience, and let her know she was not alone. Perhaps I felt it also gave some weight to the suggestions and resources I offered. If I had the chance to do it again, I may not have disclosed about my family or addressed her medical issues so directly. It may have been just as effective to say that I had known people who had had ovarian cancer without disclosing who they were.

"I later discussed the encounter with my supervisor, who initially tried to disagree with my offering of resources, saying that I was a part of Helena's mental health team and he was sure she was receiving good medical care. I bristled at that suggestion both because I believe the delineation between mind and body is a false dichotomy, and because I had seen too much cancer in my life to be content with 'good' care if better was available. Now, with some time and distance, I see that my supervisor was correct. My own fears had a negative influence on my behavior. I need to be more mindful about how my emotions influenced my approach."

It is not clear what instructions Gwendolyn received from her supervisor about this episode, but it does seem that, despite her own evaluation of the situation, she overstepped proper boundaries in responding to the client's cancer diagnosis. She allowed herself to become involved in medical decisions and even implied that the available medical resources may not be adequate for her needs. Further, she got sidetracked from her initial focus on psychodynamic theory, which calls for a greater emotional distance between a worker and client. Gwendolyn knew that her emotions might have been clouding her judgment, but even so she did not try very hard to acquire some healthy professional distance from them. This vignette provides a good example of the power of a social worker's emotions on his or her behavior.

The list of warning signs continues:

Dual relationships, or those in which the social worker interacts with the client or the client's significant others in more than one role. For example, the client or the client's significant other might be the social worker's mechanic, grocer, neighbor, or fellow church member. These situations create potential conflicts of interest. They are often unavoidable in rural settings but can occur anywhere.

Intrusion into the client's physical or technological territory. The home represents an especially private territory in which residents can exercise control and expect that visitors abide by their rules. Intrusive activity by the social worker may include visiting the client who does not want to be visited or making unannounced home visits, both of which are commonplace, for example, in child protective services work. Other types of potentially intrusive activity include phone calls, using the same social media sites as a client, or following the client on social media.

The hospital setting is one where physical boundaries must often be negotiated, since many patients are physically impaired and unable to exercise control over their "space" as health professionals come and go from their rooms. The following vignette involves Tamira, a 25-year-old Black woman who was new to her medical placement and struggled with how to observe appropriate boundaries there.

No Clothing

"John was a 73-year-old Black male veteran with Parkinson's disease and partial paralysis. He was on the spinal cord unit of the VA hospital for a colonoscopy and treatment of a probable urinary infection. I had met with him once before during a multidisciplinary team meeting, where his discharge plans were discussed. During the meeting staff had expressed the importance of John's having 24-hour care due to his risk of falling. Different options were shared, including his having multiple home health workers, having someone move in with him, or going to an assisted living facility. I had not had other interactions with John because he had been assigned to a different social worker. One day, however, I was asked to check in with him due to his social worker being out with an illness. John was planning to be discharged in three days and I was asked to see if he had spoken with a caregiver regarding his bowel and bladder care, if that person had been contacted by the nurse educator regarding compensation, and his plans for getting home. I was also to inform John that the doctor had put in a consult for his home health assistance.

"As I entered John's room, I saw that the curtains were drawn around his bed. In the past, when I had seen doors closed or curtains pulled, I checked back with the veteran later, as a means of respecting their privacy. However, I had been told recently that curtains were often pulled and doors closed due to a veteran's desire for privacy from other veterans. Rather than come back, I knocked to see if John was willing to speak. I said, 'Knock knock, John, is it alright if I come in? I'm with social work.' From behind the curtain a voice said, 'Yes, you can come in.' Unsnapping the curtain, I saw that John was lying on his bed without a shirt or pants on and his blanket pulled between his legs.

His genitals were covered but his legs and stomach were visible. Seeing that his body was minimally covered, I wondered if I should come back later. I felt uncomfortable and wasn't sure what to do, but I decided to try to ignore the minimal coverage, focus on John's eyes, and tell him why I was there.

"*I told him my name and said I was helping the social worker who usually saw him. I first asked about his transportation arrangement. John looked confused and said that he hadn't had his colonoscopy yet. I asked if they were still planning to do that during this visit and he said that he believed that they were. I told him that I would speak to his doctor about this. As I spoke, I noticed that John was trying to pull the blanket farther up over his legs. Again, I pondered if I should leave, but he was speaking to me so I figured that he was okay with me being there. Still, I wanted to accomplish my task as quickly as possible to avoid additional discomfort for either of us. I went through my list of questions, and when I asked if I could have his caregiver's information so that our nurse educator could call her, he got out his phone and, still trying to pull the blanket up some, faced the phone toward me. I tried to make out the number without moving closer because I wanted to respect his space. After getting the number, I told him that the doctor had put in a consult for home health assistance, so he should be contacted by them soon. He smiled and stated that he was looking forward to speaking to them. I asked if there was anything else I could do for him, and he said no. I told him that I would give our nurse educator his caregiver's information, speak with his doctor regarding his colonoscopy, and update him if I was given any new information. He said that would be fine. I thanked him and left the room. I was relieved to be finished because of the feeling that I had violated John's privacy.*

"*Before the interaction began, I noticed that the client's curtains were drawn, indicating he wanted privacy. This indicated a boundary. When I noticed that the client was not wearing clothing, I felt that I was violating that boundary, even though he told me that it was okay to enter. His genitals were covered but he made multiple attempts to pull up the blanket, indicating that he wanted to be covered up. It is possible that John told me to come in due to feeling that he had to, since he was the client and I was the professional. My decision to stay, even when I saw that he was not dressed, was influenced by my being told to accomplish some important tasks and having been told that drawn curtains did not necessarily mean that people wanted to be left alone. In the past, I had noticed that some patients closed their curtains so they could hear their television better or dampen the outside noise. I assumed that John would have asked me to come back later if he had wanted privacy. After walking in, though, I felt conflicted. I wanted to leave the room but I needed the information to make sure his needs were met before discharge.*

"If I could do this interaction over I again, I would behave differently. I would knock the same way, announce myself, and enter. Seeing that he had minimal clothing on, I would say, 'It looks like this is not a good time for you. I can come back later.' By stating this I would be creating space for John to ask for privacy if he wanted it. If he stated that now was a good time to talk, then I would interact with him just as I had. Regardless of his answer, my question would have given him the power to make the decision he wanted, which would keep his boundaries from being violated. In the moment, I did not know what to do, so I chose to take the client on his word and speak with him. My intentions were in the right place and I was able to get what I needed; I just wish I had made sure that my client was comfortable speaking to me."

Tamira's discomfort with this situation is understandable, given her inexperience in a medical facility. In most practice settings, social workers and their clients do not need to address issues related to physical exposure. For Tamira this represented a boundary concern related to the client's territory that she hadn't faced before. It is likely that the hospital had clear policies in place regarding staff approaching clients in their rooms. Tamira seemed to have been aware of this, although she didn't recall what the policies were. As a result, she found herself in an awkward position where her ability to interact comfortably with the client was compromised. It is good that she recognized that some patients might feel unable to refuse a professional's visit due to power imbalances, but this was a boundary issue with which she would probably become comfortable given more experience in the setting.

Now for the remaining warning signs:

Self-disclosure. The sharing of feelings, opinions, or personal anecdotes may be legitimate when used as a means to a therapeutic end (although practice theories maintain different positions in this regard), but in a negative sense it may also reflect a sharing of personal information for the worker's own benefit. A social worker who shares that he had an argument with his son may be using the client as an outlet for venting. This may put the client in the inappropriate position of being a caregiver.

Out-of-office in-person contact with clients. A social worker may be invited to, and consider attending, a client's graduation ceremony, a family's holiday cookout, or a picnic planned by a group of clients.

Referring to clients as friends. Social workers rarely interact with their clients in the same manner as they do with their friends, so referring to clients as friends can be misleading. It may cause eventual hurt to the client or discourage clients from developing their own friends.

Investigating certain details of clients' personal lives. The need to know *some* personal information about clients does not mean that the social worker has a right to know *everything*. Such curiosity may be voyeuristic at times.

Loaning, trading, or selling items to a client. The social worker may, for example, be inclined to loan a compact disc to an impoverished client with similar musical tastes or borrow an interesting book from a client.

Accepting or giving gifts. This may or may not be appropriate, depending on the setting, the intervention, the client and worker's motivations, and the value of the gift. It may be an important action to help clients practice reciprocity in relationships. Often, agencies have policies that staff must follow to establish limits in this area.

Touching or physically comforting a client. Sexual contact with a client is always inappropriate but other forms of physical touch may be therapeutic, such as comforting a grieving client with a hug. This topic is addressed in detail in Chapter 11.

Intervening Factors

The preceding list consists of possible, not actual, boundary violations. A variety of contextual factors must be considered as the social worker establishes his or her appropriate boundary conduct, with the goal being what is in the best interest of the client, or what behaviors will facilitate the client's achievement of goals. These factors include:

- The functioning level of the client (his or her ability to use good judgment in interpersonal situations)
- The client's history in relationships (patterns of behavior and his or her ability to manage differences of opinion)

- The history and dynamics of *this* relationship (what patterns of interaction have been established, and whether a boundary-crossing activity by the worker is likely to be growth enhancing or a setback for the client)
- The social worker's level of professional experience
- Cultural norms reflected in the behavior of both the worker and client.

In the following vignette an experienced 35-year-old social worker presents a boundary-crossing risk he took with a client that succeeded in enhancing their relationship.

Graduation Day

"I worked full time in a community mental health center and saw about 20 clients per week, some of them over periods of several years. The relationship was always important in long-term work and I tried to be aware of how well the client and I were connecting. I worked from an object relations theoretical perspective, which became relational at times if our work progressed to a point that it might be beneficial to discuss the affective nature of our relationship. This was helpful to some clients who had never experienced depth in a relationship. Like anybody else I developed strong feelings about my clients at times and had to be careful not to overstep my bounds, which for me usually meant not becoming too informal with them.

"One of my clients was 25-year-old single White female with a history of sexual abuse and overall family neglect named Carrie. It may not have been the best idea to assign a male to work with her, but at the time the agency had no options, and the client agreed. She was terrified of any kind of closeness and had a hard time talking in our sessions because of her overwhelming anxiety. She was fearful, not sure what she wanted, and seemed to expect rejection from me and everyone else she encountered. I don't think she trusted me for a long time, and I can't blame her, given her history. Over the course of two years, though, we moved from a position of mostly silent sessions to a relationship in which she seemed to have tentative trust in me and would confide in me at least some of the time. I believe that her self-esteem was so fragile, though, that she still didn't think I cared about her. I hoped she would come to understand some relationships could be positive.

"During our work together, Carrie had decided to attend school to become a licensed practical nurse, a decision I supported. Not only did she do well

in her courses and practicums, but she was selected to be the salutatorian at the graduation ceremony. True to form, she downplayed this accomplishment. She did not verbally invite me to the ceremony but mailed me an invitation. I had never attended a client's private event but this time I wanted to make an exception. I wanted to go partly for my own sake, in that I would feel good about this grand visual evidence of her progress, but I also wanted to demonstrate that I cared about her enough to go out of my way to share in her accomplishment. I knew this would be a boundary-crossing event, so I discussed it with my supervisor. He agreed that it would be therapeutic for Carrie if I attended.

"The event included a few awkward moments because Carrie's housemates were there, and I knew that several of them had been cruel to her, including one man who had exploited her sexually. They invited me to sit with them in the small auditorium but I said no. One of them responded, 'Well, of course you don't want to be seen with the other crazies.' I sat alone across the aisle from them and overheard a few similar comments until the ceremony began. Carrie did fine, though, and I hoped she saw me in the audience. Afterwards I waited in the parking lot just long enough to say hello and congratulations to her. I turned down an invitation from another housemate to attend their planned cookout, and then left. Carrie never said anything to me later about the event but I congratulated her one more time at our next session. I'm glad I went, and I believe it made a good impression on her about our relationship and her great achievement."

It seems that this social worker was in part trying to teach Carrie about the range of interactions that constituted a supportive relationship, which she hadn't experienced during her life of abuse and betrayal. His attendance at her graduation might have confused Carrie and made her question his intentions about her, but she had quietly indicated that she wanted him to come, and a supervisor helped the social worker to process the issue and determine that the action, while unusual, might be beneficial to her growth.

Managing Boundary Dilemmas

Developing good judgment about boundaries with clients is a process that evolves over a social worker's entire career. Listed next are guidelines that social workers (Shevellar & Barringham, 2016) and supervisors (Thomas, 2010) can use to help address boundary dilemmas.

Guidelines for Social Workers

Set clear boundaries with the client's input at the beginning of those relationships, including the scope and limits of your roles and activities.

Clarify boundaries with clients over time, as they may change. For example, you and the client may decide that home visits, not made before, are now indicated, or that the two of you will begin to address a broader range of the client's problem issues than was done initially.

Be aware of your own emotional and physical needs as much as possible and be wary of obtaining too much personal gratification at the expense of a client. Of course, all interventions should be provided for the client's benefit.

Secure the client's informed consent for all service activities. This may involve obtaining written consent for some activities but should always involve explaining the rationales for all interventions and providing clients with choices.

Be educated about the client's cultural and community standards of behavior so that you understand what boundaries are reasonable to them in those contexts.

Avoid dual relationships with clients or significant others as much as possible. When such a relationship may exist, you should assess its potential risks and benefits, discuss these with the client, and then decide whether it is feasible to continue as the service provider.

Utilize peer consolation and formal supervision routinely. Above all, seek input from persons with whom you can be honest, given the sensitivity of some boundary issues.

Refer to codes of ethics for their recommendations about boundaries.

Guidelines for Supervisors

Some guidelines for supervisors are provided here as well to emphasize that all social workers will experience boundary dilemmas and possibly make mistakes in addressing them, and it is important for a supervisor to validate the social worker's concerns. Supervision should provide a safe forum for practitioner disclosure, but because many boundary dilemmas are related to the personal needs of workers they are not always easy to discuss with another person, particularly one in a position of authority.

Supervisors should invite discussion of a social worker's boundary dilemmas in a spirit of guided exploration, where the social worker is helped to reflect on and resolve his or her concerns in an atmosphere of support rather than cross-examination, which puts him or her on the defensive. Supervisors should be sensitive to the worker's personal situation and help him or her differentiate normal emotional reactions from feelings that promote boundary violations. All social workers have a range of reactions to clients, and knowing which ones challenge their objectivity can help supervisors to be alert about boundary issues that might develop. Further, supervisors should promote clarity in staff roles. As noted earlier, with role clarity, social workers have an easier time deciding what is or is not appropriate in their activities with clients.

This final vignette from Kelly, a 25-year-old single White female who was placed at a university counseling center, provides an illustration of the role of supervision in boundary setting with clients.

The Letter

"My client, Javid, was a 24-year-old male international student from India who was in a master's program for engineering. He came to the center for help with extreme anxiety and I intended to use cognitive-behavioral interventions to assist him with this problem. Javid was close with his family, and they were proud of him for seeking a graduate degree in the United States. Last semester, however, he had to fly home due to a family emergency and as a result fell behind and failed most of his classes. Now Javid was at risk of being terminated from his program and was struggling to cope with the idea that he may lose his visa and bring shame to his family. He worried that his hard work at school would come to nothing. Javid's treatment goals included stabilization and trying to stay enrolled at the university.

"At the beginning of our second session Javid asked if I could write a letter to the dean of his department, verifying that the reason he failed his classes last semester was due to psychological distress. His dean had informed him that verification from a counselor that he was having mental health issues would enable him to retroactively withdraw from those classes and stay in the program. I wanted to do this, but after consulting with my supervisor I told Javid

that I could only write a visit verification letter, stating that I'd seen him twice but could not speak about his experience last semester because he was not in counseling then. I could not include my own opinion after the fact. He initially seemed pleased with this arrangement and I wrote the letter.

"Over the following weekend, however, Javid sent me several emails stating that my letter would not suffice because it didn't explicitly state that his mental health impacted his performance. During the time of those emails, however, I was not in the office and, per agency policy, could not respond to them. When I got back to the office, I called Javid and explained that I could not alter the letter because I was limited to what was in his records at the agency. During the first part of the following week we had several back-and-forth conversations via email and, eventually, in person about the limits to what I could provide him. Javid even came into the agency on Monday and Tuesday when I was not in (I was there Wednesday through Friday) to try to find and talk to me. He was clearly disappointed with me and I felt terribly guilty, as if I was letting him down. My supervisor was away that week so I could not consult with her.

"The major relationship issue here was my lack of clarity with Javid about the boundaries and limits of my service. I had failed to tell Javid that I can't answer emails on the weekends or when I'm not in the office, so he grew frantic, as if I was ignoring him. I was in turn growing frustrated with his persistent emails and unscheduled visits to the office. He did not seem to grasp the idea that I could not bend the rules for him. When I wrote the letter, I was already going out of my way to get it to him in a timely manner. I even got another supervisor to co-sign it because my supervisor was out of town. *I allowed his urgency to become mine and I was hesitant to enforce stricter boundaries because I felt sympathy for his situation and pulled emotionally to protect him.*

"My personal self was evident in my frustration and annoyance with Javid for the way he was trying to get me to do something I wasn't allowed to do. Still, I felt pressured to go the extra mile for Javid because I didn't want him to fail his program and risk having his visa revoked. I felt conflicted telling him that I couldn't write the perfect letter that could fix everything. It was only when my supervisor came back and talked with me that my professional self emerged and I saw the importance of abiding by agency policy. My supervisor was always reminding me to 'do less' in some ways, which seemed at times like an abdication of professional responsibility, but her point was that *social workers and clients in our setting need to share responsibility for problem situations, and that we can burn ourselves out by trying to do too much for them. It could be hard for me to abide by this 'keep a safe distance' mentality because of our professional mission to promote social justice. I knew my role was to write a letter that verified his visits, but I would have liked to do more to ensure he didn't get kicked out of VCU. I felt like I was being a bad, culturally insensitive social worker for not being able to help him more. I also believe that, under the surface, I thought that fixing this problem would prove I was competent. Actually, it was my supervisor who picked up on that aspect of my motivation.*

"If I could go back and change anything about this interaction, I would have been more clear about my role and limits as an intern during our first visit. We can help our clients in many ways but can't do everything that they may need. It's important to establish clear boundaries with clients so that you avoid confusing them or sending them inaccurate messages about your role. Now that some time has passed, I can see that my supervisor's concerns about her students possibly 'doing too much' was good career advice."

Kelly stepped outside of her professional boundaries and tried to do too much for the client, partly because she was new to the agency and did not understand or feel confident about the limits of her role. She might have used the cognitive strategy of education with Javid, due to what could be labeled his cognitive deficit (lacking understanding), and made him more clearly aware of their mutual responsibilities in the relationship.

Summary

The nature of all relationships is largely reflected in the mutual boundaries people develop related to their physical and emotional space. While boundaries can change over time, most people develop boundary patterns in their personal and professional lives. While these are (or should be) quite different when interacting with clients or friends, they reflect one's intentions about those relationships. As the dynamics of the social worker/client relationship throughout this book will be considered regarding such topics as the working alliance, use of self, relationship ruptures, the uses of touch and humor, and challenges presented by various types of clients, it will be seen repeatedly how important attention to boundaries is for establishing and maintaining positive working relationships. Appreciating that point and understanding the importance of reflecting on boundary-making processes toward that end is critical.

3
The Use of Self

Social workers, like other human services professionals, combine the *personal* with the *professional* in their delivery of services to clients. That is, social workers integrate their personal characteristics, which include extra-professional knowledge, skills, and values, with professional knowledge, skills, and values, in the formation of unique strategies for helping people. The "personal" also includes personality traits, tendencies, talents, biases, habits, and beliefs, all of which take root years before one's professional education gets under way and continue to evolve throughout one's life. Thus, while there is some uniformity to professional education in that all students and practitioners are exposed to similar curricular and training opportunities, no two social workers operationalize that material in quite the same way because of their unique personhood. Of course, the "personal" may create barriers to effective intervention when it contributes to conflicts with certain kinds of clients and practice situations, but it is helpful when it enables the worker to empathize and connect with clients. The purpose of this chapter is to explore the concept of the social worker's *use of self*, a process of developing self-knowledge that enables social workers to use their personal characteristics and experiences to enhance their work with clients.

"Use of self" was a central concept in the social work literature until the late 20th century, when the profession's focus shifted toward evidence-based practice and the importance of managerial, procedural, and task-focused interventions grew in perceived importance (Gordon & Dunworth, 2017). Still, the profession's current educational policy and accreditation standards make references to necessary practitioner competencies consistent with the use of self-concept (Council on Social Work Education, 2015). Competency #1 (Demonstrate ethical and professional behavior) includes the statements "Social workers recognize personal values and the distinction between personal and professional values. They also understand how their personal experiences and affective reactions influence their professional judgment and behavior" (p. 7). Competency #7 (Assess individual, families, groups, organizations, and communities) states in part that "Social workers understand how their personal experiences and affective reactions may affect their assessment and decision making" (p. 9). Thus, the profession requires that practitioners attend to drawing reflectively on the "self" in organizing their practices.

The use of self is loosely related to intersubjectivity, described in Chapter 1 in the context of relational theory. The latter concept helps social workers to understand how they and their clients mutually influence each other's thoughts, feelings, and behaviors in unpredictable ways during an intervention. Some of its related intervention strategies are contingent on the social worker's possession of self-knowledge and awareness. Clearly, a practitioner who effectively uses the self must possess these qualities as well. Still, the use of self does not imply that the social worker must engage in relational therapy. He or she may be partial to one-person psychology but effectively use those personal qualities to develop a positive relationship.

To begin this discussion, the following vignette from Emma provides an example of how a young, single, White female social worker's use of self was critical to her ability to effectively serve a challenging client.

The Detail Artist

"Mrs. Smith was a 62-year-old, Black, heterosexual, married female who, along with her husband, had served as foster parents with my agency for the past three years. They had parented three foster children in the past and were currently foster parents to two siblings, three-year-old Jay and four-year-old Sarah. Mr. Smith worked full time in construction and Mrs. Smith was a homemaker who stayed home with the children and served as the primary caregiver. I was the agency case manager who worked with the Smiths and conducted weekly home visits to check on the family. Most of my interactions were with Mrs. Smith. She displayed many good qualities of a caregiver, such as providing an emotionally nurturing environment, but she experienced some challenges as well due to a mild cognitive impairment that affected her memory and thinking. She had difficulty making decisions, understanding details, learning, and remembering information. As a result, her follow-through on administrative tasks, many of which were considered simple by others, was unreliable.

"Previous case managers at the agency had become frustrated working with Mrs. Smith, as she would often promise to attend meetings or complete reports and then forget about them. Her inconsistent behaviors made their jobs more difficult and held back the children's progress in various ways. For this reason I was surprised to find that my time with Mrs. Smith was a pleasant and rewarding experience. Looking back, I think it was because I have certain personality characteristics that helped me to mesh with her. I am by nature a concrete thinker who loves to get into the details of any task I am addressing. I enjoy breaking down projects into small 'bits' and watching them come together piece by piece. When working on my own school assignments, for example, I enjoyed reviewing them over and over. I used to try to disguise my task orientation, practicality, and lack of 'deep thinking' with my peers because I thought I was unsophisticated, but I have since learned that these traits serve me well with some clients, including Mrs. Smith.

"I worked with Mrs. Smith for six months as a student social worker. Initially, I was anxious because of her negative reputation at the agency. I tried to come in with an open mind, though, and while I recognized some of the challenging behaviors I had heard about, I found ways to collaborate with her to ensure that the children's needs were met. For example, I learned that she benefited from reminders about upcoming tasks and that she had an easier time understanding what was expected of her when a task was explicitly and repeatedly explained to her in minute detail. These kinds of interventions, as monotonous and repetitious (and annoying) as they might be for some people, were right down my alley. I noticed, too, that my calm and accepting demeanor helped her to relax with me.

"On one occasion, Mrs. Smith and I were working together to get Sarah enrolled in a pre-kindergarten program. Mrs. Smith told me that the program staff had asked her to attend an enrollment meeting to complete paperwork for Sarah. She was panicky because she had difficulty understanding what was being asked of her and what documents she should bring. I reached out to the school and asked if I could attend the meeting with Mrs. Smith, and I inquired about the documents that she needed to prepare. I was then able to follow up with Mrs. Smith and tell her (several times) exactly what she responsible for. I chose to talk with her only about the paperwork she needed to complete, as I had learned through experience that giving her too much information overwhelmed her.

"Later that week, Mrs. Smith and I attended the enrollment meeting with the children. A program assistant took Mrs. Smith, Sarah, Jay, and me into a room for Sarah to complete a developmental assessment and for Mrs. Smith to fill out the enrollment forms. While Mrs. Smith was working on the forms, I noticed that she became confused and stressed. I asked if she would feel comfortable with me explaining the forms to her again. She said yes and, calming down, was better able to focus. Once we completed the forms the assistant informed us of additional registration steps that would need to be addressed after Sarah was enrolled in school, including the timely submission of a physical examination report. The employee informed us that the program had a wait list and that Sarah's spot would go to another child if we were unable to quickly complete and return those forms. Mrs. Smith later admitted to me that this seemed like a judgmental ultimatum, and it made her feel panicky. I again informed her in clear and concise language what she needed to do. Once Sarah was officially enrolled in school, I visited Mrs. Smith and explained yet again what the school needed. Then I left her in charge of going to the doctor's office to get the physical report. Mrs. Smith was able to do so successfully.

"Social workers bring personal qualities of self in their work with clients. As a student, I sometimes felt like I placed too much focus on how I was applying the theories I was learning in class and tried to focus more on how my personal qualities affected my client interactions. I liked Mrs. Smith as a person because she allowed me to exhibit my natural tendencies to problem-solve. Our personalities were compatible, but I could understand why my colleagues, being different kinds of people, were put off by Mrs. Smith's repeated failures to follow through with tasks. She could certainly be frustrating in those ways.

"While I think we worked well together, I might have approached Mrs. Smith's situation slightly differently. If I had the chance for a do-over, I might spend more time preparing Mrs. Smith for any meetings and then let her take a more active role in the process to help build her confidence for working independently. I wanted Mrs. Smith to feel confident in her abilities to provide for the children, and the downside of my interventions was that they may have been too directive and maintained her dependence on providers. I tend to think that my behavior was appropriate in this case, but I need to remember, too, that with some clients I might be too directive. I guess there are benefits and limitations to all uses of self."

Emma was aware that certain of her personal characteristics helped her to connect with and gain the trust of an insecure client. Her love of structure, attention to detail, desire to nurture, and patience had been parts of her persona long before she decided to become a social worker. Emma had a natural inclination toward cognitive-behavioral interventions that helped her connect with clients who did not easily engage in reflection. It is fortunate, too, that she was aware that these same characteristics might be problematic in other contexts. She was uncomfortable with ambiguity and, more significantly, had a tendency toward control that would be disempowering for some clients. Her decision to focus on her use of self as part of her professional education was constructive, especially because it made her aware of her strengths *and* limitations as a provider.

With this example as a starting point, it is now important to consider the nature of the "use of self" concept, including the nature of this "self" that a social worker is using.

The Self

Defining the self is not easy. There is no consensus about what it is, if indeed it is anything continuous over time, and whether there is a "core" self (Kaushik, 2017). Thinkers from the fields of psychology, theology, sociology, philosophy, and social work have struggled for generations to articulate the essence of the self. It is variously conceptualized as a soul (constant through life and perhaps transcending physical being), an unfolding potential (as in self-actualization), an organizing activity (such as the ego), a cognitive structure, a shared symbolic experience (developing through interaction with others), and a flow of experience (existential and postmodern perspectives) (Gray, 2010; Rogers, 1986; Goldstein, 1995; Early & Grady, 2017; Denzin, 2001; Burston & Frie, 2006). The self is certainly multidimensional, and the concept of a *self-system* is thus probably more accurate.

Despite its complexity, making an effort to know one's "true" self, however one understands it, is a part of reflective practice and a precondition to using the self effectively. For the purposes of this book a self, or self-concept, can be defined as a person's knowledge of his or her physical, cognitive, emotional, and behavioral characteristics (Broderick & Blewitt, 2020). This self, or portions of it, can be largely but never completely identifiable by the individual. There are, for example, *known* and *unknown* aspects of a self, including characteristics that are known to oneself and to others (the public self), known to oneself but not to others (the private self), unknown to oneself but known to others (blind spots), and unknown (at least readily) to oneself or to others (the unconscious) (Ruch, 2010). An ideal state of self-knowledge would be one in which the last two conditions, blind spots and the unconscious, did not exist, although that is unrealistic. While never fully attainable, the development of self-knowledge is a process that continues over the duration of a career.

The way that one perceives the self is dependent in part on what other people are present in the external environment. That is, during an interaction, the characteristics of the other person draw out responses that highlight certain aspects of one's self but not others. In the previous vignette, for example, the client's lack of organizational ability drew out the social worker's love of structure.

The Use of Self in Practice

The *use of self* refers to the social worker's combining of professional knowledge, values, and skills with aspects of the personal self, including personality traits, belief systems, life experiences, and cultural heritage, toward the goals of being authentic with clients while honoring the values of the profession (Liechty, 2018). The self is a filter or medium through which one's professional knowledge, attitudes, values, and skills are conveyed. The social worker who consciously uses the self becomes able to know and integrate the personal self into the style and technique of a professional in the service of a client. This is why the personal self is a major determinant in one's choices of practice theory. It requires the integration of what one knows as a practitioner (including knowledge and techniques gained from professional education and training) with who one is as a person in the room with the client (including relational dynamics, personal belief systems and psychology, and personality traits), and how these all influence the therapeutic encounter.

Several small qualitative studies have investigated how practitioners understand this concept. In one study completed in Australia, participants ($n = 7$) described the use of self as an essential factor in the practice relationships they strived to develop with clients (Reupert, 2007). They elaborated the meaning of the concept as being a kind of ultimate integration of theory and practice enacted in the worker–client relationship. They all acknowledged it as central to social work values and the change process. In an Ontario, Canada, study, practitioners ($n = 10$) identified specific helpful aspects of themselves used in practice, including self-disclosure, using humor, and being a role model (Adamowich, Kumsa, Rego, Stoddart, & Vito, 2014). Their rationales for using self-disclosure with clients included normalizing client experiences, establishing credibility, building rapport, and providing education. In their self-reports, however, the social workers fell on a continuum from suppression of the self (denying that it has any influence), to selective use of the self, to extensive use of the self. Women used the self most extensively. Interestingly, the social workers tended to reject relational models of the self (which acknowledge the client's influence on how the social worker experiences and utilizes the self) in favor of individualistic perspectives. One researcher conclusion in this study was that social workers seem reluctant to report ways in which the self might negatively impact their practices and instead constructed a definition of self they would *like* to have. There is no reason to doubt that these were good social workers, but on this final point they seemed to possess only a partial sense of self.

This next example features Chris, a middle-aged White male social work student who had been a Methodist minister before becoming a social worker. He describes how his background prepared him well for using the self effectively with a particular kind of client.

True Stories

"Larry was an 89-year-old hospice patient residing in an assisted living facility, and I was his social worker. Larry was experiencing the early stages of dementia and had a history of several strokes from which he had partially recovered. He was a widower whose only remaining family consisted of an adult son who lived in another state. Larry had been a real estate salesman before retiring and had an outgoing personality, being quite talkative and enjoying telling stories. He often admitted to feeling lonely and displayed symptoms of depression such as hopelessness, guilt, and remorse over his past life choices. He admitted that his relationships with his mother, wife (both deceased), and son were not positive and had produced mostly pain and anxiety for him during his life. He was especially bitter toward his wife, whom he felt had only used him as a source of money. He would like to have made different choices in his life and wondered if there was still time to make any changes in the brief time he had left so that he might be more at peace with himself.

"Larry and I met weekly for four months. In our early meetings it was difficult for me to do anything but listen due to his extreme talkativeness. His stories

often include references to famous people he claimed to have known many years ago, including Generals MacArthur and Eisenhower, Howard Hughes, and former members of the mafia. It was often difficult for me to end sessions, as Larry would continue to talk even when interrupted. I would have to resort to standing and walking toward the door before he would accept that a session had to end. Eventually he began to allow more of a dialogue, although he still dominated our conversations.

"One interesting session began with Larry telling me about some dating relationships he had before meeting his wife. These included a woman he met in his hometown, but he focused more prominently on film star Jane Russell, whom he claimed to have met through a mutual friend in Hollywood. He was surprised that she became interested in him romantically. He described in detail their first date at the famous Chinese Theatre and others, telling me that he eventually ended the relationship because Ms. Russell was less mature than he was. She was allegedly quite upset at his leaving and had to withdraw from a film project as a result.

"This and many other of our sessions centered on my listening to Larry and trying to find spaces in the conversation to interject questions. I often doubted the truth of his stories but recognized that, factual or not, there were underlying truths in the things he shared with me. He had always had a difficult time with family relationships, beginning with his mother and continuing through to his wife and son; I thought his stories were constructed as distractions to his life struggles and ways for him to believe that his life had been full of drama, with himself as a heroic figure. They did help me to understand him. My role was to facilitate Larry's life reviews to bring his lingering regrets to a better resolution and to help him explore his current relationship with his son before he died. I tried to help him find new ways to interact with his son that would be constructive so that he did not feel so mired with guilt. I do believe that Larry came to terms with his negative interpersonal qualities and he had one short visit with his son before the end that he reported as pleasant.

"I think my personal qualities were especially helpful in my work with Larry. While I utilized theories and interventions from my courses, I was also aware of my life experiences that influenced my interactions with Larry, whether or not I was consciously aware of them at the time. One aspect of my personal style that was useful with Larry came from interpersonal patterns I had observed during my years as a Methodist minister. I had learned in my religious studies about the 'confessor' style of taking a church member through a reflective process that leads to self-forgiveness in order to move forward through *a problem. I noticed in my seminary studies that this confessional style was natural for me, although I developed it more fully in my ministry. It seemed to be beneficial with many of my hospice clients, including Larry, who tended to express much regret about his past behaviors. I found that it was useful early in our relationship to simply listen to what Larry was saying and reflect on it between sessions to guide my future interventions with him. My confessor style also affected my reactions to his tall tales. I was skeptical as to the facts regarding many of his stories but knew from my preaching experience that one should not let the facts get in the way of the truth of a story. Facts and truth are two different things and Larry was expressing truths that overshadowed the facts. He was describing how he had wished to present himself, and aspects of himself that were probably real but had been suppressed, as his anger was dominant. Other social workers may have been impatient with and dismissed his tall tales.*

"Still, it was a challenge for me that Larry dominated our sessions with his storytelling. I wondered then if I should try to develop a more assertive style and rely less on my client's direction in conversations. On the other hand, I learned a lot about him by listening. I still work on my assertiveness, but I believe that my approach was useful in working with Larry, who eventually had a partial reconciliation with his son."

As in the earlier example, this social worker was consciously aware of certain personal characteristics that helped him connect with a client who might have been overwhelming and even seen as delusional to another social worker. Chris's patience and curiosity about what lay behind the client's surface messages were natural traits that seemed to work well in his hospice setting. He had an affinity for narrative interventions as he gently guided his client to a reauthoring of his life story toward the goal of imagining new possibilities for future action.

The Self and the Social Worker's Style

One aspect of a social worker's use of self comes across both consciously and inadvertently in his or her *style* (Siporin, 1993). Style refers to a person's mode of functioning; ways of enacting given areas of behavior that are unique in an individual. It is a distinctive "how" of action, with characteristic features of expressing and relating to others within various social roles. A personal style is the "signature" of a person, in dress, appearance, gestures, language, diction, tone, rhythms of speech, and the use of time and space. One develops a personal style over time and, partly unconsciously, forges an individual identity to project a personal presence. The setting in which a social worker meets with a client may also become a part of his or her style, especially when it is personally crafted (such as how an office is furnished and decorated).

A *professional style* is a collective type of behavior characteristic of members of a profession. All social workers, for example, present themselves in ways that honor the profession's values: being accepting of all people as worthy or respect, seeking to enhance competence, and being alert to issues of social justice, as varied as those presentations may be. Any social worker's style is a combination of personal and professional styles, and one's style of practice expresses some of the qualities of the practitioner as an individual. In order to demonstrate genuineness, social workers should try to communicate in ways that feel natural but also that a client can readily understand. The uniqueness of every practice situation unfolds when the distinctive styles of the social worker and client coalesce. Some professionals attempt to display an entirely professional style by adopting ways of dress, speech, affect, and behavior that they believe will capture the essence of a desirable professional demeanor. While a person can probably never suppress all aspects of his or her personal style, some social workers hope to achieve high levels of detachment and objectivity in this manner, while others are drawn to a more casual presentation.

Developing the Use of Self

Developing an effective use of self requires ongoing self-monitoring, reflection, professional development, and supervision. While there is no standard formula for developing an effective use of self, several examples are included here, all of which differentiate the process of acquiring technical knowledge and self-knowledge.

One pair of authors describes two stages of learning that are significant to a professional's development, beginning with adherence to technical skills and moving toward the development of a unique, authentic style (Schneider & Grady, 2015). They maintain that the use of self involves combining the self of *what one knows* (training, knowledge, and techniques) with the self of *who one is* (personality traits, belief systems, and life experience). They include the concept of the "unconscious use of self," which involves the practitioner's becoming more aware of how his or her unconscious processes intersect with the client's and how this intersection plays out in the practice encounter. In this way, some of what has been unconscious becomes conscious. The social worker's receptivity to this dynamic fosters movement into a state of being as opposed to doing. He or she becomes more comfortable with the self and how it is projected in the practice situation. This level of presence requires authenticity and the integration of the social worker's personality, skills, and respect for the unconscious processes that unfold in all relationships.

In the first stage of learning, the student complies with academic instruction, internalizing and using the basic interventions taught by the school. The student also learns the ethical virtues of intervention, including respect, appreciative curiosity, and the attitude of not-knowing, or being open to a client's presentation without making theoretical assumptions in advance. This stage captures technical learning; that is, what to say, when to say it, and how to organize an intervention. Once a beginning level of mastery is achieved, the student is ready to move to the second stage, where what is learned is reorganized. Elements of practice that do not fit the social worker's self-system are abandoned. At this point, learning does not necessarily mean adding something to one's repertoire but at times letting go of something. This stage is more about learning to live with uncertainty, which is a break from the comfort of following a routine structure. It involves taking risks but also feeling confident in one's ability to manage risks by making intervention decisions that are appropriately based on each client's presentation. More individualized practice techniques are created through the professional's personality.

Edwards and Bess (1998) add specificity to the "stage two" process just described by recommending that social workers avail themselves of self-inventory exercises. These can take the form of written journals, listings of personal traits and behaviors that come naturally to the person, and statements about what the person enjoys about being a social worker. Nonprofessional pursuits can enhance one's growth as well, such as participation in the arts.

Elaborating on the possible content of a self-inventory, Dewane (2006) presents five operational uses of the self, all of which can be developed through a social worker's written reflections on:

Personality traits—Why am I in this field? What personal needs does my work fulfill? What traits do I bring to my work, for good and for ill? What do I enjoy about being a social worker? If a client resists my direction, how does that affect my behavior, emotions, and work? If I were to be anything other than a social worker, what would that be?

Belief systems include views of human nature, the meaning of life, and explanations of pain and suffering. The social worker may consider: What is my view of how the world works? What traumas or crises have shaped my worldview? How do I solve my own personal dilemmas? Is there congruence between my personal philosophies, those of the profession, and those of my clients? Do I project my worldviews onto my clients? How does my worldview contribute to or hinder my development of relationships with clients?

Relational dynamics include the elements of client empathy, authenticity, understanding all relationships as being unique, and self-empathy. The social worker may consider: What is my natural interpersonal style? Am I introverted or extroverted? Does my natural interpersonal style help me to convey empathy and positive regard? How do my clients perceive me? Am I capable of accurately conveying my internal experiences and feelings about others?

Anxiety—Understanding one's experiences of anxiety is important, as the ways in which one responds to anxiety can have great impact on the work being done. The social worker may consider: What makes me anxious in my work with clients? How do I experience anxiety in the work? Do I talk more when anxious? Do I tend to withdraw? Do I seek collegial assistance when I perceive that anxiety is affecting my work?

Self-disclosure is the social worker's sharing of personal information about "here and now" experiences with a client or his or her life outside the office. It may or may not be appropriate in a given instance, but it is always to be done in service to the client rather than to help the social worker get a need met. The social worker may consider: For whom, and for what reason, do I engage in self-disclosure? Can I justify its use? Am I willing to risk sharing personal failings in the service of my clients? Is my self-disclosure always for the benefit of my clients and not myself? Is this ever a boundary-crossing exercise on my part?

The following vignette provides an example of a social worker's struggle to decide whether to reveal her sexual minority status to a client who shared that status and had not been able to develop relationships of trust with her previous heterosexual practitioners. Lia understood that revealing this characteristic to her client might create its own problems in their ability to work together but ultimately decided that it was a risk worth taking.

The LGBTQIA+ Community

"Corinna was a 20-year-old White cisgender female who identified as pansexual. She had been diagnosed with post-traumatic stress disorder stemming from the verbal, physical, and sexual abuse she experienced nearly every day by her parents until she was emancipated at age 17. Corinna was an intelligent and motivated individual. She graduated high school with honors, currently was a sophomore in college, and had kept consistent part-time employment since age sixteen. Corinna expressed pride surrounding her pansexual identity but reported experiencing significant bullying at the Adolescent Growth Center, where she now lived, for her identity and physical appearance, which she described as masculine. Corinna was most comfortable in men's clothing and she did not use makeup. Once she was emancipated Corinna entered our Independent Living Program, where I worked in a case management role. The program was designed to help young adults aged 17 to 21 who came from unstable housing transition into successful adulthood. While Corinna and I worked together, she experienced frequent panic attacks, difficulty sleeping, hypervigilance, and flashbacks.

"Corinna had a disorganized attachment style, as evidenced by a lot of push/pull dynamics from her in our work together. For example, she would oscillate between canceling sessions and wanting to come in multiple times a week. Corinna and I were scheduled to weekly until her 21st birthday, four months away, at which time she would be terminated from the program. She initially expressed distrust for new people, including myself. However, with time, I believe that we established a good relationship.

"Corinna and I had met twice before this session without developing much evident rapport. She expressed distrust in me and would not say much else. During our third session, Corinna shared some of her homophobic experiences at the agency but quickly shut down and said, 'Never mind, you wouldn't get it.' I asked her what I wouldn't understand. She stated that I wouldn't understand what it is like being gay in this world. I paused for a moment to think about how to respond. I openly identify as queer and had experienced much

homophobia in my own life. I didn't want to make the session about my identity and experiences, but I did want her to feel that I could relate to her.

"While I paused, Corinna expressed wanting to have one person who 'gets it.' I asked what it would mean for someone to 'get it.' She paused and then said they would have to be gay. I asked her what it would mean to her to work with someone who was gay. She paused again and then asked me directly if I was gay. I asked her what it would mean to her if I said no. She shrugged her shoulders and said that it wouldn't make a difference because neither is anyone else she works with. Then, I asked her what it would mean to her if I said yes. She said it would make her want to work with me because I would understand her. I nodded my head as I thought about what to say next.

"I decided to tell Corinna that I identified as queer. I went on to explain while we both shared an LGBTQIA+ identity, and there is solidarity and community in that identity, it does not mean that I have the same experiences as hers. I explained that only she has her own experiences and that she is the expert in them, regardless of our shared identities. I asked her if what I was saying made sense, and she nodded. We paused again; I wanted to give her space to talk or process in her own head for a moment. She then said with tears in her eyes, 'I get what you're saying. I'm glad to know I'm not the only one here.' With that comment, I believed that I made the right choice in self-disclosing.

"I had faced a dilemma about whether to disclose my gender identity to this client. I had to figure out what the potential positive and negative effects would be on our relationship if I did so. I decided self-disclosure would more than likely strengthen our relationship, and I doubted that it would have much potential to do it any harm. The research shows that LGBTQIA+ individuals do not report the same levels of safety or effectiveness within the therapeutic setting as individuals who identify as cisgender and heterosexual. The perceived safety and effectiveness of services are reported to be significantly higher within therapeutic settings that tailor services to LGBTQIA+ identities. When a social worker has a personal experience that echoes that of their clients, it makes them more sympathetic to the client and gives them a more empathetic understanding of their situation that leads to a better relationship. All of this indicated that my work with Corinna would most likely be effective if I tailored my intervention to be LGBTQIA+ specific and share that I hold an identity in that population.

"I believe that my use of self had positive effects on the therapeutic relationship as evidenced by Corinna's statement following my disclosure. I later brought up this encounter with my supervisor, who agreed that the disclosure *appeared to be helpful. Furthermore, although there was always the potential for a negative effect to arise in the future, my supervisor and I also agreed that we did not anticipate any such effects. Although there was no way for me to predict the future of my relationship with Corinna at that moment, after several months it seemed that the disclosure served to strengthen our relationship and ultimately make our work together more effective."*

This vignette provides an example of how the use of self can influence the decision to self-disclose about certain personal aspects of one's life. Lia had been utilizing person-centered intervention and realized that her ability to be authentic with Corinna required her to reveal herself as queer. It is generally not advisable for a social worker to become this personal in self-disclosure, because the client may come to rely on the social worker as a friend and advocate regardless of the behaviors that the client might exhibit, but in this instance it does appear to have been therapeutic. Still, it is admirable that Lia and her supervisor remained aware that negative outcomes were possible and should be monitored. While it is unknown what interventions Lia subsequently provided, she might have used her self-disclosure as a basis to initiate relational interventions, as Corinna may have been inspired to share her personal challenges more deeply and benefit from experiencing Lia's emotional responses.

As a final example of self-development, faculty at a university in Spain implemented a formal reflective learning model to be addressed in students' education prior to the start of their practical work experiences to help them develop self-knowledge and a professional identity, which together potentiate the effective use of self (Pallisera, Fullana, Palaudarius, & Badosa, 2013). The three components of the educational model were:

Constructing personal life paths—understanding how one's experiences influence how life paths are shaped and how educational experiences affect one's actions, expectations, and relationships; and exploring personal motivations for wanting to help others

Attending to the self in practice relationships—exploring skills that lead to the construction of honest relationships in professional life; listening and empathy as the basis for relationships; analyzing challenging issues that may arise in practice; boundaries; and personal prejudices that influence relationships with clients

Exploring professional identity—developing the ability to analyze and understand one's cultural competence; understanding how stereotypes, sexism, and prejudicial elements may be transmitted; exploring the image of the preferred professional identity; and identifying and analyzing underlying assumptions attributed to professionals in the field.

Instructors utilized a variety of educational activities to cover these topics in the curriculum, such as reading and analyzing the life stories of other professionals as a basis for reflection and then producing personal stories and experiences to be shared with peers for their feedback.

The next vignette recounts the story of Erica, a 27-year-old Asian American female student who was experiencing negative feelings about her client but through self-examination was able to locate the source of those feelings and in turn use her natural inclinations toward advocacy for the client's benefit.

A Battered Man

"Mr. James was a 56-year-old White male who came to reside in our domestic violence emergency shelter after being abused by his girlfriend. He had a history of homelessness and had been involved with the police several times in the past for domestic issues, both as a victim and perpetrator. Mr. James reported that he had experienced frustrations in trying to gain independence from his perpetrator/girlfriend. Most recently she allegedly stole his wallet and thus he had no money, identification, insurance card, or social security card. He was accepted into our shelter for purposes of safety and to receive case management services for help in establishing a life without the perpetrator. I was assigned to work with Mr. James.

"When I first heard about and then saw Mr. James, I felt confused. While I had worked with survivors of domestic abuse in the past, they had all been female. Mr. James was a large man, seemingly able to take care of himself, and it was hard for me to believe that he was a victim. Because he had been a perpetrator of violence in the past, I wondered if he was claiming to be a victim as a defense against his own abusive behavior, which I had heard of some men doing. It was in this state of skepticism that I began working with Mr. James.

"In our first encounter, I entered Mr. James's room to give him a bag of food, toiletries, and aspirin for his injuries. I was surprised to see that his injuries were significant, as his head was wrapped in a bandage and his eyes were

swollen. To build rapport, I made small talk with Mr. James by asking how he was doing and if he had everything he needed to feel comfortable. He began talking to me about the difficulty he was having processing everything he had been through while also trying to adjust to this new space. He was concerned about his identification and benefit cards being stolen and that the injuries to his eyes were preventing him from using the phone to make calls to have the card replaced. Mr. James was also concerned about the whereabouts of his perpetrator and stated that he was unsure how to get in contact with the police to get answers to his questions. Because I was there partly in an advocacy role, I offered to assist Mr. James with these phone calls, an offer he gladly accepted.

"*I have always been a natural advocate for the underdogs of the world, and this is probably the main reason why I became a social worker. Realizing that I was having mixed feelings about Mr. James as a legitimate client of our agency, I decided to delve into advocacy activities on his behalf as a way of compensating for my partly negative reaction to him. Noticing that Mr. James had a sense of humor also helped me feel better about working with him, because I like to make jokes. Mr. James once joked with me about smelling burning from his brain from working too hard on his paperwork before I came to help. I responded, 'I knew I smelled smoke in the hallway. I thought you were roasting hot dogs.'*

"*After arranging to have his benefit card replaced and leaving a message for the police officer involved in his case, I checked in with Mr. James about how he was feeling both physically and mentally. He was relieved to have the phone calls taken care of but stated he was 'not doing so hot' mentally. After some gentle questioning, he opened up about the long history of abuse he had experienced, including being stabbed and needing surgery for a broken nose. It was clear that Mr. James was uncomfortable speaking about a topic that made him feel vulnerable, and he apologized repeatedly for becoming tearful. He added that 'men shouldn't have to deal with this stuff.' By that time, I was feeling guilty for having judged Mr. James negatively. My assumptions about the client had changed by now and I was able to respond to him with empathy.*

"*When working with Mr. James, I ultimately drew upon my professional and personal styles. From a professional side, I engaged him as an expert of his own experiences and tried to focus on the factors that were influencing his situation. Both are characteristic behaviors of members of the social work profession. My personal style showed in my utilization of small talk to build rapport with Mr. James. It was my personal choice to build our rapport by engaging the client in conversation about various carefree topics and engaging what I perceived to be his appreciation of humor. His body language showed that he felt relieved when we joked together.*

"*I was eventually able to use my empathetic sense of self to help develop our relationship. Not only did I become able to listen actively and maintain positive regard, but the combination of Mr. James's physical injuries and his tearful, vulnerable admission of years of abuse and embarrassment almost caused me to break composure and become tearful myself. One of the most important parts of the self I bring to practice is my belief in survivors and desire to make them feel special after being manipulated and victimized. I became a strong advocate for Mr. James's interests with the courts, housing authorities, and various government agencies with which he had to deal to get back his lost resources.*

"*The relationship dynamic of a male experiencing intimate partner violence is not the most common. Mr. James often mentioned his embarrassment being a man experiencing violence. Fortunately, my lack of previous experience assisting male survivors of violence and the initial anxiety surrounding my willingness to be helpful was unknown to him. I tried to remain cognizant of my gender identity as a female and how, given my historical distrust of men who claim abuse, that could have negatively influenced our relationship. It was helpful to me to remember that Mr. James was an expert on his own experiences and pull from my academic knowledge of the dynamics of violence to become supportive of him. I should say, too, that my agency supervisor was helpful in me recognizing my negative countertransference and identifying natural strengths that would help me overcome it. I was pleased that I was able to move past my anxiety of working with a male survivor and build a strong working relationship with Mr. James.*"

Erica appeared to be comfortable working with the client population of domestic violence survivors and had developed a clear stance of advocacy regarding their needs. While some of her technical skills (knowledge and values) were evident in this vignette, her ability to effectively use her "self" was temporarily compromised by her admitted distrust of men who claimed to be abuse survivors. She did not have experience with such men in her practice setting, so despite her awareness (in the Pallisera et al. formulation) of the personal motivations for her work, and her professional identity as an advocate, she had not attended to the possibility of holding personal prejudices toward men who alleged abuse. Fortunately, Erica became aware of this blind spot though self-examination and the help of a supervisor and addressed it in time to become an effective service provider for Mr. James. It is interesting to note that, while continuing to work with her client in a person-centered manner, she decided to become a fierce advocate for him as a way of compensating for her earlier mistake. Erica could further utilize Dewane's (2006) personal inventory outlines to reflect on other personality traits that may help and hinder her caring capacity, better comprehend her belief systems about the dynamics of abuse from the perspectives of both genders, and better comprehend her relational style—specifically, how different types of clients may perceive her.

Summary

Social workers benefit by being aware of how their personal characteristics contribute to their effectiveness in relationship development with clients over and above their use of formal theories and intervention strategies. This "self," which contains these personal characteristics, can be understood as a filter or medium through which one's professional knowledge, attitudes, values, and skills are conveyed. When one has an understanding of these characteristics and how they can be utilized to promote one's practice effectiveness, one is engaging in the "use of self." Of course, personal characteristics can also get in the way of being responsive to the needs of clients, which is another reason why understanding the "self" is critical. Self-awareness is a process that begins during professional training but should command the attention of social workers throughout their careers. Several sets of guidelines were provided in this chapter to promote the constructive use of self. A part of self-awareness involves attending to one's personal style, or nonverbal manner of presentation to clients that includes tone of voice, posture, mannerisms, and other automatic behaviors. These habits or predilections often escape one's own scrutiny and can perhaps be best perceived with the help of significant others or by watching oneself working on camera. However it is developed, the constructive use of self maximizes a social worker's capacity to engage with clients.

4
The Working Alliance and Cross-Cultural Competence

There are many ways that social workers can attend to the development of positive relationships with their clients, including, as has been discussed in the previous chapters, using appropriate practice theories, establishing appropriate boundaries, and learning to constructively use aspects of the self. Another strategy that can facilitate positive connections with clients is monitoring the *working alliance* (Horvath & Greenberg, 1994). This is a pan-theoretical concept that promotes a collaborative stance between a client and practitioner and is associated with positive intervention outcomes. The working alliance has been researched since the 1970s and has been shown to be a valid means for practitioners of all disciplines and theoretical perspectives to assess the quality of their relationships with clients over time (Zilcha-Mano, Eubanks, Muran, Safran, & Winston, 2018). Many research instruments have been developed to measure the concept (Doran, 2016), but it can also be less formally assessed by practicing social workers. The purpose of this chapter is to review the concept of the working alliance and illustrate how it can be established and monitored. Later in this chapter we will explore the concept of *cross-cultural competence* in relationship development, which is critical for alliance development.

The Working Alliance Defined

The concept of the working alliance has been developed in research studies that ask practitioners and clients to independently rate the perceived quality of their connection at various times during an intervention. Results of those studies indicate that the alliance includes the following three factors (Fuertes, Toporovsky, Reyes, & Osbourne, 2017):

Forming an emotional bond encompasses a set of practitioner activities that includes acquiring informed client consent for all interventions, utilizing physical space that the client considers to be comfortable, allowing clients (at least initially) to talk about problems as much as they wish, and providing responses that feature empathic reflection, strengths-based feedback, and feelings validation.

Worker/client goal consensus refers to the parties collaboratively drawing up a problem or goal list that they both believe is appropriate to the client's needs. In this process the social worker encourages the client to elaborate on his or her own goals, articulates them in the client's own words, provides feedback on their practicality and their falling within the purview of the social worker's expertise and resources, and perhaps helps the client to rank their importance, which can help them determine where to begin.

Task collaboration involves engaging the client in specific intervention tasks, activities, or procedures that are understood by both parties to be logical means of solving problems and achieving goals. The timing and pacing of these tasks must be appropriate in the context of the client's motivation and capabilities, and they must be consistent with the client's lifestyle, worldview, and expectations.

It is important to note that children do not discriminate multiple measures of a working alliance, as adults do (Roest, van der Helm, Strijbosch, van Brandenburg, & Stams, 2016b). Rather, they tend to develop a global feeling about the practitioner based on that person's general presentation. The therapeutic alliance is generally captured in one-dimensional ratings, such as, "I like when my mentor is around." Developing alliances with children will be discussed in detail in Chapter 7.

From the perspective of the client, actions that promote the working alliance provide evidence that the social worker cares, is competent, and is interested in his or her welfare. Interestingly, however, while shared worker/client perspectives about the alliance are associated with positive relationships, research indicates that there is often a low association between their respective ratings (Heinonen et al., 2014). More specifically, and perhaps surprisingly, practitioners are poor predictors of their clients' sense of alliance. Social workers should thus not assume that their own views of the therapeutic alliance are shared by their clients. Further, during an ongoing intervention the working alliance may, and probably will, fluctuate. One implication of this point is that it may be useful for social workers to "check in" with their clients occasionally (depending on the length of the intervention) about each person's perceptions of the quality of their collaboration. Clients may not offer such feedback unless invited.

It may seem logical that tending to the three components of the working alliance will promote constructive collaboration, but some limitations to the validity of the working alliance as a guiding framework have been identified (Doran, 2016). Some argue that the alliance may only be a measure of client cooperation, a sign of acquiescence rather than collaboration. It can certainly be productive at times for the two parties to negotiate their work in a manner that includes conflict and perhaps even some lingering mistrust on one or both sides, as this can prevent complacency from setting in (Moeseneder, Ribeiro, Muran, & Caspar, 2019). It is also argued that the alliance, especially when assessed later in the intervention process, might be a result of positive outcomes, not a predictor of them. The focus in this chapter will be on the nature of the alliance in the early part of intervention, and attention to the topic of managing ruptures over time will be addressed in Chapter 5.

Practitioner Characteristics and the Working Alliance

Because practitioners and clients may assess the working alliance differently, some studies have investigated the impact of the practitioner's personal and professional characteristics on the alliance ratings of both participants. Several are reviewed here to illustrate the point (Heinonen et al., 2014; Savaya, Bartov, Melamed, & Altshuler, 2016). Regarding the practitioner's personal characteristics, relational styles that feature a composed, responsive presence; a capacity for empathy; and an ability to communicate concern predict symptom reductions for clients in both short-term and long-term work, but they do not necessarily predict positive client-reported alliances in longer-term interventions. (In this review, short-term interventions were described as those that lasted no longer than 20 sessions—not really "short.") It seems that a practitioner's engaging and affirming relational style is well suited for short-term alliance building, but over time client-reported alliances are based more on the practitioner's ability to implement constructive interventions (which is, of course, appropriate). The client rates the alliance higher when the social worker demonstrates an ability to adapt to the client's needs and manifests the skills needed to help him or her overcome any intervention challenges that arise over time. For some clients who anticipate a long-term relationship, a practitioner's initially engaging and affirming style may not produce a strong alliance if the client feels that he or she is being drawn prematurely into an intense exploration of his or her problem issues.

Practitioners' ways of managing relationships with friends and family (such as how open, forceful, or private they experience themselves) tend to predict how they will experience their relationships with clients. Further, a practitioner's self-confidence, work enjoyment, and positive levels of satisfaction in his or her personal life often correlate with positive alliances with clients. These characteristics do not necessarily correlate with strong client-rated alliances, however. On the other hand, the opposite of some of those practitioner characteristics, such as the experience of professional distress (which predict his or her low alliance ratings), do not necessarily correlate with negative client-rated alliances. It seems that social workers can at times effectively prevent their lack of confidence and enjoyment of the work from being conveyed to the client in a way that affects the client's perception of the alliance.

Practitioners sometimes have negative feelings about a client, of course, and based on the above reviews it appears that those feelings cannot always be overcome by self-rated advanced relational and practice skills, as clients often pick up on their negativity. This suggests the importance of the social worker's self-awareness and monitoring of any possibly negative verbal and nonverbal messages when providing interventions. It has been shown that experienced practitioners who are aware of their negative feelings about a client can contain themselves in a way that does not harm the alliance.

These findings about worker/client alliances and their occasional disparity are intended to remind social workers that they should never make assumptions about the quality of their collaboration without addressing the topic over time. The two vignettes that follow provide examples of how social workers try to develop the working alliance as defined in this chapter. The first example features a social worker who successfully cultivated the three components of the alliance, but the practitioner in the second example was not successful in doing so.

The Ambivalent Client

> *"My name is Angela, and I was a 24-year-old single White female when I worked with Heather. My client was a 21-year-old single White cisgender female in her final year of study for a social work degree. She had begun*

receiving counseling services from my agency two months ago, reporting a depressed mood that negatively affected her interactions with family members and romantic partners. Heather's family history featured parental conflict and separation, parental and sibling substance abuse, and domestic violence. She had not been in counseling before but said that her depression had been worsening since her senior year of high school. She added that there was significant depression among her nuclear and extended family members. None of them were psychologically minded and they all relied on Heather, the social worker, for emotional support, which she described as draining. Heather said that it was a recent breakup with a boyfriend that prompted her to finally seek help.

"Heather and I met weekly for one hour and had completed seven sessions thus far. She spoke about her childhood issues, academic stressors, and current depression, as well as the abrupt and distressing end to her most recent relationship. Heather was elusive about why the relationship ended, although it seemed related to a 'bad event' she often alluded to but would not describe. Because her commitment to counseling seemed tentative I was careful to develop a working alliance with her. I used our first few sessions to join with her and validate her feelings of worry, sadness, and anger. We processed her feelings of abandonment, inequity, and betrayal in all her relationships. Slowly, and in pieces, she started to refer more frequently to the 'bad event' and her resulting symptoms of restless sleep, crying episodes, never feeling safe, memory problems, guilt, and dissociative symptoms when she starts to think of the event.

"Prior to our most recent session we hadn't met for three weeks due to the school's holiday break. In that session Heather seemed more upset than usual and talked continuously, with pressured speech. After speaking for a while without a break (or seemingly a breath) she said, 'I feel like I just don't want to stop talking.' I said, 'I'm glad to hear you want to talk to me today, but if you'd like you can slow down a bit.' She let out a sigh, nodded, met my eyes, and smiled. I prompted both of us to take a few deep breaths and 'see what comes to mind.' Heather followed the rhythm of my breathing for a few deep breaths, and then we made eye contact. I raised my eyebrows and leaned forward, nonverbally prompting her to continue. Heather said that she might have been so talkative because she had been looking forward to this session for weeks. When driving to her appointment, she had decided that we would talk about 'the really bad thing that happened.' Heather then admitted that she had been raped four months ago by an acquaintance. I could see that this disclosure was a point of major anxiety for her. I validated her anxiety and asked for her consent to continue talking with her about the topic. She agreed, and we went on to further explore her mixed feelings about addressing the issue. While overwhelmed at first, Heather eventually calmed down.

"Noting that we had about 15 minutes left in the session, I asked Heather if she wanted to talk more about the assault next week. She said, 'Yes, but I'm pretty scared, honestly. I've never spoken about it without crying, and I haven't told anyone all the details.' This had been her goal for seeking help, although it had taken until now for her to say so. I assured her that it was safe to process her emotions in our time together. I assured her that she was the only person who could tell this story, and that she could tell me as much or as little as she wanted, and that we could take breaks and make the space as comfortable as possible for her.

"Regarding tasks for Heather to pursue in the coming week, I asked if she could identify anything that would be soothing for her in our next session. After some deliberation, Heather identified that having soft jazz music playing would be helpful. She had described music as her 'outlet' and was involved with the local live music scene. I told her that was a great idea, and we decided that she would make a playlist of soothing music and listen to it every day as a way to relax herself. Next, she asked if she could take her shoes off and sit more comfortably on the couch during our next session. I told her that she could do so, and that she could dress more comfortably, too, if that would be helpful. Heather then asked if she could bring something to eat or drink with her, and I assured her that she could. We confirmed that we would start to unpack and process the sexual assault in our next session.

"The key relationship issue in this encounter was our working alliance. I believe that my intervention approach was to use person-centered intervention as well as some behavioral principles of trauma-informed care. I listened with empathy, regarded Heather as the expert in her experience, and summarized her statements into thoughtful reflections. I was particularly intentional in fostering a sense of safety and choice for her, setting the expectation that we would discuss concerns at her pace, and ensuring that we could take breaks at her discretion. I demonstrated to Heather that I valued collaboration with my clients when I asked for her thoughts about how we could set a comfortable environment. Additionally, I maintained a nonjudgmental stance as she shared her experience with me."

Angela consciously set out to attend to all three components of the working alliance with Heather, but she had the sensitivity to suspend the pace of her planned strategy when she noticed that the client was having trouble articulating details of an event that might represent her most pressing problem. She worked hard to engage with her client, utilizing person-centered and trauma-focused interventions, but held back on assuming the nature of Heather's ultimate goals until the client was ready to risk sharing the details of the critical incident. Even so, Angela was able to solidify their alliance by creating a safe environment that facilitated her client's willingness to trust. Once that happened, Angela patiently invited Heather to articulate her own goal and subsequently supported it. Angela's attention to the process of task development was also characterized by her giving Heather the opportunity to suggest appropriate tasks.

The next vignette provides an example of how *not* to develop a working alliance, as a rigid adherence to a preordained session structure prevented the student practitioner from connecting with her client. Taylor, also a 24-year-old white female, came to the session with an agenda that ignored the standard practice of "starting where the client is." In doing so she failed to make sustained empathic contact or promote collaboration with her client on goals and objectives. Fortunately, the social worker's mistakes, which were based on her inexperience, did not appear to create a significant rupture in the relationship.

The Agenda

"Miranda was a 54-year-old White, heterosexual woman, self-referred to the agency with a complaint of 'an overwhelming sadness I just can't shake.' After conducting an assessment, I diagnosed her with major depressive disorder, single episode, and posttraumatic stress disorder. Miranda had experienced several traumatic incidents during her life, including the losses of her mother at a young age, her husband six years ago, and her father a year ago, along with the stress of being diagnosed with cervical cancer two years ago (she was currently cancer free). Miranda was experiencing complicated grief because she had avoided grieving the losses of her husband and father. She wanted to work on reducing her depression and anxiety and getting through her grief. Her main supports included her aunt, children, and sister, although she reported feeling like a burden to them.

"Miranda was the first client I had ever seen on my own as a social work student. This was also her first time attending therapy. My agency was short term in focus, usually limiting practitioners to six sessions with clients. We were encouraged to use cognitive-behavioral interventions so that we could clearly track evidence of client progress during our work. Early on, Miranda said she felt comfortable with me, which eased my anxieties about being able to connect with her. However, I also felt anxious that maybe I was not able to help her as much as an experienced therapist could. Our first two sessions focused on rapport building, goal setting, and education about what she could expect from therapy. Miranda was emotional in our sessions but often mentioned that she felt better afterward.

"I felt pretty good about the nature of our relationship in those first sessions, but during our third meeting I experienced a setback. At this point we had finished up the 'official' assessment protocol so I had no script to guide me. I have always been an over-preparer and felt as though I needed to have several different topics and activities prepared to present to a client. I was anxious about wanting to provide Miranda with the help she needed in the time provided, and I calmed myself by doing too much pre-session prep work. Of course, this meant I wasn't able to be flexible in letting Miranda take the initiative in our meetings. This proved to be problematic in the third session. Miranda came in upset, sharing that she had just gotten a call from her doctor after her six-month cancer checkup. He told her she would need to come in for more tests because they 'found something.' She was also stressed about her recent job loss, stating that she no longer had health insurance and was wondering how she would be able to care for herself if her cancer was back. Miranda was upset—and I wasn't ready for that!

"While my client was expressing her fears, I was experiencing my own anxiety about trying to keep the session 'on topic' as I had planned. I took notes on everything she said, but instead of attempting to meet her needs in that moment and showing empathy for her pain, I continued to be preoccupied with my own list of things to accomplish, such as completing a coping plan form that she could reference for the next few weeks while I was on break. The session ran over by thirty minutes because, although I let her talk, I eventually insisted that we complete those other items.

"The relationship issue that emerged in this encounter was the absence of an alliance. We were on separate pages, so to speak, due to my behavior. Miranda came with her needs for the session and I had my own agenda. I became anxious that I wouldn't have enough time to get through my items and I let that feeling dominate the session. I believe that I came off as stiff and impersonal rather than showing the empathy she needed. Miranda was cooperative and said that she had no problem with having a longer session to get through my 'session checklist,' but looking back I feel guilty that I pushed aside her needs of the moment, which were to process the new stresses in her life. While she did not complain I know I could have been more helpful than I was. Additionally, I worried afterward that she might come to anticipate that kind of structure in future sessions and decide that she should not come with her own agenda.

"A social worker can never fully prepare for a session because she can't know what the client will bring. I could not know that Miranda had gotten a frightening call from her doctor and lost her job. My professional self wanted to stay organized, but letting go of that structure would have been better for building my relationship with Miranda. Since then I have learned how to find a balance between structure and flexibility in my work, and that short-term interventions need not be rushed. Looking back at this encounter I realize that the content I brought was less important than the emotional support that the client needed. I should have trusted that there would probably be time to address the client's goals and tasks during that hour, but if not, that was okay."

It is common for beginning social workers to prepare for their sessions with a structured agenda, partly because it makes them feel safer and better focused. Still, the practitioner should always "start where the client is," knowing there is no way to predict what the client will bring. Taylor wanted to develop the working alliance by formally attending to its three components but became flustered when her client was not "cooperative" with the process. In fact, while she espoused the use of cognitive-behavioral interventions, it does not appear that in her haste she provided any real intervention. While Taylor concluded that her mistake did not irreparably damage the relationship (based on her memory of their subsequent sessions), it is possible that the client was uncomfortable with the disjointed process. Taylor also mentioned that she took a lot of notes during this encounter, which itself can distract a social worker from fully attending to a client.

Cross-Cultural Competence

Developing working alliances with clients, or constructive relationships by any definition, depends in part on the social worker's grasp of the impact of their cultural backgrounds based on such characteristics as race, ethnicity, religion, economic status, age, sexual identity, and health status. When social workers and their clients come from different perceived backgrounds, they should try to understand how their clients experience the world with regard to the following:

- How do they experience and define their problems?
- How do they identify the sources of those problems?
- What are their primary emotional experiences?
- How do they move from the experience of a problem to a selection of goals?
- What do they believe are the appropriate steps to take to achieve goals?
- Who should be involved in the problem-solving process?
- What is the proper role of the social worker?

Being able to thoughtfully answer these questions demands that social workers address their cross-cultural competence.

For social workers to develop productive working relationships they must be able to adequately comprehend their client's perspectives on the world. The word *adequately* is used here because it is impossible for one person to fully understand another person's perspectives. All people are unique, and social workers should never assume that they are on the same page (so to speak) as their clients, even when they share surface similarities. On the other hand, relationship development is often more challenging with people who possess evident characteristics quite different from one's own. A social worker's ability to connect with clients of various backgrounds is often referred to as *cross-cultural competence* (CCC), a capacity that is never fully achieved but requires lifelong professional dedication (Cox, Sullivan, Reiman, & Vang, 2009).

CCC refers to a social worker's capacity and willingness to be attuned to a client's culturally imbedded experiences, investigate the relevant details of that client's experiences, and share with the client some of the social worker's own relevant cultural experiences, to create shared moments of understanding (Lee, 2011). It is best understood as a dynamic and relational process rather than a "one-way" activity. That is, CCC arises *between* a social worker and a client and attends to each person's understanding of the other rather than being a static trait of the social worker. As a part of this process, the practitioner must be willing to share information about his or her own culture as well as seek to understand that of the client. In this way the client becomes an active participant in a shared process of understanding, which facilitates mutual trust and respect. CCC also works against any tendencies toward defensive behavior by either party that might be rooted in distrust and that can compromise all facets of the intervention.

Considering CCC in the context of the working alliance, a client who is "different" may wonder (regarding bond and trust), "Can this social worker understand me? Can I trust him or her?" and (regarding compatibility of tasks and goals) "Can we work together effectively?" There are many ways in which social workers can develop greater cultural competence, and many books are written about how to better understand members of diverse populations (e.g., Sue, Rasheed, & Rasheed, 2016). The process described here is based on a conviction that social workers must always be curious about perceived differences without making stereotypical assumptions about members of diverse groups. (For example, one might erroneously expect that a rural American adult will have negative feelings about Middle Eastern immigrants, or that a conservative Christian will be anti-gay.)

In the development of one instrument used to measure CCC (Bernhard et al., 2015), five essential factors emerged that social workers can usefully apply to their work:

Motivation and curiosity. This refers to a social worker's determination to be open to exploring characteristics of a client that might represent a significant difference between them, as opposed to downplaying the relevance of any such differences to the relationship-development process. If a heterosexual male social worker meets an openly transgendered male client for the first time, he might decide to actively investigate (although not necessarily at the beginning) some of the client's perspectives on sexuality and stigma rather than passively wait for the client to offer them. The social worker may assume that such a conversation is necessary to know how to help the client and, in turn, it allows the client the opportunity to share any concerns about their differences.

Attitudes. This refers to the social worker's tolerance and respect of differences, and his or her observation of professional values that ensure the preservation of a sense of dignity when interacting with a "different" client. The social worker must engage in ongoing self-examination to ensure that personal biases, which all people possess, are not making the process of connection more difficult. One example of this process is a female social worker's effort to maintain a constructive working attitude toward an adult male who has engaged in sexual violence toward another female despite her tendency to dislike such persons.

Empathy. This is a desired characteristic in all social worker/client interactions, of course, but in this context it suggests that the social worker puts himself or herself in the client's shoes in an effort to understand the client's emotional experiences related to difference, and then conveys that understanding to the client. For example, a social worker tries to understand as much as possible the emotional experiences of an aging individual whose family is trying to convince him of the need to move out of his home to an assisted living facility against his will.

Only the final two elements of cross-cultural practice, presented next, include factors related to knowledge and skills. The first three factors pertain to a social worker's need to observe values that are emphasized throughout professional development. CCC is thus not only a matter of learning about different cultures but a willingness to explore it with a client so that the two parties can come to an enhanced mutual understanding.

Knowledge and awareness, the fourth factor, refers to culturally specific knowledge gained through reading, taking courses, or other professional-development activities. This is a process that should occupy a social worker's entire career. For example, if a social worker has a Latina client and has little knowledge of or experience with members of that culture, he or she can set out to become educated about its typical perspectives and traditions. This trait is illustrated prominently in the second of the following vignettes.

Intervention skills, the final factor, refers to the social worker's ability to incorporate knowledge of a client's cultural perspectives into a treatment plan that reflects those perspectives. For example, it is said that members of lower socioeconomic groups often look to professional helpers for practical, task-based assistance with specific problems rather than seeking a more reflective, holistic interpersonal experience (Andrews, Griffiths, Harrison, & Stagnitti, 2013). A social worker who comes to understands this (after working past any stereotypical assumptions) will be able to serve that client well by addressing the relationship and providing interventions that fit with these expectations.

In summary, CCC helps to mediate the working alliance. The social worker attempts to attune to the client's cultural voice, open sensitive dialogue on cultural differences, and balance the client's and his or her own perspectives about problems, tasks, and goals. Social workers with greater CCC will also be more responsive to ruptures when they occur and will be able to initiate appropriate repair processes, using the experience to consolidate the alliance. (This process is illustrated in the first vignette below.) CCC can provide corrective emotional experiences following a rupture when the social worker demonstrates that he or she can tolerate the client's resentment of a misunderstanding.

The following vignettes describe efforts by two social workers to develop CCC with clients who grew up in cultures quite different from their own. The first social worker was only partially successful in this task, despite his efforts, while the second practitioner experienced major success with the relationship following a rupture. Both examples illustrate how acquiring cultural competence can be quite challenging. The first vignette comes from Roger, a 27-year-old single White male social worker who had difficulty developing a working alliance with Dan, a 28-year-old single second-generation Chinese American graduate student.

The Pre-Med Student

"Dan was working toward admission into medical school but was having difficulty concentrating on his studies. He was in danger of failing a course he needed to pass to stay on track for medical school admission. He came to the counseling center to get help managing his anxiety related to that task and to some family conflicts. Dan described the source of his tension as having to deal with perceived personal slights from several friends, his sister, and his mother. Dan told me that he needed help learning how to get these people to behave more responsibly toward him so that he could focus more clearly on his own studies.

"I learned that Dan was the older of two children (his sister was 22) born to a couple who had grown up in Taiwan and moved to the United States before the children were born. His father was a surgeon and his mother a homemaker, and they had divorced when Dan was seven. He and his sister had lived with their mother since then and had only occasional contact with their father. Dan tried hard to be a good son and brother but held firmly to the position

that others should always accede to his directives. He believed he was always 'right' in decisions he made about his mother and sister (regarding where they lived, how his mother spent her time, and what kinds of friends and career choices his sister should make). Regarding his friends, Dan felt that whenever there was a conflict it was always their fault. He gave an example of a friend who had arrived more than 20 minutes late on two occasions for scheduled social outings. The second time Dan demanded that the friend apologize for being insensitive, and when the friend did not do so to Dan's satisfaction, the relationship ended. These kinds of disruptions were common in his life. Dan's family and friends often did not accept his admonitions, so he wanted to learn from the social worker how to better help these other people see that he was always 'rational' in his behaviors.

"I thought that I knew some basic Chinese family cultural characteristics, but I also read up on the topic in a book. It appeared that Dan had internalized the values of his culture; he understood that without his father being present he (as the oldest son) needed to assume responsibility for the well-being of his mother and sister while also achieving high social status for himself. What I didn't understand was the extent to which this responsibility could control the life of the male figure. I shared these observations with Dan, but he was not interested in discussing them in much detail, saying only, 'In my family I'm responsible. That's the way it should be.'

"As our relationship got under way I empathized with Dan's position and tried to help him address his concerns, and I did not take a position on the appropriateness of his goals. In an effort to avoid challenging his assumptions about his family responsibilities I first utilized a reflective style of intervention, encouraging him to consider the balance of his responsibilities to himself and to his friends and family. I soon became concerned about Dan's rigidity in his attitudes toward others. He liked to process his experiences with his mother and sister from week to week, and I routinely reflected to Dan the difficulty of his competing demands related to his desires to help his family lead safe and productive lives and becoming a medical doctor. Before long Dan began challenging my nondirective feedback. 'This is all too vague. I want to know what you think I should do here.' 'How can I approach my sister so she won't be so defensive about my input?' 'I tell my mother she shouldn't speak to my dad so often, but she keeps doing it. How can I get her to stop?'

"Dan understood the difficulty of balancing his desires for personal advancement with his need to care for two adult family members, but he seemed to distort the motives of others as oppositional rather than expressions of their *own personal inclinations. In recognizing Dan's rigidity as in part related to a cultural value, I shared this point with him and tried to help him reflect on the possibility that the behaviors of others toward him might not be intentionally oppositional, but indicative of differences of opinion, and that perhaps Dan could reward himself for his well-meaning efforts while recognizing that one's influence over others cannot be absolute. I patiently reminded Dan, 'You are in a difficult situation, trying your hardest to do the best for your family, and it's frustrating that you can't find ways to help them understand your concern for them.' 'It hurts you to see other people move in directions you believe are not good for them.' 'You feel strongly that certain people should do what you suggest even though they disagree.' Despite my responses, which I believed to be empathic, Dan became increasingly frustrated with me. 'I thought you were a professional. Why can't you come up with some solutions?'*

"Dan always came back to the position that he was 'rational' and others were 'irrational.' I decided to begin using cognitive interventions because he had a practical, concrete perspective about his situation. For example, I helped him devise several behavioral strategies for concentrating better on his schoolwork. Still, he accused me at times of being incompetent for not answering his questions concretely enough, and after six months of regular meetings brought up the idea of terminating: 'Maybe I should see another counselor.' I responded, 'I do think that your concerns about your family and friends are legitimate, and I'll continue to try to help you consider how you might deal with them in ways that are true to your sense of responsibility and also your own goals.' But Dan disagreed with most of my input regarding how he might implement change activities and eventually decided to terminate with me. I hoped he would eventually perceive that his influence over others was limited and that people have different ideas regarding what is best for them. During our final session together he said to me, 'I don't know if I've gotten anything out of this, but I appreciate that you tried.' It was a nice comment, but I was still frustrated that I had not been able to help Dan resolve his problems. In retrospect I also regret how frustrated I was with Dan's rigid presentation, which resulted in my feeling tense during many of our sessions.

"I often wonder how well I had understood Dan from a cultural basis, despite my efforts to do so. He never wanted to talk about his culture when I raised the topic, suggesting to me that it wasn't germane to his issues, but if I had a greater awareness of Chinese cultural family life, as well as ways in which his mother and sister may have stopped observing some of those traditions, perhaps I could have developed a better alliance with Dan."

Roger was certainly aware of the cultural differences between himself and his client, and he tried to learn about Dan's culture so that those differences would not become an obstacle to his ability to be helpful. Roger was motivated and curious, had a respectful attitude toward his client, was empathic, and intentionally developed knowledge about his client's culture. He tried to tailor his intervention strategies to be compatible with Dan's worldview. Still, those interventions were ultimately not helpful to the client. It cannot be known for certain what might have been more helpful in Roger's quest for cultural competence, but there are at least two possibilities. First, he might have had more open discussions with Dan about their differing perceptions of the client's problem in an effort to find more common ground, and second, he might have tried harder to accommodate his client's desire for more directives to address the problem, even though that went against Roger's general collaborative orientation.

This second example—by Kat, a 30-year-old middle-class White woman—has a more positive outcome but again illustrates the difficulty of acquiring cultural competence and then understanding how to use that new knowledge constructively with a family that represents, for the social worker, a diverse population.

The Patriarch

"I was a second-year social work student placed in the Children's Care Center, a program located in a major metropolitan hospital with many specialized medical services. Many of the patients, who came from around the state to get their unusual and complex medical needs met, did not have extensive resources, including transportation. It was my job as a case manager to work with the children and their families to make sure they attended all their appointments at the hospital and followed through with prescribed home health care procedures.

"The El-Masri family was referred to me when their six-year-old daughter Lateef came into the program because of losing much weight. She was found to have several serious health problems, including a previously undetected heart defect, a rare muscular disorder, and a failure to thrive condition. Sadly, Lateef had been born with these medical conditions. The El-Masri family was African; Lateef's parents had lived in Egypt and moved to the United States only three years ago. Lateef was in and out of the hospital during the year

I worked with the family (there were no siblings) and the doctors wanted me to make sure that the parents understood the child's medical conditions and needs. The doctors, I should add, maintained a strictly formal relationship with the couple.

"I had an extremely difficult time engaging the family and building trust with them. Dad was a biologist with a research firm; he was often unavailable for our meetings at the hospital or their home, so I didn't get to know him for a while. Mom was always available, however, and when the child was in the hospital she was always at her bedside. I had most of my initial contact with mom, who for some reason always seemed standoffish and withdrawn, not seeming to take my input seriously. Neither mom nor dad wanted me to attend their daughter's medical appointments, although doing so was a requirement of my job. I noticed that when dad was able to attend he would often yell at the doctors, sometimes looking as if he might become physically aggressive with them. I did not understand why these intelligent people were so oppositional, so I decided to go to the library and read about the family's cultural background.

"I found some material in a book about multicultural counseling about the specific area of Egypt where the parents had lived. I learned that theirs was a highly paternalistic and male-authoritarian society, which helped me realize that I had been going about establishing a relationship with them all wrong. I had been trying to connect first with the mother, but instead I should have been prioritizing dad's involvement, even though he was less accessible. So, for the next few months whenever we were all together I intentionally spoke only to him, and never to his wife. (I made a point of attending every appointment when he would be there.) When he could not attend an appointment, I called him promptly afterward to let him know what had transpired. Because dad was a highly educated biologist I started communicating with him from that perspective, using language and metaphors that he would understand, given his limited grasp of English. I began to share my curiosity about their backgrounds, asking him and his wife many questions about their culture, which they seemed to appreciate. Once I gained his trust, dad became open to my meeting with his wife alone. She, too, warmed up to me, seeing that I was showing her husband proper respect. I was eventually able to help them understand the severity of their daughter's illnesses and how attention to the prescribed therapies at home would maximize her recovery chances. I was also able to provide some supportive counseling to mom as she was grieving the loss of a normal, healthy future for her daughter.

"Still, we had setbacks. At one time I learned that they had been feeding their daughter orally at home instead of with a gastrostomy tube (inserted into the stomach), as they should have been. They did not accept that their daughter could not eat in the 'proper' way, and I had to explain repeatedly the danger in which this placed their daughter. (She would fail to digest the food and continue losing weight.) They still did not adjust their actions. We had a few tense meetings about this and at one of them I had to become confrontational, seeing that their cognitive deficits (lack of knowledge about the implications of their behavior toward Lateef) was putting their daughter at risk of death. I explained that I might need to call Child Protective Services to intervene on their daughter's benefit, which might result in her temporary removal from the home. This did not sit well with them, of course. During this time, at one of our tense meetings, mom had brought me a Christmas present because she knew I celebrated the holiday, but before the meeting ended she asked for it back. I felt awful and had a hard time sleeping for a few days afterward. But I remained consistent in my practice and my interest in their culture. I still called dad after every meeting, showed up to appointments, and helped mom to process the medical information. Eventually I was able to help them see that they wanted their daughter to get better and the best way to do that would be to use the gastrostomy tube on a regular basis. Lateef then began gaining weight.

"It was difficult to walk the line of building rapport, being culturally sensitive, and reinforcing boundaries needed for the child's safety. As our conflict about the feeding tube was resolved, we processed one day how betrayed they had felt by me, in a constructive and calm manner, and we were able to put the rupture behind us. I never again felt that I might need to call Child Protective Services. Lateef would always be a medically complex child, but she was gaining weight and receiving all the therapies she needed. I also think that I helped mom cope as she grieved for her daughter and had to make many major decisions after the shock of not having a healthy baby. This helped her become better able to care for Lateef and reduced some of her depression.

"After graduating I took a full-time job elsewhere, and I told the El-Masri family of my departure two months in advance. They both cried, and I did, too. I helped them transition to another social worker and educated that person about the family's cultural norms. This was one of my favorite families ever for many reasons, but I was mostly pleased to have made a connection with them despite our cultural differences. I think it was my own research and open curiosity with them that helped this to happen."

What is so impressive about this vignette is that the social worker started from a position of no awareness about her family's culture, but with a determination to become culturally competent she not only educated herself with books but also invited the family to educate her. Her willingness to learn and to understand seemed to have convinced the family of her integrity, and they finally became receptive to the doctor's recommended tasks as presented by her. Dad's "scientific" mind made him amenable to behavioral interventions regarding his child, which he eventually came to accept. Notice, too, that the issue of cultural differences did not change the social worker's dedication to the welfare of her primary client (the child), even if it meant inviting conflict with the family.

Summary

The concept of the working alliance, with its three operational components of the worker/client bond, agreement on goals, and agreement on intervention strategies, provides a practical means for social workers to monitor the quality of their relationships with clients over time. Such monitoring can be done with formal instruments, but the social worker's inviting clients to provide regular feedback on their perceptions of the quality of the three components may be an effective way to proceed. Attention to cultural or other significant worldview differences between the social worker and client is a part of facilitating a collaborative relationship, and this can be ensured through CCC, which features the five elements of motivation and curiosity, attitudes, empathy, knowledge and awareness, and skills. Not every professional relationship can be collaborative, but these tools can help to increase the likelihood of its occurrence.

5
Relationship Ruptures

The social worker's first task with clients is to develop a positive relationship, but as the intervention progresses he or she faces the ongoing challenge of sustaining that relationship so that the client can experience a positive environment for working toward his or her goals. As with all relationships, however, despite the practitioner's best efforts, conflicts and misunderstandings may develop between the two parties that can threaten their bond and possibly undermine the work being done. As one example of the ubiquity of this threat, most trauma clients in one study reported that they had been angry with their social workers, and perceived that their social workers had been unjustly angry with them, at least once during those relationships (Dalenberg, 2004). The term *relationship rupture* refers to any event in direct practice that contributes to a deterioration in the social worker/client relationship once it has been positively established (Safran & Muran, 2000). The purpose of this chapter is to help social workers to become more skillful in identifying and repairing ruptures so that the relationship can resume in a productive direction.

Some relationship ruptures are more significant than others. For example, a small and temporary rupture might occur when a client reacts with anger to the social worker's momentarily forgetting his or her first name, and a major rupture might occur when a client feels betrayed by a social worker's breach of confidentiality. Still, practitioners should never make assumptions about the severity of a rupture without addressing it with the client. For some clients the first example might indeed be devastating. A rupture's threat to the future of the relationship can only be determined in context, and what is emphasized here is the importance of the social worker's attending to all such perceived occurrences, as they may all have some effect on the quality of the relationship.

It is quite possible to repair ruptures, and doing so can sometimes result in a *better* working relationship (Cash, Hardy, Kellett, & Parry, 2014). That is, when clients (and their social workers) learn that they can effectively resolve interpersonal conflicts with a significant other, they may develop greater confidence in the durability of relationships in general. In the repair process feelings are expressed and accepted, the rupture is resolved, and the relationship may be strengthened, hopefully with clients transferring their learning to other relationships. This new awareness also provides clients with an appreciation for the "personhood" of the practitioner as well as the self and helps them become aware that they can be accepted and valued even as fallible human beings. For clients with chronic interpersonal problems, this can be quite a revelation.

The following vignette is provided to give an example of a relationship rupture. It is the story of a 26-year-old White male social worker's experience of a rupture that was sudden and severe, and about which he was not sure how to respond. Fortunately, the social worker (Kevin) was able to salvage the relationship with his client Trevor, a 28-year-old White male with schizophrenia, although prior knowledge about the repair process may have helped him to do so sooner.

No Medication!

"I was upset with myself for the way I handled an incident with one of my clients, even though, fortunately, there was no lasting harm done. I had already seen Trevor six times over six weeks at the community mental health center, and despite his chronic mental illness, the intervention had been going well. I enjoyed working with clients who had schizophrenia and felt that I was good at establishing relationships with them. I was pleasant, listened well, was calm, and wasn't pushy about their setting goals quickly. My experience was that people with schizophrenia often felt pressured by practitioners to make changes in their lifestyles too soon, and as a result they didn't engage well with those persons. Trevor came in each week ready and eager to talk about his daily activities and get my thoughts about how he was doing. He was delusional about many of the people he encountered in his neighborhood, but he stayed out of trouble, so rather than confront his ideas I tried to help him organize his days in a structured, more productive manner.

"Clients with schizophrenia are accustomed to practitioners trying to get them to take medications. If my clients were agreeable about doing so, that was fine with me, but if they weren't I often didn't push the issue, especially if their behavior not causing problems for themselves or others. I hoped that they would eventually agree to take meds, but I thought this would most likely happen if

they were given the choice and time to think about it. That was the situation with Trevor. He didn't think he had a mental illness and didn't want to take medications. I initially urged him to consider doing so and he said he would.

"Trevor lived with his parents and spent his time in their basement making furniture that was amateurish and certainly not salable. He believed that he could make money selling the stuff. He had delusions about being a world-famous physicist but generally kept these to himself, although he "meditated" about "altering spacetime" for several hours each day. In response to Trevor's ideas his parents had encouraged him to see a counselor about career options and he had reluctantly agreed to do so. His parents were of course concerned about their son and the seven-year illness that left him a social isolate outside the family. They wanted him to take medications, which he had done once before with some positive results, but Trevor was not willing. For the time being his parents were happy that he would at least see a counselor. After a few visits Trevor relaxed with me and seemed to enjoy our meetings. I was pleased to earn his trust and tried to help him organize his time in such a way that he got out of the house more often and considered getting a part-time job for spending money. I would label my approach as both reflective, as Trevor enjoyed analyzing his relationships with his family, and behavioral, toward his expansion of productive daily activities. Trevor seemed to value my feedback about his concerns.

"Then I screwed up. I got a call from dad before our seventh session (Trevor had given permission for me to talk with dad) who was upset about his son's increasing agitation. Trevor was becoming more openly angry with his mother and that morning had lashed out at her after she confronted him about being lazy. Dad's concern was so strong that I agreed to talk with Trevor about medications again. Later that day, partway during our session, I said something like, 'Trevor, I know I said I wouldn't talk with you about medications again, but I got a call from your dad, and I tend to agree from what he said that your anxieties are getting higher and you might do something you regret. I think you should see someone about medication, and I can help make that happen.' What happened next completely surprised me. Trevor stood up, shook his index finger at me angrily, and shouted, 'You said we weren't going to talk about that again! You promised! I trusted you! You're a liar!' And he stormed out of the office. I was stunned and not sure what to do. I had never seen Trevor upset like that.

"I was mad at myself afterward for basing my decision to take up the medication issue on his father's concerns rather than my own. I hadn't even asked

Trevor about the morning incident with his mother. Not knowing for sure how to proceed, I decided to do nothing and give him time to cool off. I thought it would be destructive if I reached out while he was still angry. I waited for five days and then called him. I did not mention the incident of the previous week but said, 'Hi, Trevor. Tuesday is our next appointment, but I wasn't sure if you were planning to come in. Will you?' He hesitated for a few seconds before responding, 'Not yet,' and then he was quiet again. I felt badly and only asked, 'Can I call you next week?' He said, 'I guess so.' When I called him a week later he agreed to come back in.

"When Trevor and I met, two weeks after the rupture, it seemed like business as usual in that he was pleasant and talked about his activities of the previous week. He didn't seem to be thinking about what had happened between us. The session went on like this for about 10 minutes, when, during a natural break in the conversation, I said, 'Trevor, I wanted to ask you about something that happened the last time we met. You were upset with me for bringing up the topic of medications when I told you earlier that I wouldn't.' Right away, Trevor tried to apologize: 'Yeah, I know, I'm sorry. I was having a bad day. I shouldn't have gotten mad.' He was taking responsibility for his outburst, but I didn't want him to do that because it wasn't fair to him. I wanted him to understand that it was okay for him to be angry about it. 'I'm not upset with you, Trevor. You had a right to be angry. I promised I wouldn't bring up medications, and then I did. Your dad was worried about you, but I could have talked with you more about that first. I'm sorry I did that.' Trevor seemed to appreciate my comments, and responded, 'Okay, thanks, I'll remember that.' I added, 'I might bring up things or make comments from time to time that bother you, even though I wouldn't do that on purpose, but if you ever get angry with me, that's okay. I hope you'll be able to tell me about it.' Trevor appeared to take this all in and again he responded, 'Okay, that'll work. That's good.' Then he raised an unrelated topic on which we focused for the rest of our visit.

"Looking back on this episode, I was aware of the rupture as soon as it happened, but I made a mistake in that I didn't make a stronger effort to acknowledge it to Trevor until the next time we met. I could have apologized before he got out the door. The rupture was due to my own change of heart about medications after speaking with his father and I wanted him to understand that he had a right to be angry with me. He seemed to accept my support of his position, which was a relief to me. That was the extent of our repair process, and it worked out okay, but it could have gone either way, and I wish I had *been more proactive about addressing the issue. I should add that, to my utter surprise, about four months later Trevor raised the topic of medication himself and said that he'd like to try using it again. I referred him to a psychiatrist and he accepted a prescription that seemed to help him."*

Kevin survived this rupture, but he may have done so more constructively if he had understood the relationship rupture concept more fully, including the steps that can be followed toward resolution. These topics are addressed next.

The Dynamics of Relationship Ruptures

Relationship ruptures originate in social worker behaviors that for some reason are off-putting to the client. The reasons for such ruptures include:

- The client's feeling caught unprepared to address a topic initiated by the social worker (for example, challenging a substance user's denial too soon)
- Confusion or ambivalence about the intervention process
- The aftermath of any confrontation, even when it may be considered by the social worker to be therapeutic (Couthino, Ribeiro, Hill, & Safran, 2011). Confrontations by the practitioner are more likely to produce ruptures and result in early client terminations when they occur early in the relationship (Locati, Rossi, & Parolin, 2019).
- The social worker's perceived failure to be empathically attuned to a client regarding a particular topic (such as minimizing the depth of a client's grief over a lost pet).

The social worker may or may not be aware of the occurrence of a rupture, as there are many ways in which clients might manage it. The two general types of client responses are the *confrontational* and *withdrawal* modes (Safran & Muran, 2000). In the confrontational response, the client reacts to a social worker's comments or behaviors in ways that are visible, with active objections or displays of anger. In the previous case illustration, Trevor stood up, made an angry comment to his social worker, and walked out of the office. In the withdrawal response the client does not display any obvious emotional reactions to the rupture but as a result becomes less actively involved in the intervention process. The client may lose trust in the practitioner. In one study of relationship ruptures clients in the withdrawal mode either shifted the topic of conversation or avoided it with distracting comments (Eubanks, Lubitz, Muran, & Safran, 2019).

Ruptures resulting in client anger are more likely to be resolved when the social worker does not challenge the validity of that reaction but seeks to maintain connection with the client by attributing the event to problems in the relationship rather than the client (Walker, 2008). By accepting responsibility in this way, the worker demonstrates that he or she can make mistakes. In general, a social worker who is attuned to the client's overall level of engagement may notice when a rupture has occurred and address the issue immediately. Of course, a client's changed affective presentation may be due to something other than a rupture, such as a life event unrelated to the intervention or sensitivity to a topic being discussed. For example, a client who has recently been reprimanded by her boss may come to the session in a state of agitation that is unrelated to the professional relationship but plays itself out in a tense interaction.

While all clients are unique, studies indicate that some types of clients demonstrate shared tendencies in their rupture responses. In one literature review trauma clients were found to report that the most ineffective practitioner responses to their anger were a perceived absence of a clear response or a switch from a typical pattern of encouraging emotional expressions to questioning their relevance (Dalenberg, 2014). For example, the social worker may openly wonder why the client is "overreacting." Positive client responses were related to the practitioner's taking some responsibility for the client's anger and teaching the client that expressions of anger are possible in a good relationship. In a study of 105 clients from a university mental health clinic it was found that the negative outcomes of relationship ruptures were the clients' feeling disengaged from and distrustful of the practitioner, with an increased level of distress and less hope that their problems can be resolved (Bartholomew, Gundel, & Scheel, 2017). While these are serious outcomes, a successful repair process could restore the client's hopes for improvement and even provide the client with a greater sense of resilience.

Another literature review found that the parents of children with emotional and behavioral problems often experience ruptures with social workers in part as a defense against their feelings of shame and guilt about the part they have played in their children's difficulties (Baldwin, 2014). Practitioners need to be sensitive to this pain and perhaps raise with the parents the normality of those emotions during the repair process. When the child experiences a rupture, he or she is often reluctant to raise the topic, believing, in accordance with his or her internalized social norms, that the adult (the social worker) should take responsibility for identifying and addressing it (Manso, Rauktis, & Boyd, 2008). Social workers who work with clients experiencing severe mental illness, who tend to interact with a variety of service organizations and providers, face a greater-than-average risk for alliance ruptures (Yerushalmi, 2015). Those clients are usually engaged with various professionals in diverse contexts and, given their range of needs and different levels of motivation to achieve them, they often experience goal ambiguity. Ruptures can occur when they experience an empathic failure from any practitioner who fails to adequately understand the stresses they face within the system. They may also engage in splitting behaviors among different helpers, coming to favor some more than others. Ruptures can occur in any of those settings.

Steps in the Repair Process

Despite the many circumstances that can surround relationship ruptures, the process of their repair follows the sequence described next, although not all of the steps will be followed in every case (Baldwin, 2014; Hill & Knox, 2009; Keenan, Tsang, Bogo, & George, 2005; Moesender, Ribeiro, Muran, & Caspar, 2019; Safran & Muran, 2000; Yerushalmi, 2015).

> *Acknowledge the rupture and respond empathically.* If the social worker perceives that a relationship rupture may have occurred, he or she should ask the client about the possibility in a welcoming manner. If the social worker is mistaken, there is no harm done and the effort reminds the client that the social worker wants to understand him or her as clearly as possible. In the process of acknowledging a rupture a client may express anger, disappointment, or hurt; minimize what occurred; or try to take responsibility for it. The social worker's empathic, accepting reaction will hopefully encourage the client to express the needs that were threatened by the perceived event. The practitioner might even prevent ruptures by reminding the client on a regular basis that his or her thoughts about, and reactions to, the intervention are always welcome.

Consider the alliance dimension that is affected by the rupture. Because the working alliance, as discussed in the previous chapter, incorporates the three dimensions of worker empathy, agreement on goals, and agreement on tasks, it may be helpful for the social worker to assess which of those, if any, is the source of the rupture, so it can be specifically addressed. The rupture may also be due to a misunderstanding between the participants that is unrelated to the three dimensions.

Explore the process by which the rupture occurred. Once a rupture has been identified, the social worker should guide a reflective process with the client in which the events leading up to the rupture are reviewed and understood. This requires clear and direct shared communication, with both parties involved, so the social worker must be careful not to dominate the process too assertively and not to react defensively to any accusatory client comments, even if they seem inaccurate. Some ruptures may be rooted in a client's longstanding disappointment with how the social worker is conducting the intervention, so the discussion may cover numerous events that have occurred over a period of time.

Identify the part that each person played in the rupture. The social worker must recognize that the occurrence of a rupture is not the client's "fault" in the sense that, for example, the client simply misperceived some action of the social worker. Most relationship ruptures involve the behavior of both persons. That is, the social worker has behaved in a way that was distressing to the client, even though that result may not have been intended. The social worker should admit that he or she had a role in the process, not only because it is true but also because it relieves the client of any perception of being "wrong" or "less than" and invites the client into the process of examining what happened between them without feeling blamed.

Investigate the characteristic of the client and social worker that contributed to the rupture. This step requires a shared reflective process including how the rupture relates to the client's or social worker's accidental misuse of words, interpersonal patterns, underlying needs, psychological characteristics (although any such factors should be addressed in concrete terms to ensure clarity), concerns related to the unequal power in their relationship, or perhaps cross-cultural misunderstandings (as described later in the chapter). The social worker may acknowledge, for example, that his or her wish to move the client too quickly through an intervention led to an underestimation of the client's ambivalence or lack of confidence.

Summarize the discussion and check the accuracy of the emerging understanding. The social worker must check with the client often during these reparative conversations to make sure that they are understanding each other as accurately as possible. Recalling that some clients withdraw emotionally following a rupture, the social worker may need to draw the client out and remind the client that his or her feelings are always respected.

Negotiate a resolution to the rupture. While the social worker may lead the conversation, both parties should share ideas and consider a variety of solutions to the rupture—ways to internalize their new understanding of the relationship and adjust their ways of interacting. This might resemble a process of problem solving, whereby a variety of possible solutions are considered and discussed until a viable resolution is agreed upon. The social worker, for example, might agree to in the future explain her reasons for asking certain personal questions about the client before doing so. The client may in turn agree to try harder to express his or her discomfort with certain questions. The practitioner must take the initiative to revisit the issue if the strategy turns out to be unsuccessful.

Go forward with the relationship and interventions. At some point attention to the rupture must end and the parties should move ahead with their work. The repair process might proceed rapidly or take several sessions to resolve. It must be kept in mind, however, that even if both parties agree that the episode is resolved, it may take the client time to regain trust in the social worker if that has been violated. In many cases, however, the relationship will be strengthened, with each party experiencing a heightened mutual respect as they have successfully addressed and resolved a sensitive issue.

The following vignettes provide examples of how the steps of rupture repair can be implemented. The commentaries are provided in part by the student social workers themselves. The first illustration was written by Brianna, a 27-year-old White female placed in a family practice agency.

The CPS Report

"I worked with a couple that included Maria, a 62-year-old White female, and her husband Mike, a 61-year-old White male. The couple had been clients of the behavioral health unit at my agency for one year, and of the agency's medical clinic for several years. Both Maria and Mike suffered from major depression, while Maria also suffered from post-traumatic stress disorder related to an assault by a former partner ten years ago. I had been working with them from a cognitive-behavioral theoretical perspective to help them learn and implement new behaviors that would help to alleviate their distress.

"The couple, who were both physically disabled and had experienced periods of homelessness at times, had agreed eight months prior to babysit three-year-old Brooke, the daughter of a family friend, to obtain additional income. Shortly after this agreement the child's mother began leaving Brooke with the couple for extended periods of time, often overnight. At the time of this meeting, Maria and Mike reported that they had not seen Brooke's mother in four weeks and were concerned that she was engaging in prostitution. The couple loved watching Brooke, however, and stated that she was like a granddaughter to them, 'the light of our lives.' Her presence brought them joy, helped both of them to manage their depressions, and improved the quality of their marriage.

"Maria and Mike, however, lived in what they themselves referred to as a 'shack,' with broken wooden floorboards that exposed the dirt ground underneath, no running water, and at times no electricity, as their landlord 'doesn't pay the bill.' Maria had previously reported that she bathed Brooke on the floor so that the water could drain directly onto the ground. Due to Brooke's apparent well-being, myself and my supervisor initially agreed not to involve Child Protective Services (CPS) in the case. The couple was informed, though, that if these conditions persisted a call would need to be made to CPS in order to uphold ethical standards of care. Maria and Mike both expressed understanding this and said that they wanted the best care for Brooke.

"Having worked with this couple for four months, it was evident to me that Brooke had brought joy to Mike in particular. During our sessions, to which they brought the child, Mike often held Brooke and kissed her cheeks, smiling and stating, 'I wish we knew you sooner.' The couple recently admitted, however, that Brooke's mother had not been paying them for their services, which resulted in a greater financial hardship for them. Additionally, during our previous session, the couple expressed concern that they were unsure of when

Brooke had last seen a pediatrician. Though Maria and Mike had attempted to take Brooke to the medical provider at this agency, they were told that given the laws of confidentiality, this would not be possible without her mother's written consent. They were told that they had one week to contact Brooke's mother and obtain written consent for her to see a doctor. If they were unable to do so, I would need to contact CPS, given Brooke's need for a well-child checkup. The couple expressed their understanding and stated that they would contact Brooke's mother immediately.

"At the following session Maria and Mike again presented with Brooke, who appeared to be well groomed and clean, with no evidence of malnourishment. The couple stated that they were able to obtain food for Brooke from a food pantry that was willing to supply them given their current circumstances. They added that they were able to visit the local Goodwill to buy Brooke clothing since, as Mike stated, 'she's growing like a weed.' Mike again presented in bright spirits and was doting on Brooke. After further questioning, Mike admitted that he bought Brooke new clothing instead of getting food for himself and Maria. He was able to obtain an emergency bag of food from the same food pantry that assisted them with Brooke's food, but this was offered as a one-time service. Regarding Brooke's need for medical care, Mike reported that they had been unable to connect with Brooke's mother since our previous session. She had promised to bring written consent to allow Brooke to be seen by a pediatrician but had not done so. Despite numerous attempts to contact the mother, Mike reported that she had not answered or returned their phone calls.

"I decided that I needed to involve CPS in the situation, as it was apparent that Brooke was still unable to visit a pediatrician and the couple would be unable to consistently provide for Brooke's needs. When I informed the couple of this decision I did my best to be nonjudgmental by acknowledging their efforts to provide good care for the child. Maria stated that she understood but Mike did not agree. Despite Maria's attempts to contain her husband, Mike became irate, shouting at me that he no longer wished to be serviced by this agency because Brooke was 'everything' to them. He complained that it was unfair that CPS was being called, as he had done 'nothing to deserve this.' After allowing a moment for Mike to gather his thoughts, I tried to reiterate the importance of Brooke being appropriately cared for, as well as the process of mandated reporting. I explained to the couple that they demonstrated a strong ability to tend to Brooke's emotional needs, and it was evident that they deeply cared for Brooke, but it *was also critical that Brooke be physically cared for. Mike did not accept this response, standing up to leave and stating that he would 'never come here again.' Maria tried to apologize and express her understanding of the process, and then she followed her husband out.*

"I was distressed by my need to contact CPS, which appeared to result in broken trust from Mike's perspective. Still, I was aware of the need for safety and security of the child and had previously expressed my role as a mandated reporter to the couple. I felt that I would not be loyal to the couple should there be a negative outcome for the child because of Brooke not receiving medical care. I felt as though I had little choice but to contact CPS. I did emphasize that contacting CPS was not an accusation that this couple was incapable of providing for Brooke, but to ensure that Brooke was able to be cared for both physically and emotionally. Still, I felt terrible.

"To my great relief, the couple returned the following week. Mike was calm and apologetic, and stated that he had been nervous and reacted without considering his actions. I was relieved by his comments but felt that it was important to process what had happened at the end of the last session. He agreed to do so. I acknowledged that we had had a major disagreement but that I understood his position, given how hard he had worked to be a good surrogate caregiver for the child. I suggested that it may have seemed that I was not crediting his devotion to the child and was judging him harshly. I reviewed with the couple the process of our mutual efforts to make sure that Brooke received proper care and that it was the natural mother's unreliability that 'forced my hand' and led to our rupture (although I didn't use that word). Mike had already expressed the part he played in the rupture, so I added that while I had tried to be clear with them about the possibility of contacting CPS, perhaps I had not adequately talked them through the process of what would be involved in such an investigation, and the possible outcomes, some of which might be favorable to the couple. Mike stated that he understood now that within my role as a mandated reporter I was left with no choice but to contact CPS. I reminded Mike that his angry reaction reflected his great care for Brooke, and my own actions were not personal but based on my requirements as a professional. I said that given those factors I saw no reason why we might not resume our relationship constructively. As a final effort toward resolution I focused on Mike and Maria's strengths as 'grandparents' to Brooke, while continuing to note the importance of Brooke receiving medical care, which is what we both wanted."

Brianna had addressed all eight steps in the repair process and experienced a relatively quick positive outcome with Mike, because he came to the session aware of the part he played in the rupture and wanted to "make up" with the social worker. The couple was able to resume working constructively with Brianna right away. (The child, by the way, was taken into custody by CPS while the agency located and began working with the mother on her suitability as a parent.)

The next vignette includes a similarly positive outcome and comes from Meaghan, a 23-year-old White female with a special interest in working with children.

The Reluctant Talker

"Daryl was a nine-year-old White male in the third grade who lived in a single-family household with his seven-year-old biological brother, foster mother, and foster father. Daryl had been removed from the care of his biological parents one year ago and been placed in the custody of the County Department of Social Services. Since then, he and his brother had been in the care of several foster families. Daryl's foster parents sought services from my counseling agency because of his frequent emotional outbursts, which included physical violence. During these outbursts he hit and kicked his foster parents in addition to breaking and throwing various objects. Daryl also struggled regularly with sleep due to nightmares and encopresis. These symptoms suggested that he may have been sexually abused. Daryl had been diagnosed with post-traumatic stress disorder and attention-deficit/hyperactivity disorder (ADHD). He took one medication for his ADHD and another to help him sleep at night.

"I began working as Daryl's individual intensive in-home counselor after his previous counselor was removed from the case. I worried that Daryl might resent me for replacing the previous counselor but we quickly built rapport through our playful interactions. During our first month, Daryl and I mostly played games to strengthen our relationship and create a safe space for him to talk about his emotions and past traumas. Eventually, we were able to discuss Daryl's emotional outbursts toward his foster parents. I could tell he was reluctant to talk about this by the way he would hide his face when the subject came up. He often said that he didn't want to talk about feelings in general or talk at all. I had a feeling that Daryl's reluctance to talk was related to his suspicions of sexual abuse from his father. After I shared a therapeutic story about a boy getting his mouth stolen,

which is a metaphor for sexual abuse, Daryl disclosed that his mouth had been stolen a few times, but he did not elaborate.

"Our rupture occurred after six weeks together when I felt that we had a strong relationship. He was finally talking about the sadness behind his angry outbursts. Although he still was having outbursts after visits with his father, we were able to practice grounding techniques for preventing them. Because Daryl had become more verbal, especially about 'getting his mouth stolen,' I felt that he might be able to talk about his abuse history if I begin pushing him more about those events. Knowing that this would be risky, though, I think I unintentionally abandoned my normal congenial personality style and took on a more rigid persona for that meeting so that I might be able to keep us on the delicate topic when talking about Daryl's traumas. Only later did I realize that I came into our session with my own agenda: to get Daryl to talk in detail about his traumatic events. By doing so, I violated an existing value we had established, which was to maintain the office as a safe and predictable environment for him. As the session went on, and I continued to be insistent in my questioning, it was obvious that Daryl was becoming more and more uncomfortable. He began hiding his face behind a bean bag and redirecting my attention toward his toys in an attempt to avoid the conversation. Eventually, I relented and asked Daryl if he would feel more comfortable writing a letter to me about his 'mouth getting stolen.' He agreed to do that and talk with me about it the following week.

"As soon as the session ended I began to feel anxious. I recognized that I had probably pushed Daryl harder than I should have. I later learned that Daryl had what his foster parents called a 'two-day temper tantrum' afterward, and they had needed to go to respite care for the weekend. When Daryl's foster mother described the situation to me over the phone the following Monday, I felt at fault. I doubt that he would have had such an intense emotional outburst if I hadn't pushed him so hard.

"Later I talked about this encounter with my supervisor. I had videotaped the rupture session, and she pointed out that I had not been my normal self that day, as evidenced by my facial expressions and body language. She concluded that I was stuck in my head rather than being emotionally present. I think that because Daryl was still having emotional outbursts after his visits with dad, I was feeling insecure as his counselor. I felt like I was failing him, which led to me pushing harder than I should have and violating our established pattern. Her main advice for me was to resume my previous demeanor with Daryl and to be patient with his process.

"Still, at our next session, I made another mistake by asking Daryl at the outset if he had written the letter I suggested. That assignment had been a part of our rupture episode, of course, in that I had asked him to write about feelings he didn't want to share. I guess I hoped he had decided to disclose some of his secrets after all, which was presumptuous of me. At least I should have waited to see what he brought to the session. Daryl said that he did not have time over the weekend to write anything, and I assured him that it was okay.

"Then I addressed the rupture. I began by acknowledging the tension of our last meeting and apologized for upsetting him by asking so many questions. I said that it was not fair of me to push him as hard as I did when he wasn't ready. I told him that I had been imposing my own goals for his therapy onto him, which wasn't appropriate. I told him that it was my mistake, and there was nothing wrong with how he reacted. (His reaction to me had been one of withdrawal, as he had tried to change the subject and move near the toys.) I was pleasantly surprised that Daryl responded by saying that he was scared to talk about certain things out of fear of getting his dad in trouble. I told him that was fine. I then attempted to recreate our sense of a safe environment by letting Daryl know that he could talk to me about the past only if and when he was ready. I repeated this statement several times that day because I wanted to be sure he understood it. Because Daryl was a quiet boy, and because he always had a hard time talking, I knew that I needed to lead the process of addressing the rupture. For the rest of the session, we talked about his outburst from the previous weekend while playing his favorite games. It seemed that were moving on. Also, his comment about not wanting to get his dad in trouble seemed to indicate that he still trusted me.

"I think my apology to Daryl was helpful in resolving the rupture. As a child, it is likely that he did not receive many apologies from adults. By doing so, I think I was able to reinforce trust between us."

It is clear that Meaghan was responsible for the above rupture because of her perceived need to take on a more assertive persona to successfully lead her client through a difficult but important conversation. She took control of the session, which was out of character for her and ran contrary to her desire to create a safe space for her client. When this did not seem to help the process along she became impatient and probably seemed to Daryl like other authority figures in his life. While Meaghan felt that the relationship was salvaged, it is possible that Daryl might have anticipated similar behavior from her when other sensitive topics emerged and withdraw again. In fact, Meaghan began the follow-up session with her own agenda before recognizing her mistake again. This may have represented an automatic behavior that she needed to address in her supervision.

Ruptures and Repairs in Cross-Cultural Intervention

In cross-cultural practice, misunderstandings, and thus ruptures, are inevitable. In fact, one literature review indicates that cross-cultural relationships are associated with shorter interventions and poorer outcomes because the parties do not fully understand one another and thus make mistakes in communication or make errors in judgment (Keenan et al., 2005). Micro-ruptures, characterized as mini-breaches in some aspect of the relationship, a slight negative shift in relationship quality, or an ongoing problem in establishing one, are especially common in the early sessions when the parties are getting to know one another. The ruptures may be due to cultural misunderstandings regarding role expectations, the process of problem articulation, the negotiation of goals, and the meaning of communications from either party. Ruptures may also be due to the nature of one's professional practices; that is, whether they are consistent with the client's belief system. These ruptures can be repaired in the same manner as any others, although the parties may spend more time discussing their cultural backgrounds toward the goal of greater overall understanding.

The final vignette in this chapter concerns a client with a somewhat unusual cultural background that was foreign to the social worker—he had been a longstanding prisoner in the criminal justice system and thus was indoctrinated in that institution's unique cultural practices. The social work student, Lizzie, a 27-year-old Black female, had been placed in the jail where Jason was currently housed and had to negotiate a relationship with the 34-year-old White male who had spent half of his life behind bars. Lizzie, by the way, hoped to pursue a career in criminal justice social work.

The Tough Exterior

"Jason was incarcerated at the jail where I was placed for possession of cocaine, assault, carjacking, and speeding. He had previously spent 12 years in prison for an assault and battery against law enforcement charge. Three of those 12 years were served in solitary confinement because he stabbed and

killed another inmate in self-defense during a fight. Long ago, when Jason was only 12 years old, he accidentally shot and killed a friend with his father's handgun while they were playing in the garage, and he spent the next six years in the juvenile justice system at a detention center. Jason had thus been a 'free man' for only two years of his adult life. Only two years after completing his 12-year prison sentence he had been arrested for the previously noted charges. He was now facing a sentence of 90 years to life.

"I was one of the jail social workers. I first met Jason after finishing a session of my anger management class, which featured behavioral interventions. As I walked back to my office, Jason approached me in the hallway. He asked what I did as a case manager and if I could help him. He explained that he had felt intense anger since he was a kid and did not know how to handle it. He told me he was interested in joining my anger management class so I invited him to come. He also shared with me that his sister had died while he was incarcerated and he had been unable to attend her funeral. At that time, I had been formulating a curriculum for a grief and loss group, so I assigned Jason a related exercise that I thought might be helpful. I asked him to write a letter to his sister, focusing on the guilt and anger he felt about her loss. A week later I saw Jason again to check on the status of that exercise. He had completed the task, and as he read the long, emotion-packed letter out loud to me, tears streamed down his face. It was quite touching. I decided that he might benefit from the grief and loss group, which was focused on emotional expression and personal reflection, and he agreed to come to that as well.

"Jason had been attending both groups for a few weeks when we experienced our rupture, and it was largely due to my impatience with him. I had observed that while Jason was good at sharing his feelings with me one on one, he was less able to do so in group. Instead he came to the groups late, goofed off, and interrupted other members with distracting, sarcastic comments. Essentially, he was acting as the 'class clown.' I realized that he was putting on a façade for his peers to try to impress and frighten them, but most of them were merely annoyed with his antics. They rolled their eyes or sighed loudly, but that had no effect on his behavior. He was, in short, a negative force in the group. He puffed up his chest, talked about how he had been 'up the road' (in prison), used derogatory language about other members, and berated his peers as being inferior for not 'seeing the shit [I've] seen.' The other clients and I were becoming frustrated with Jason's behavior.

"Despite my many verbal warnings in the groups and in our private meetings (where he always behaved appropriately), Jason continued to act up. One day *in the anger management group Jason came 30 minutes late and after he sat down he made a derogatory comment about someone's contribution. I guess I was fed up with his antics, and while I hate to admit this, I lost my temper. I turned to Jason and told him sharply that he could not come to group late, which was already a disruption, and then create other distractions. I said, 'Jason, you come in here and screw around while we are trying to process some intense personal stuff about anger and where it has gotten us in life. That is unacceptable! If you don't want to be here, don't come. This class is for people that take it seriously.' I immediately regretted what I had done. I knew that Jason needed to get this message, but it was inappropriate for me to deliver it in front of the group. He said nothing but I could see hurt in his eyes when I finished. No one else said anything. Jason stayed, but he scowled in his seat and did not make eye contact with anyone for the remainder of class.*

"After the group ended I took Jason aside and we discussed what had happened. He said that it was unfair for me to single him out like that, and that it could have been handled better between the two of us. I told Jason I agreed and apologized for the way I behaved. I did, however, explain my frustrations with his behavior again, and I mentioned that it surprised me because he had done such good work with me one on one. Jason said that he accepted my apology and then told me something that I hadn't considered. He explained that he could not be as vulnerable with his peers as was with me privately, because they might later use his vulnerability against him. While I did not think that was necessarily true at this facility I am sure it was true in the prisons where Jason had stayed. I realized, too, that the severity of Jason's institutionalization had contributed to his lack of understanding of how to act appropriately in a classroom setting. He was a 34-year-old man who had retained much of the immaturity of the 12-year-old boy who accidently shot his friend. At that point, Jason and I had only been working together for two months. I had not fully considered what 'survival behavior' in prison was like, and as a result, I misunderstood the reasons for Jason's behavior and confronted him in ignorance. The bond we had developed had been threatened because of the blunt and berating tone I used when confronting him in the group.

"Our working relationship fortunately survived this rupture because we talked it out. I acknowledged my part in the rupture as a failure of empathy and he admitted that his behavior in the groups was unhelpful to himself or anyone else. Despite his limitations Jason was a forgiving soul when he felt that the other person was trying to be helpful, and we worked together well afterward."

> "When I started working with Jason, I was naïve. I thought that by working with him one on one I could help him process his grief about losing his sister and the many years he lost to incarceration, but there were other elements at play. Jason had been institutionalized, which put him in a constant state of survival mode. While he was a total goof in the pod (the public social area) and with his peers, no one doubted that he could seriously injure or even kill someone who crossed him. Once our rupture was resolved Jason and I worked together for another five months, and while I think I had a positive effect on him, I have since become more aware of the many factors working against him in the jail setting, which is a lesson I carried with me. I can put all my energy into helping these guys, but at the end of the day, they are still locked up. Their priority is to survive, and processing past traumas or losses is secondary to that fact.
>
> "Before I left the setting Jason was transferred to another jail for acting inappropriately in the pod. Ironically, not long after the transfer he was released from jail. The charges against him were dropped due to the death (by natural causes) of a key witness. Still, I could not help but think that he would end up back in the system soon. His behavior was erratic and inappropriate in serious situations, and he had few supports in the community. I hope I am wrong about that."

This story provides an illustration of how cross-cultural competence can help to prevent relationship ruptures. Lizzie had little awareness of prison culture and was thus operating from a position where she had expectations about group behavior that were unrealistic in that setting. She was fortunate to meet a client who, while being a member of that culture and behaving as such, also had the ability to be sincere in private situations and thus was able to educate her about the constraints inherent in the setting where he lived. From that point on Lizzie had a better understanding of prison culture and, despite the many obstacles to effective social work intervention there, might have been a greater positive influence on her clients. Given the cultural tendency of prisoners to hide their feelings, it is hoped that she was able to develop better ways of stimulating emotional sharing in her grief group.

Summary

Any significant, ongoing practice relationship includes the possibility of a rupture, or a lessening of trust and positive feelings due to a misunderstanding or conflict. These incidents are normal and even to be expected in a close relationship and can happen for a variety of reasons. They are perhaps even more likely in cross-cultural working relationships. At their worst, ruptures can destroy a working relationship even when reparative measures are taken. Social workers should always be alert to the possibility of ruptures, noting any significant negative changes in a client's session behavior, and be prepared to take the lead in addressing them so that the relationship can be mended and the intervention can proceed. While ruptures are usually not desirable, it has been found that they may at times strengthen practice relationships if the parties learn, perhaps for the first time, that a constructive relationship can survive such an experience. The purposes of this chapter have been to illustrate the nature of relationship ruptures in social work practice and provide a systematic means of resolving them.

6

Relationship Endings

Terminations and Transfers

Each of the preceding chapters has focused on the process of relationship development between social workers and their clients. This chapter focuses on the endings of those relationships. Termination is a process in which, when actively addressed, practitioners and clients can bring their work to a mutually understood and hopefully satisfactory conclusion. A transfer is a termination coupled with the assignment of the client to a new practitioner. Whether the ending of an intervention is managed well can at times make the difference between successful and unsuccessful outcomes for both the client and the social worker. A successful termination is one in which the client achieves his or her goals and feels prepared to move ahead and both parties achieve a sense of satisfaction about the work that has been done (Walsh, 2007). The purpose of this chapter is to review how social workers can utilize their relationships with clients to constructively process their separations, whether they be due to a termination or a transfer.

Types of Terminations and Transfers

There are many types of endings in direct practice (Westmacott & Hunsley, 2010). They may be:

Unplanned and initiated by the client (due to perceived gains and a client's reluctance to request an ending, dissatisfaction with the absence of perceived gains, taking advantage of an opportunity to drop out during involuntary treatment, or dissatisfaction with the practitioner's intervention methods);

Planned and premature, initiated by the social worker (when the client demonstrates a lack of expected progress without a perceived potential to make future goals, will not adhere to an intervention plan deemed

reasonable by the social worker, abuses agency policies or boundaries, or engages in other types of unacceptable behavior); or
* *Mutually planned and addressed* (agreement that the client's goals have been sufficiently achieved, the social worker's need to observe time limits, a decision that he or she is not competent to help a client and thus arranges for a transfer, the practitioner's leaving the setting, the client's requesting a new social worker, or an expected death of the client as in hospice work).

Social workers can proactively address all of these situations except for those involving client dropouts.

The Social Worker's Tasks During the Termination Process

While a social worker's actions during termination may differ depending on his or her theoretical perspective, the practice setting, and the client's needs and personal characteristics, common tasks for ending include (Walsh, 2007):

- Deciding when to actively implement the process
- Anticipating the emotional and behavioral reactions of both parties
- Attending to the reactions of both parties
- Reviewing the client's gains
- Generalizing the client's learning
- Articulating the client's remaining needs
- Planning for goal maintenance and relapse prevention
- Linking the client with external supports
- Evaluating the intervention
- Resolving the worker/client relationship and setting limits on future contact.

This final item refers to reviewing the nature of the worker/client relationship over time and its relevance to goal attainment. All people can benefit from utilizing social supports as sources of ongoing functional stability, so it may be important to review with clients what, if anything, they have learned during the intervention about relationships as resources.

Sometimes a termination can be facilitated by the social worker's use of *rituals*, defined as activities that are appropriate to a special occasion. The purposes of rituals in termination are to celebrate the end, acknowledge the significance of the shared experience, and provide a constructive transitional experience for the client. Examples of rituals will be discussed throughout the chapter.

What follows is an example of a termination provided by Janet, a 24-year-old White female social work student, that was largely successful, although she was troubled about not being able to attend to the process as thoroughly as she would have liked. The student attended to many but not all of the common tasks of termination as described earlier.

The Miracle Child

"The Murphys were a middle-class White family including two parents, Darcy and Mark, and their two children, Tom (16) and Haley (14). Haley had been admitted to my pediatric intensive care unit after she passed out and had a seizure while at school. Once admitted, it was found that Haley had anti-NMDA receptor encephalitis, an autoimmune disorder where antibodies essentially attack the brain. The disease features neurologic deficits and psychiatric symptoms and its prognosis is uncertain. Prior to admission Haley was perfectly normal, but suddenly she was mostly unconscious and tended to be combative during her brief periods of lucidity.

"I was assigned to work with the family, to help them adapt to this new and sudden diagnosis and prepare for their future in coping with it. I spent most of my time with Darcy, who was struggling with guilt and anger about her daughter's condition even though the doctors assured her it was no one's fault. I also assisted the family with coordinating their visiting accommodations since they lived several hours from the hospital. The biggest stressor that the family was experiencing was not knowing if Haley was going to survive, and if she did survive, what her quality of life would be.

"I developed a good relationship with Darcy during the family assessment. I wanted to include both parents in the task but they were not comfortable leaving Haley alone in her room, so dad stayed behind. We didn't meet in her room because Haley might be aware of conversations happening around her. During the assessment Darcy expressed anger toward her daughter's school. On the day Haley was admitted she had complained of head pain related to

noise and lights in the classroom but her teacher had only instructed Haley to sit outside in the hall, where she experienced the seizure. I validated mom's feelings and reassured her that Haley was receiving appropriate medical care. I had meetings with Darcy every day I was there, about 10 times in all, and I regularly checked on the rest of the family. Darcy said that it helped her to process her overwhelming emotions with me. Mark was quieter and more stoic and preferred to stay with his daughter. I had no verbal interactions with Haley but nonetheless became attached to her, as I visited her bedside each day.

"Haley's condition slowly improved over four weeks' time and then she surprised everyone by making a full recovery. She was walking, talking, and acting like her old self, and was going to be discharged home instead of to a rehabilitation center. She was doing so well that the nurses began calling her 'miracle Haley.' I was only at the hospital three days per week and was not aware that Haley would be going home until I came in one Wednesday. That morning I saw Darcy in the hallway with a young girl. I had no idea it was Haley, as I had only ever seen her unconscious. I was shocked to see her standing there talking like a typical teenager. Darcy was beaming and told me they were going to be discharged that day.

"I was excited about Haley's progress but also disappointed, because I felt that Darcy and I were not quite finished with our work related to her developing coping strategies about her daughter's condition. Of course, there were other things for me to take care of that day to help the family transition to home, including preparing their family medical leave application. While doing this I enjoyed seeing Haley in her room playing on her phone and giving attitude to her parents. Darcy and Mark both expressed gratitude to me while Haley kept saying she wanted to leave as soon as possible because her friends were coming over to the house.

"At one point I pulled Darcy outside of the room and tried to summarize with her our work together, recounting her progress from being angry and fearful to accepting what had happened and dealing with realistic anxieties about Haley's future. I advised her to consider outside counseling for the family but, unfortunately, I soon had to move on to seeing my other patients. I did make it a priority to see Haley and her family again, briefly, when they walked off the unit.

"This was the first time in the pediatric intensive care unit that I had been able to follow a case from beginning to end. It was a positive, powerful experience for me, but I was sorry that the termination occurred so quickly. I thought,

> *like everyone else, that Haley was going to be in the hospital for at least a few weeks longer. My termination with the family was adequate under the circumstances but I would have appreciated a few more opportunities to speak with Darcy and Mark, to help them anticipate challenges with Haley's health status and look up counselors in their area for referral purposes. If I could change anything, I would have liked to have had more contact with Mark and their son Tom. They were experiencing the same emotions as Darcy, but I was only able to focus on her because of my limited availability."*

While Janet felt generally good about the termination, she was not able to attend to several of its components. She was able to successfully link the family with needed resources, review Darcy's progress, make them aware of their remaining needs, and engage with them in a planning process, but she was not able to proactively implement that process over a period of time, have time to anticipate and attend to the emotional reactions of the family and herself, generalize their gains, evaluate their work together, and process their relationship. But this was a remarkable outcome, and it seemed that the unfinished aspects of the termination might become significant only if symptoms of the daughter's disorder recurred. It is surprising and unfortunate that the hospital social work department did not include post-discharge follow-up contacts with clients as a part of its work, which might have helped Janet to address her remaining concerns with the family. One other point made clear in this example is how the opportunity to spend more time in the termination stage would have been good for Janet herself, perhaps bolstering her sense of professional confidence and competence.

Now that we have reviewed some common tasks of termination, it is important to consider more fully an element that was demonstrated in this vignette; that is, how the parties may be emotionally affected by the process.

The Worker/Client Relationship and Termination

The quality of the worker/client relationship can be assessed in part by exploring their mutual feelings during the termination process (Weil, Katz, & Hilsenroth, 2017). During a successful termination those feelings, whether openly expressed or not, should be largely positive. They may each take pride in their accomplishments, experience an enhanced sense of competence, and feel encouraged to enter other relationships (the social worker with new clients, and the client with supportive others outside the agency). Sadness can be a positive feeling, too, if the parties will miss each other, and even relief, when it signifies that the work has been challenging as well as productive. Of course, in some working relationships that are largely formal and task-focused, the issue of feelings may not be highly relevant to either party.

Other feelings may indicate that there are, or have been, problems in the relationship. The social worker may feel disappointed or even guilty if the intervention has not gone well. If the social worker feels ambivalent about the ending process, or has personal problems dealing with separation, he or she may try to avoid or delay the topic, deny its significance, focus on its technical elements, or even offer additional contact inappropriately. The client may collude in those actions and may choose to drop out, initiate disruptive acting-out behaviors, bring up old problems or introduce new ones, and in the case of transfers, test the competence and dedication of the new worker (Knox et al., 2011). Factors that influence these problematic reactions may include the cultural traditions of either party or their learned coping styles.

It is important for practitioners to remember that in termination situations where they are leaving an agency, they are managing multiple transitions with clients and colleagues, and their feelings about leaving the agency, positive or negative, can affect how they process endings with clients. For example, if a student social worker is looking forward to leaving a field agency, graduating, and starting a paid job, he or she might be less sensitive to the emotional reactions of his or her clients (Siebold, 2007).

Many of these themes are illustrated in a study featuring interviews with 92 student social workers and 48 practitioners in Israel about their own, and their clients', reactions to termination (Baum, 2007; 2005). The researcher considered three situations: those in which clients initiated the termination, the practitioners did so, or the process was mutual. The clients who initiated termination sometimes felt that their goals had been achieved but they were just as often dissatisfied with the intervention, and as a result they experienced lower levels of optimism, accomplishment, and hope than the clients who had terminated in the other circumstances. On the positive side, those clients experienced some feelings of pride because they had taken control of the intervention process. Practitioners in these situations reported positive feelings when they perceived that the intervention had been successful, but they also experienced a distressing lack of competence when it had not been a success, especially when the ending was abrupt.

Clients whose terminations were initiated by their practitioners experienced hurt and anger if they did not feel that they had met their goals. They experienced the most self-doubt and hurt in situations where the intervention was terminated abruptly, they perceived little choice in the matter, or they felt that it had been a failure. If the ending was forced at the end of a field placement or when the practitioner was leaving the agency, clients reported significant loss experiences. Practitioners also had negative feelings when the self-initiated ending was due to a perceived failure of the intervention, but this was balanced in part by a positive sense of having been proactive when an intervention was not going well.

Clients who were said to end the intervention mutually with their practitioners also expressed feelings of significant loss. In fact, the strength of those feelings suggested to the researcher that joint terminations may not always reflect clients' wishes and needs. That is, practitioners who reach termination decisions together with their clients should not always assume that the ending is coming at the right time for the client, who may be agreeing to the plan without necessarily endorsing it, deferring to the expertise of the practitioner.

The researcher also inquired about the feelings of both parties during terminations where the quality of the relationship was believed to be a central element of the intervention. In all three circumstances relationship centrality was a mitigating factor to any negative feelings, in that both parties experienced some positive feelings as well as negative ones, reflecting the ambivalence many people feel when ending important relationships.

Overall these findings suggest that practitioners should, when possible, include the client in the decision to terminate and ensure that the process leaves enough time for clients to reflect on and express the feelings that accompany it. When this is not possible, it is important that practitioners be aware of their clients' range of possible reactions and try to anticipate and mitigate any feelings of distress that may emerge.

This mix of feelings is illustrated in the following vignette, written by Sonya, a 22-year-old single Asian American social work student.

Going Home

"Mr. Mark, as I called him, was a 60-year-old White single male admitted to the inpatient hospice unit with final stage lung cancer. Mentally, he was fully

functional, but the cancer caused him much physical weakness and fatigue. He was most upset about his loss of autonomy. Following Mr. Mark's 30-day reassessment a discharge plan was formulated to send him home. He was no longer eligible for inpatient care as he had stabilized, and he indicated that he would like to return home, where he lived alone. He knew that his extended family would oppose his living alone, but he was determined to do so. Mr. Mark was being sent home with hospice, referrals to community resources, and medical equipment from physical therapy.

"I had been assigned to work with Mr. Mark at his admission and visited him weekly for psychosocial support and resource development. Per my supervisor's idea, I suggested that he submit a request to the Dream Foundation, which granted final wishes to people who have a terminal illness. We brainstormed about this and I helped him submit a request for a laptop computer to help him learn architecture and be able to enjoy the visual arts. His wish was granted; it was a special moment in our work together.

"At a tense family discharge planning meeting with his son and ex-wife, Mr. Mark kept insisting that he would return to his home, against his family's wishes. Later he asked me to prepare a list of apartments in the area and get information about transportation (as he couldn't drive anymore), meal delivery services, and socialization opportunities, which I did. Mr. Mark would be leaving on a Monday, so I had to finalize my work and say goodbye the previous Friday. Throughout that week I reminded him that I would not be there on Monday, so he would not be surprised by my absence. Ironically, due to our good relationship and my fondness for Mr. Mark I felt nervous about the termination and waited until the end of the day to say goodbye.

"I had seen Mr. Mark earlier that day to give him the resource packet I put together. I told him I would come back later to say goodbye. When I returned, I asked how he was feeling about going home; he said he was looking forward to having time to enjoy his hobbies. He already had his drawing books stacked and ready for packing. He was excited to show me the equipment he was going home with—a walking cane and wheelchair from physical therapy. He said that he wasn't worried about anything, but I knew him well enough to pick up on his anxiety. I didn't push him to reveal his feelings, though. I didn't want to detract from his high hopes.

"Mr. Mark wanted to get a cup of coffee so I walked with him to the kitchen. On the way, we ran into a few nurses who greeted him warmly. I remarked that the nurses had grown fond of him and that we would all miss him. He responded, 'Do you really think so?' and I replied in the affirmative. When we got back to the room, I reminded Mr. Mark that this would be the last time I would see him before his discharge. I told him that I enjoyed working with him, wished him the best of luck, and shook his hand. He thanked me for my help and said he couldn't have done it without me. He was becoming misty-eyed, and I could feel my own emotions welling up, so I hurriedly told him that I thought he was a good person before I left.

"The feelings I had for Mr. Mark made the termination difficult for me. When he became tearful I physically withdrew, because I didn't want to get upset in front of him. The awkwardness I felt led me to leave more quickly than I had planned, and I regretted this afterward. I also regretted not pressing Mr. Mark some about challenges that might come up at home and how he would manage them, such as preparing meals and doing laundry. We had already talked about resources in the community that he could use, but I knew he was not keen on receiving help from outside organizations. Mr. Mark tended to believe that people who voiced concerns about him did not want him to be successful. Still, I should have raised my concerns with him about his likely challenges.

"For the entire week I had felt nervous about saying goodbye to Mr. Mark. I had grown attached to him and invested in trying to help him achieve the best possible outcomes. I was hoping we would be able to care for Mr. Mark again, that he would return to the inpatient unit when he experienced a further decline. I tried to minimize my concerns about his discharge even though I knew he might not function successfully at home. But Mr. Mark had wanted to go there and it was my duty to respect his right to self-determination.

"The nature of termination in hospice is complicated because one cannot predict if a person will ever be discharged. As such, I gave little thought to Mr. Mark's discharge until it was imminent. I wanted to share a dignified and professional ending with him although I wasn't sure how to do it. With little previous experience I tried not to become overly emotional as I thought it would be inappropriate. It was my hope to honor our work together by letting him know that I enjoyed working with him and hoping he would have a successful future.

"About a week after Mr. Mark left, I found out that he had passed away. He did not take his medications correctly, became confused, and fell. He was admitted to an inpatient facility for respite but unexpectedly died there. After learning this, I felt guilty about Mr. Mark's discharge. I knew something bad could happen to him, but I didn't think it would happen so soon. I started to wonder if I had been neglectful in my duties by not advocating more that he *consider a group home. I also wondered if I had made him feel neglected when I didn't stay with him during his tearful reaction to our goodbye. I do think that my work with Mr. Mark demonstrated my care for him, and he was able to grasp that."*

Sonya appears to have done a good job of helping Mr. Mark prepare for termination, especially given that it happened rather abruptly. While she admits that she might have been better prepared for this development if given more time, she attended to its details responsibly. The only thing she was not ready for was her own and the client's emotional reactions. Even as the process unfolded she was aware that her feelings about Mr. Mark led her to avoid addressing some important post-discharge challenges he would likely face, and sharing her positive feelings about him more openly, which may have been important since he doubted his likability. This probably reflected Sonya's patterns of behavior in her personal life and was something she could address in supervision. The sadness and guilt Sonya felt on learning of his death, however, would probably have occurred regardless of how thorough the termination had been.

Because termination involves the ending of a relationship, one that may have been significant for the client, the process can sometimes be guided by attention to attachment theory (described in Chapter 1) and what it suggests about the client's interpersonal needs following the end of a supportive relationship (Zilberstein, 2008). Securely attached clients will likely make a smooth transition from the professional relationship. Avoidant and ambivalent clients can also be successful in fulfilling their needs for supportive relationships, but they may experience related anxieties and benefit from termination-stage assistance with those tendencies. The social worker should consider revisiting some of the relational work addressed in previous sessions. For example, with anxious-ambivalent clients termination sessions might be an ideal time to revisit their propensity to engage in "people pleasing" behavior. The social worker can remind those clients of this self-defeating pattern and help them learn to engage in relationships without sacrificing their own needs. Avoidantly attached clients often suppress their negative feelings during separations and have difficulty acquiring confidence to undertake the challenge of developing new relationships. They might benefit from the social worker's assistance in practicing how to prioritize emotional sharing with others. Disorganized clients may become so overwhelmed by issues of loss that they need help in structuring their lives as a means of coping with their scattered emotional responses.

Some attachment issues are unique to children (Shilkret & Shilkret, 2016). Those with strong parental supports may cope well with termination because they have those resources on which to rely. Children without such attachments may be devastated by the loss of an attachment figure and benefit from processing their sense of loss as well as feeling supported in their efforts to connect with other people. In addition, children's cognitive understandings of their internal and external worlds differ from those of adults. Their cognitive abilities grow as they mature but they remember their internal states, relationships, and environments differently at different ages. For children to become able to grasp and remember the gains of therapy as they age, it may be helpful for them to be given concrete reminders of the experience, such as pictures or written stories, which they can later review from a more advanced developmental level.

The following vignette describes Rebecca's difficult termination with an adolescent client who had significant attachment deficits.

Three Strikes

"Richard was a 15-year-old White male who had been in our Family Services Residential Treatment Program for one year. He had a diagnosis of reactive attachment disorder (RAD). His admission was due to unruly and sometimes violent behavior at home. He had many insecurities related to having been born into a neglectful family and then feeling lost in his adoptive family. Richard's adoptive family, which he entered when he was three years old, was blended, including children from the parents' previous marriages and other adoptees. In total there were 11 children in the family ranging from 9 to 47 years old, with five still living in the home.

"Richard's behavior improved while in our program as he learned more socially appropriate coping skills and developed some emotional awareness. He was working toward the goal of overnight passes and, in a few months, discharge. Richard had been on my caseload for six months, from the time I began my field placement at the agency. I was a 22-year-old White single woman with little experience but a career goal of working with children. Richard and I met weekly for counseling sessions related to his coping behaviors and I facilitated

the therapy group in his cottage that was intended to help the boys develop better social behaviors.

"I was only six weeks from ending my work at the agency when Richard's behavior began to regress. The treatment team thought this was because he had been in the program for longer than anticipated, and his primary social worker and family therapist Natalie had left the agency several weeks ago. I saw Richard more than Natalie did, but he had a stronger attachment to her. After she left he became quieter and more aggressive and engaged in some self-harm cutting behaviors. The reason for his extended stay was that his parents had been slow to complete the necessary steps to bring him home. Then, a week after Natalie left, for reasons unknown to our staff, Richard's parents notified the agency that they had decided to relinquish custody of him. He had believed he would be going home soon. And now I was intending to begin my own termination process with him. This was a terrible situation for Richard.

"It had initially been difficult for me to build rapport with Richard. He often presented with a flat affect and could be apathetic and disengaged, seeming not to care about anyone or anything. His response to my questions during our first weeks together was often 'I don't know' or merely to shrug. He struggled to verbally identify or discuss his emotions. In the beginning of our work together, I spent time 'chilling' with Richard, talking about music or basketball, with the goals of building rapport and providing a stable adult presence. I was kind of a tomboy and felt comfortable playing outdoor games with him. We connected on that basis and eventually I introduced a basketball game that involved asking each other questions with every basket we made. This structure helped him to talk about his fears.

"Over six months our relationship progressed to the point where I could get Richard to verbalize feelings and he frequently sought me out for support. However, in the last month or so he mostly talked about wanting to go home and being with his mom. Easily angered, he began walking into classrooms and throwing chairs or walking the halls and kicking windows and breaking fire extinguisher boxes. When I asked how I could help him, or when I gave him the option of going outside or to the gym, he kept quiet. It was difficult for me because I couldn't be sure what was going on inside him. I assumed he was upset about not going home and because he had lost Natalie. The situation was even more upsetting for me since learning of his parent's decision to terminate custody rights and knowing that my departure was coming soon.

"I was planning on telling Richard six weeks before I left that my internship was ending. He knew I was a 'therapist in training' but we hadn't discussed *my leaving in a while. My plan was to tell him on a Friday, but the day before we learned of his parents' decision to relinquish custody. I had already been hesitant about discussing termination because I knew he was struggling with Natalie's departure. I had assured him then that I would be available to help him in her absence. I felt terrible that now I was going to have to tell him that I was leaving soon. He was being abandoned on three sides.*

"*When I went to get him for that session, he was sitting in the back of a classroom with a laptop listening to music. He didn't look up when I called his name. This avoidant behavior was typical of Richard when he was upset. After a few seconds of silence, I told him I needed him to talk to me, even though he might not want to. He responded with a shrug and continued looking at his laptop. Children with RAD don't often seek help or respond to comfort when they are sad or in pain. In some ways Natalie had fulfilled the role of his caregiver and he wasn't going to seek soothing from others. I was unable to convince Richard to come to my office for our meeting. I didn't pressure him and decided not to bring up our own termination that day. I told him we could talk after the weekend and that I was there for him if he changed his mind. I felt guilty saying this and was furious with his parents for giving up on him. I didn't think I was a great social worker but I knew I was a genuine support for Richard. My weekend was ruined because of how badly I felt.*

"*I'm highlighting this episode of not talking with Richard about my leaving because it was the worst emotional experience I had in that field placement. I know that termination is a process as opposed to a single event, and how the process unfolds affects whether the relationship is viewed in a positive or negative way. I hadn't thought of termination as a major issue for me to manage until I learned of Natalie's departure and his parents' plan. I was afraid that the rapport we'd built over the last six months would be ruined because in the end I turned out to be another adult who left him.*

"*Things did improve from that point regarding my ability to implement a thoughtful ending process with Richard. I was determined to support him consistently until the end and encourage him to express his feelings to me. I told him that Monday that I was leaving and spent the next six weeks reminding Richard about the skills he had developed, providing him with support, reminding him how much I cared, and trying to teach him about the importance of trusting at least a few people. I gave him the time and space to express any anger or fear and to grapple with any sense of loss. He became more verbal toward the end, even though he mostly expressed frustration about his future. I was willing to withstand Richard's emotional rejection of me and try and focus on the positives of our experiences. I was later able to transfer Richard to another student who was beginning a year-long internship just before I left. I spent a lot of time with her describing Richard's situation. I don't know how that relationship unfolded, or how long Richard was in the program, but I felt good that I attended to the transition as carefully as I could."*

It is unfortunate that adolescents with RAD must exist in a social services system where additional relationship ruptures are likely. These terminations feed into their deep trust issues, but it is possible that "curative" relationships can develop with caring staff and foster and adoptive parents. Richard's attachment disorder meant that he had great difficulty forming supportive relationships with anyone. He rarely sought or responded to comfort when upset, had limited positive affect, and endured episodes of fear that resulted in acting-out behaviors due to his history of emotional deprivation and inconsistent parenting. Knowing this helped Rebecca persist in being supportive of him, as demonstrated in the final paragraph of her vignette, in her efforts to provide a consistent relationship even as he had to endure several losses. It is unclear whether Richard was able to internalize any of her caring and eventually become able to trust other caregivers, but that was her hope.

Social workers often end their relationships with clients in the context of transfers, arranging for their clients to resume intervention with another practitioner. This process can have additional effects on the original relationship as well as the client's capacity for goal achievement.

Client Transfers

A transfer is a termination coupled with the assignment of the client to a new practitioner. Transfers usually occur because the primary practitioner is leaving the agency or program, but they can also occur when the client requests a new social worker or the social worker believes that the client may benefit more from working with a different practitioner. The fact of the transfer suggests that the client is still in need of services and is thus in a vulnerable position, which makes the process sometimes delicate. In fact, while recent data are not available, one study showed that between 10% and 60% of transfers are *not* successful, in that the client ends treatment soon afterward (Wapner, Klein, Friedlander, & Andrasik, 1986).

Clients may experience a range of reactions unique to a transfer, in addition to those prompted by termination, including anger toward the departing practitioner; frustration about having to start over; and concerns about the likelihood of making additional progress, the new practitioner's use of a different approach, and not being liked by the new practitioner (Clark, Cole, & Robertson, 2014). The new practitioner may also be faced with several challenges, including dealing with displaced client anger, comparisons to the former practitioner, and a period of testing by the new client. The transferring social worker may also experience anxiety about exposing another practitioner to his or her work.

There are several predictors of transfer success, including the client's success with previous transfers and a period of practitioner overlap (Williams & Winter, 2009). To help ensure a successful transfer the new practitioner should acknowledge and process the client's feelings about the change, encourage (at first) the client to talk about the former practitioner, communicate a willingness to work with the client, demonstrate that he or she knows a lot about the client (is prepared), and be aware of any feelings of competition with the previous practitioner. The new practitioner should resist any temptations to blame the former practitioner or any others if problems ensue with the client.

What follows are guidelines for a constructive transfer process, based on the theme that clients are more likely to feel encouraged when the process is handled professionally and with the primary practitioner's active involvement. The transferring social worker should attend to the following steps (Clark, Robertson, Keene, & Cole, 2011):

Take responsibility for the need to make the transfer rather than attributing it to external factors (such as "I couldn't turn down this other job offer" or "My field placement is ending so I have no choice"). Even if such factors are true, citing them gives the impression that the social worker may be trying to avoid all responsibility for the significance of its effects on the client.

Inform the client of the need for the transfer in a timely manner and with a plan of action that demonstrates that the client's needs are paramount. It may be difficult to determine how much advance notice should be given about a transfer, but it should certainly not be announced during the final session.

- *Encourage the client to process related feelings and concerns related to the transfer,* so that they may be resolved as much as possible in advance of the event.
- *Assure the client that he or she is worthy of continued intervention.* Some clients may feel that arranging for a transfer is too much trouble for the practitioner, especially if the process takes time and involves several steps, and perhaps they should take the opportunity to end their interventions.
- *Demonstrate that the referring social worker will have an active role in the process.* This communicates to the client that the new practitioner, even if he or she has no choice in the matter, is eager to understand the client's needs.
- *Facilitate client input into transfer options, if possible.* That is, the client should be invited to give input into what kind of practitioner (gender, experience, interest areas, preferred intervention approach, etc.) he or she would feel comfortable with.
- *Review with the client his or her remaining goals.* This serves to bring closure to their work together and indicates that the new practitioner will be clear about the client's priorities.
- *Speak confidently, and provide relevant background information, about the new practitioner,* so that the client feels that the new practitioner will be able to help him or her.
- *Relay any client concerns about the transfer to the new practitioner prior to the transfer,* so that the new practitioner can prepare to address them.
- *Hold one or a few sessions, at least in part, with the new practitioner, if possible.* When a new practitioner is not yet available a supervisor can temporarily step in and be a source of continuity during the client's waiting period,

These themes are illustrated in the following two vignettes. The first one describes a transfer process that took place during the client's first visit with her assigned social worker, and the second describes a client transfer that occurred one year after they began working together. In the initial case, *23-year-old Caitlin describes her work with Alice, a* 30-year-old army veteran whom she saw for an intake assessment at the Veterans Affairs (VA) hospital.

One Visit and a Transfer

"A primary care doctor at the VA hospital asked me as a mental health provider to see one of her clients because of concern for her well-being. The client, Alice, presented with symptoms of major depression and endorsed recent suicidal ideation. Her symptoms interfered with her sleep and her ability to perform her job as a school security guard. When I met with the veteran, she was guarded in her responses and demonstrated closed-off body language. When I asked about her symptoms, it took some time for her to share the struggles she had functioning in her daily life. Soon, though, she began to explain how she lost her mother and her brother in the past year, which prompted a decline in her ability to cope. She then shared that her mother's boyfriend raped her several times over a period of years growing up and her mother never believed her. She described feeling a guilty sense of relief when her mother passed away because of their tumultuous relationship and the emotional burden she carried because of the lack of support she received. Alice also described how she was sexually assaulted by her sergeant in the military. She shared insightfully how she believed the increased severity and duration of her symptoms was related to the loss of her immediate family members. She had only received therapy and medication intermittently through the VA and while in active duty.

"This was my first meeting with the client. Alice had not been engaged with any mental health support at the VA for the past year and a half. She was not contacted after her last session and never reached out for additional help. She endorsed having a few therapy sessions with different providers on and off in the past five years and felt they were helpful. She also shared that in the past she took an antidepressant drug with success. Though I had only met with her for a short time, I felt Alice began to trust me and was willing to share intimate parts of her life that had been burdening her. She was candid with me about her concern that she'd hate to endure switching providers and losing contact with a source of help again. This pattern had created an emotional barrier that prevented her from getting longer-term support in the past. I knew I needed to tactfully navigate her treatment planning.

"Given the client's history of complex traumas, I knew that I might need to transfer her care depending on what I decided was clinically appropriate. I made sure I provided validation and reassurance that the way her treatment plan would be initiated would ensure she was in the most appropriate level of care. Once she began to open up to me, about 10 minutes into our session, she shared that it was painful for her to share her story to several people due to her difficulty trusting others. Her last termination reinforced some of her beliefs about not trusting people and feeling unworthy of getting help. This sentiment was complicated by the family dynamic of growing up with a mother who refused to believe her daughter was raped by her own boyfriend. I knew then that the level of treatment my team and I could provide would not be clinically adequate to support this veteran so I would need to address the topic of transfer with her in this session. I knew that this news would be frustrating for Alice to hear.

"If her treatment plan and its execution did not get carried out in a streamlined manner, I feared that Alice would not only terminate from seeing the appropriate provider at the VA but that she would not be able to regain faith in getting mental health support anywhere. I do believe that I managed this challenge pretty well. I soon understood that Alice's needs were more than our level of care could treat, and I carefully explained that although she and I had met and discussed her symptoms and past traumas, I could not be her provider for the long term. In response, she rolled her eyes and said, 'See?' But after I explained that our session was a treatment planning meeting meant for evaluation, she appeared to be relieved. It took my explaining the process in different ways and offering reassurance for Alice to trust that she would be taken care of. This transfer was difficult for me because I felt it was in my hands to develop a good relationship with the client in a short amount of time. Still, I had to work within the model of care that the VA used in addressing clients' mental health issues. I hoped that the barriers of a large government hospital and possible waiting time would not make for a troubling transition for this veteran.

"The unique nature of how the VA provided mental health care only allowed for one or two sessions prior to a veteran's transfer to a higher level of care, if necessary. I was clear with Alice on how treatment is carried out in this setting so that her expectations could be managed. I informed her that given her history of sexual trauma and current depression, she required a higher level of care so that her needs could be met most appropriately. I assured her that her transfer was solely for the purpose of getting her more appropriate care that could lead to her better symptom improvement, and not because she wasn't worthy or that we didn't have time for her. I informed Alice that she would likely have to repeat her story to another few individuals in the assessment process and restated that I appreciated her willingness to share her story with me. I told her that I could see her one more time before her intake to ensure that she felt supported in the interim, but after that session her care would be managed in the mental health specialty unit with providers trained to support veterans with a history of sexual trauma. It seemed that Alice understood the process and knew by the end of our session that she was not being 'tossed around.' Though setting up future meetings with the new provider is recommended to facilitate continuity of therapy, this was not feasible due to the way the VA's transfer process was structured.

"I think the best thing I did in this session was to not focus on how or why the veteran lost touch the last time she engaged with treatment but reassure her that now we had a plan in place to ensure she would receive the appropriate level of care. I left her with my contact information and my supervisor's contact information and set up one last time to meet with her. I didn't want her to think she was forgotten about and I didn't want over a month to go by without her engaging with someone prior to her intake in the specialty clinic. I believe something I also did successfully was maintain my confidence throughout the session. I exuded faith in the transfer process and didn't leave room for the client to believe I doubted the possibility of a constructive transfer."

Caitlin managed this sensitive transfer well and seems indeed to have communicated with her client in a confident manner about how the process would ultimately work out for the best. In fact, she skillfully organized the meeting so that it was both an intervention and a transfer discussion. She assumed responsibility for the transfer by admitting that it was her professional opinion that Alice would require more specialized services than she herself could provide. Caitlin raised the issue of the transfer relatively early in the meeting, not long after noting that the client was developing a positive attachment to her. Caitlin welcomed Alice's reactions to the news, did not get defensive, reviewed her goals, and reminded Alice that she was worthy of ongoing care—in fact, a more intensive level of care from the agency. Unfortunately, due to the nature of the VA bureaucracy Caitlin was not able to offer Alice an active role in the transfer process or any practitioner overlap. She would, however, relay Alice's concerns to the new practitioner in the notes she would write about the session.

This next vignette is from Matt, a 35-year-old White male social worker, and illustrates themes arising in the transfer process after a long intervention and also the use of a ritual to assist in the termination.

The Long Goodbye

"I worked most of my career with persons who have the serious mental illnesses of schizophrenia, major depression, and bipolar disorder. Most of these clients received long-term intervention because they took medications and required ongoing monitoring and support to control their symptoms and enhance their quality of life. These were always my favorite clients, and I followed some of them for many years. I understood that developing a strong relationship with them was key to their remaining in treatment, because most of them had few relationships and often felt marginalized by others. I genuinely enjoyed them, so relationship development usually wasn't hard for me.

"The few times I left an agency for another job, I put a lot of thought into transferring the clients who I knew would miss me. Not all my clients fell into that category, but some did, and I knew that my leaving put them at risk of dropping out of treatment. I always thought about my colleagues and tried to match their personalities with those of my clients, although I had no scientific basis for this process. As an example, when I was leaving one agency after accepting a job in another city I needed to transfer Marci, a client I had known for three years. She was a 40-year-old divorced schoolteacher with schizoaffective disorder who had to be hospitalized against her will following a psychotic episode featuring delusions of persecution. She was referred to my agency after the discharge and had initially been furious with me and the agency physician, threatening to sue both of us for making her accept counseling and medication (although we didn't). While most of her delusions remitted, her paranoia persisted, and it took six months of biweekly meetings focused on person-centered and reflective interventions before she fully accepted me as a supportive person who cared about her.

"In trying to engage with Marci I had agreed to home visits, and in the process I became acquainted with her mother, father, and two sisters. They were frightened about Marci's mental status when she became psychotic so I provided all of them with education about her illness and its treatment. They came to see me as a family resource. Marci and I eventually worked together very well toward her returning to part-time teaching and a medication regimen that was helpful and included few adverse effects. Everyone in the family was feeling better. So, when it came time for me to announce my departure from the agency, it was a blow to all of them. I told them of my decision to leave the agency two months before I left, right after I had accepted the other job. They were all sorry to see me go and gracious for my assistance, which felt

good. I believe that my early announcement of the need to transfer gave Marci plenty of time to adjust to the idea of a new practitioner. (She had indicated that she did not want to terminate from the agency.)

"Regarding the transfer, I asked Marci if there was a type of practitioner she might like to work with, but she had no preferences. I considered the other eligible staff at the agency and decided on Libby, a social worker and nurse. Libby was 40 years old and had a friendly but formal manner with her clients, which I knew would suit Marci. She knew a lot about mental illness, was accustomed to home visits (unlike some staff), was knowledgeable about medications, and knew the community well so that she could make appropriate referrals. I felt like she would be a good fit for Marci and the family, and she was agreeable. I talked with Marci about Libby during one of our meetings, describing her work experience and my own good relationship with her. Three weeks before we terminated I brought Libby in and described the history of my work with Marci. They each asked some questions of the other to get acquainted, which seemed to go well, and I let them set their own first appointment for one month later.

"My final meeting with Marci was based on a ritual I had developed with clients I had seen for a long time. I suggested that, to celebrate our work together, we do something out of the ordinary that she could choose for our last session. Clients usually liked that idea but often weren't sure what to pick, so I usually suggested dining out for lunch. I had assessed that such an outing with Marci would likely be pleasant and involve little risk. Marci was agreeable and picked a nearby restaurant. We had a nice time and I felt that the outing added a sense of specialness to our final meeting. Marci wanted to pay for both of us but I didn't let her. Other ending rituals that I shared with clients included walks in a park, shopping trips to the mall, or listening to music in my office. I never spent more time in these activities than I did in a regular session, and they always occurred during my office hours. None of them were extravagant, and in my view none were inappropriate. They left both the client and me feeling good."

This transfer went very well. Matt was proactive in introducing the topic of his leaving and the need for a transfer, and Marci was invited to give input into the decision-making process, even though she didn't have many suggestions. All the people involved (Marci's family) were quick to share their feelings of sadness about Matt's departure, and he and Marci had plenty of time to get used to the upcoming change. Matt validated Marci's worth by clarifying that he was going to put much thought into an appropriate replacement, and he did so, eventually being able to secure the agreement of his first choice to work with the client. It appears that Marci had been functioning well for some time, which made the transition easier and allowed for the introduction of a closing ritual, which affirmed the significance of their long relationship for both of them. It is important to note, too, that Matt suggested a ritual activity that he believed would be appropriate to the nature of their relationship, and not something that might be awkward for either of them.

Summary

All relationships involve a process of coming together, being together, and separating, and people ascribe different meanings to each step in the process. Thus, client terminations and transfers can be delicate processes with some clients. The purpose of this chapter has been to provide social workers with specific steps for promoting successful endings with their clients. Early learning about separation sets a pattern for how people experience endings, as transitions stimulate reenactments of prior experiences and influence their success or failure. In direct practice the social worker's management of terminations and transfers can at times ensure the client's maintenance of goals and positive momentum for a better life, especially when the relationship has been significant to the client. Successful separation depends on having enough of one's needs met to be able to take better care of oneself, so helping clients appreciate their gains is essential. Social workers should try to include the client in decision-making during a termination or transfer, as people usually feel better when they have some control in the process.

7
Relationships with Children and Adolescents

The processes of forming working relationships with children and adolescents are often different than those with adults because of their physical, psychological, cognitive, emotional, and social stages of development. Additionally, children and adolescents are at risk for many unique problems that bring them to the attention of social workers, due to their dependency on and vulnerability to harm by adults. Their problems may be related to an absence of adequate family support and appropriate adult models, exposure to unhealthy social systems and traumatic situations, attachment issues, and difficulties with emotional regulation. Peer conflicts can also create distress for youth. Further, while children and adolescents are dependent on adults to get most of their needs met, they are often distrusting of adults, including social workers and other social services professionals. The purpose of this chapter is to consider how social workers can engage with members of this population and develop relationships with them based on trust. Many examples of working with children and adolescents have been included in previous chapters, but some of their unique characteristics are considered here more fully.

Children

The chapter begins with a brief review of common developmental processes experienced by children and adolescents. Human development in middle childhood (ages 6 to 12) promotes their capacity for successful interpersonal interaction (Broderick & Blewitt, 2019; Charlesworth, 2019). Their thinking enters the concrete operations stage, characterized by a gradual development of logical thinking, although this is initially limited to concrete events rather than abstract ideas. Children can best relate to and communicate about things they directly experience. They begin to develop some rudimentary control over their emotions, attention span, and problem-solving capabilities. Their working memory improves and memories become more clear and durable. Children learn to interact socially; their emerging perspective-taking ability facilitates their development of friendships and, as a part of that process, conflict regulation skills. They are exposed to a variety of peers and group norms for the first time and develop the concept of team play.

The child's beginning self-concept typically emphasizes his or her positive attributes. It is only in later childhood that social comparison begins, which can result for many children in a lowering of their self-esteem. The development of positive self-esteem results from the child's ability to be successful in distinct realms such as academics and sports. Conscience develops before middle childhood, although it is also typical for children to lie and engage in physical aggression. The latter behavior decreases in middle childhood as children develop more prosocial skills. Qualities related to a child's popularity include having good social skills, cognitive and academic competence, and emotional adjustment. Children with fewer social skills are more apt to feel rejected or marginalized and tend to be either more aggressive or withdrawn. Children's primary areas of interest and influence include their families and schools, and they tend to be distrustful of outsiders. The two sexes tend to spend their time separately from one another due to their perceived differences in biology and peer interests.

Some implications of childhood development for client engagement are that they are concrete thinkers, have limited social and conversational skills, can become aggressive when frustrated, and tend to distrust outsiders while maintaining family loyalty, regardless of the quality of those ties. They may take a long time to open up to a social worker, and they may initially be more comfortable participating in activities than talking during their interactions.

Adolescents

Significant developmental changes continue through adolescence (Broderick & Blewitt, 2019; McCarter, 2019). The physical growth of teens includes the onset and eventual completion of puberty, with hormonal changes prompting the development of romantic interests and sexual activity. Cognitive development features a new capacity for abstract thinking and the ability to contemplate the future. The emotional brain evolves more quickly than the rational brain, however, which helps to account for their mood instability and a tendency toward risky behavior, a characteristic that does not peak until late adolescence. Unfortunately, the psychosocial stresses associated with adolescent life lead to a significant incidence of depression.

Adolescents experience dramatic changes in their social orientations featuring a new sense of the importance of relationships and movements toward independence. It is a period that includes role experimentation and a sharpening of vocational and leisure interests. Identity formation, the process of determining who one is and where one is going in life, is a major task of adolescence. There is a reduction in the strength of parental influence on behavior, with an increase in conflict with parents and a sharp increase in the strength of peer influences. Their decision-making is influenced more by social situations than absolute principles, and some of their negative peer influences can lead toward substance use, crime, and bullying. Adolescents do, however, develop a capacity for empathy.

Adolescents tend to distance themselves, at least temporarily, from the cultures in which they were raised. In high school they tend to fall into one of five crowds—the socially popular kids, the athletes (jocks), the dropouts, the high academic achievers, and the average kids—and they follow the influences of their respective crowds. Relatively few adolescents are well rounded enough to interact comfortably with more than a few of these social groups. They also tend to become less academically motivated and more secretive.

Some implications for relationship development include the adolescent's emerging capacity for abstract thought, the reduction in strength of family influence and rise in significance of peer influence, fragile self-esteem, continued emotional lability, and preoccupation with sex. Their absence of trust with adults makes relationship development with professionals a slow process.

Building Working Alliances with Children

Most studies of the working alliance, discussed in Chapter 3, focus on the three elements of engagement, collaborative goal setting, and agreement on tasks. Studies have shown that children, however, do not discriminate multiple measures of the working alliance (Roest, van der Helm, Strijbosch, van Brandenburg, & Stams, 2016b). Instead, they evaluate the alliance based on a global feeling about the practitioner's general presentation. What children perceive as a therapeutic alliance is generally captured in one-dimensional ratings such as, "I like when my mentor is around, helps me achieve my goals, understands me, listens to me, allows me to talk to other group workers, has enough time for me," and "I can discuss anything with my mentor; we work well together."

Developing positive relationships with children requires that social workers take time to get to know and interact with them on their own terms. This principle was borne out in a qualitative study in the United Kingdom that included interviews with children ages 5 to 18 years and their social work staff (Whincup, 2017). The researchers found that effective social workers took as much time as was necessary to build relationships with their clients, and they maintained a patient approach when moving into the more formal activities of conducting assessments and providing interventions. As we will see, intervention was most effective when the engagement process was coupled with some type of activity, such as games, play, and art. Both the children and professionals highlighted the importance of getting to know one other and added that this involved some degree of reciprocity in terms of sharing information—not necessarily personal information, but the social worker's willingness to talk about his or her interests and general life activities. A positive correlation was identified in the study between time and trust, defined as the child's willingness to share aspects of his or her inner life with a professional.

Studies consistently demonstrate the positive impact of the worker/child and adolescent alliance on intervention outcomes. A meta-analysis by Murphy and Hutton (2018), which included 29 studies and 2,900 clients and included measures of symptom severity, global functioning, and emotional distress, concluded that the effect of the client-rated alliance on outcomes reached 8% to 12%, which is consistent with studies of adults. These findings emphasize the value that regular monitoring of the client-perceived alliance can have in service delivery. The authors add that relationship development with this population requires the practitioner's ability to repair ruptures, as they may occur frequently.

Smaller-scale studies of various types of child and adolescent clients support the above findings. For example, evidence of the significance of the worker/client relationship is found in residential settings. One such study found a positive correlation between treatment alliance and client motivation (Roest, van der Helm, & Stams, 2016a) although more restrictive settings and longer-term stays were associated with lower alliance ratings (Roest et al.,

2016b). Other studies in those settings have found positive correlations between child and adolescent perceptions of group climate and alliances with designated staff mentors (Strijsbosch, Stams, Wissink, van der Helm, & Roest, 2018), Relationship continuity and the maintenance of a home-like atmosphere is also important (Swan, Holt, & Kirwan, 2018). Another study found that a strong working alliance in residential care was associated with fewer trauma symptoms in adulthood, measured several years later (Ayotte, Lanctot, & Tourigny, 2017), although the presence of more externalizing problems before treatment was associated with lower client-rated alliances (Ayotte, Lanctot, & Tourigny, 2015). A study of inpatient adolescents at a psychiatric facility found that an effective alliance need not follow a linear path, as it can withstand disruptions (Balkin & Schmit, 2018).

Adolescents who have experienced trauma may face special challenges in developing a treatment alliance due to their vulnerability to negative emotional states and problems with trust. Still, it was demonstrated in a study of children in a Canadian clinic that strong positive alliances were commonly developed with these clients (Zorzella, Rependa, & Muller, 2017). A similar study of youth with post-traumatic stress disorder (PTSD) in Germany found that the working alliance was a stronger predictor of outcome than the clients' initial treatment expectations (Kirsch, Keller, Tutus, & Goldbeck, 2018). Some studies have suggested that an alliance is more likely to result in positive client outcomes when coupled with certain types of intervention for PTSD. Adolescents in a Philadelphia program demonstrated better outcomes when the alliance was paired with exposure (a behavioral intervention) compared to client-centered therapy (Capaldi, Asnaani, Zandberg, Carpenter, & Foa, 2016). Likewise, in a study of youth in Norway, the alliance contributed more strongly to positive outcomes in trauma-focused cognitive-behavioral therapy (CBT) than the unspecified supportive interventions (Ormhaug, Jensen, Wentzel-Larsen, & Shirk, 2014).

Several literature reviews and small-scale studies indicate that children and adolescents with anxiety disorders who are treated with CBT require a positive therapeutic alliance with their providers to fully benefit from those interventions (Crawford, Frank, Palitz, Davis, & Kendall, 2017; Whitehead, Jones, Bilms, Lavner, & Suveg, 2019), including anxious clients with autism spectrum disorder (Kerns, Collier, Lewin, & Storch, 2018). In a school-based CBT program for adolescent depression, it was found that the initial alliance, developed in the first two sessions, was important to predicting client progress (Labouliere, Reyes, Shirk, & Carver, 2017).

Some studies have looked at the therapist's comfort level with clients and its impact on the relationship. One study focused on practitioners' anxiety levels about working with children and found an inverse relationship between their anxiety and the therapeutic alliance (Scherer & Ng, 2017). A study of practitioners in an English substance abuse treatment program also found that their stress levels were inversely correlated with the alliance (Daniels, Holdsworth, & Tramontano, 2017).

Given the evidence that good working relationships are possible, although challenging, with children and adolescents, it is important to consider how practitioners can best facilitate those relationships.

Strategies for Relationship Development with Children

Numerous studies have attempted to identify specific practitioner behaviors that further or hinder alliances with children (e.g., Creed & Kendall, 2005; Fjermestad et al., 2012; Hawley & Garland, 2008; Purswell & Bratton, 2018). Their findings can be summarized as follows:

Use activities, games, and toys. Both children and adolescents are often more amenable to engaging in activities than in talking to professionals, at least at the beginning. Those who regularly work with children typically have repertoires of resources that they use for that purpose. The social worker can further promote collaboration with the child by using words such as "we" and "let's" when designing activities and setting goals, which communicates a desire for collaboration. Some practitioners note that actions such as "secret handshakes" and using the "sunglasses" technique (letting the child wear sunglasses sometimes prompts then to be more disclosive about feelings) are a part of this process.

What follows are two examples of the power of activities in developing connections with children. The first comes from Angela, a 25-year-old Black female.

Hoops

"Zeke was a 10-year-old White male who attended our middle school program with an individualized education program (IEP) for an emotional disability. He lived with his maternal grandparents. I had regular individual counseling sessions with Zeke, primarily to provide him with coping skills to use when his anger was triggered in school. Zeke had recently had an altercation with staff and classmates and had been placed in a higher-level security section of the school. Zeke enjoyed physical activity. If he was participating in a physical activity when I came to see him, he refused to see me until the activity was over.

"Since I knew this was important to him, I started offering to play basketball during our meetings. Zeke was happy to do so and always tried to beat me in H-O-R-S-E while talking about his past week and any challenges or successes he may have had. I think that my getting involved in the game with Zeke allowed him to be more comfortable with me and with our conversations. My supervisor said that it was important to not let children win games on purpose if you can help it, because it provided them an opportunity to experience and deal with losing. Zeke and I were about equal in our shooting abilities and I sometimes beat him, which always surprised him, but he took well. The setting helped us to communicate without the pressure of being in a therapy room. This was a good example of working with children through methods that are fun and less formal. I tried to provide Zeke with a safe environment where he could talk about his challenges if he wanted, but he could also talk about his interests and anything else outside of his problems. When we first worked together he had very little to do with me and often would not speak at all, but this soon changed. The use of games also allowed Zeke to practice his communication skills with me. In fact, when I left at the end of the semester, he said he would miss our talks as much as the basketball."

Angela's work with Zeke was based on cognitive-behavioral skill-building interventions, but before initiating those strategies she understood the need to patiently develop a relationship of trust with him through nondirective activities.

The second example is provided by Michael, a 23-year-old White male who also worked with emotionally disturbed youth.

In the Garden

"While I was in graduate school I worked as a direct care staff member at a group home for adolescents. One of our residents was Donald, a 15-year-old boy from El Salvador. Donald was separated from his father when he was found to have been abused by him several years ago. He was eventually diagnosed with attention-deficit/hyperactivity disorder and struggled to regulate his emotions. He had a low frustration tolerance and had many aggressive outbursts that got him into trouble in all areas of his life. Donald functioned best when engaged with hands-on tasks. He was a fast and enthusiastic learner who took pride in his independence and ability to do things without assistance. Our work focused on his developing skills to regulate his emotions and interact appropriately with his peers. The best initial idea for working effectively with this sullen young man was to offer to teach him about gardening, an area in which I had experience and he was interested. Donald enjoyed all of it, and after my instruction he often went to the garden alone to weed out some of the lettuce so the plants did not crowd each other. Through this activity we developed a strong relationship. We mostly talked about growing vegetables, but he could also talk about his hopes, dreams, and worries, partly, it seemed, because he didn't have to look directly at me. Donald did well in our program. Later, he expressed an interest in cooking, and I showed him how to make scrambled eggs."

Michael's work with Donald was largely reflective, as he helped his client develop confidence and a sense of self-worth through activities focused on the mastery of skills that were not directly related to his presenting behavioral problems. Their positive relationship emerged from their joint attention to gardening tasks and Michael's investment in helping Donald pursue these new interests.

Other relationship development strategies for use with children include:

Customize the session to the child; find common ground. This includes learning about the child's likes and dislikes and incorporating that information into the interventions. For example, if a child enjoys music, talking about or listening to music can be a productive means of helping the child feel comfortable and more willing to share his or her thoughts and feelings. Using stories is another means of focusing interactions in a manner with which clients can relate.

Maintain a playful attitude. This goes beyond the use of activities to convey an overall sense of fun. One student remarked, "I am shameless when it comes to earning a client's trust through play. I'll get down on the floor and imitate an alligator to get a playful reaction that can help to develop our bond. Whatever works, I'll do it." It is also important to attempt to mirror the child's energy level. Many children engage well with a high-energy practitioner, although others may be intimidated by such an approach if it seems aggressive.

Validate the child's perspective. This is a process of recognizing and accepting the child's hesitance or ambivalence about being in treatment and being proactive in making that a part of the conversation. It also involves being able to take the child's point of view about whatever challenges he or she has been experiencing and how that might explain his or her reluctance to trust.

Frequently provide hope and encouragement. The practitioner should demonstrate a consistently positive attitude about his or her work with children and their potentials, perhaps more overtly than with older populations, and focus as much on their positive behaviors as the negative ones.

Go conversationally where the client takes you. This suggests allowing for flexibility in the session plan or structure. It is most important that the social worker is attentive to the client's mood and is willing to facilitate the client's conversing about any topics of his or her interest regardless of where the practitioner hopes the interaction will go. This strategy is consistent with that of the social worker's being patient with the client's difficulty with addressing sensitive topics.

Practitioner behaviors that have a negative impact on the relationship include pushing the child to talk before he or she is ready, being too formal in one's session behavior, not following through with promises to the child (such as failing to provide expected rewards or to bring certain items to a session), talking at inappropriate levels to the child (either above or below his or her developmental level), and excluding children from conversations with adult caregivers when they present in a session.

Many of these points are illustrated in this vignette, provided by Dorinda, an inexperienced 23-year-old White female who had a career interest in working with children.

The Uptight Social Worker

"Michael was an 11-year-old Black male sixth-grader at a midsized public middle school. He lived in a house with his mother, Ms. Bishop, who worked as a support staff member in a legal office, but he had no other close family. Michael's father and Ms. Bishop were separated and had a contentious relationship. Michael had spent time at his father's house on weekends until four months ago, when his father abruptly terminated all contact with him. In their current household routine Ms. Bishop arrived home from work at 8 each evening, leaving Michael alone at home from 3 p.m. until then. On Tuesdays and Thursdays, Ms. Bishop arranged for Michael to spend time with friends.

"School staff contacted me about Michael early in the school year. On the first day of school he ran out of his classroom and through the hallways, with administrators and teachers chasing after him. He refused to talk about what had prompted this action once he stopped running, and afterwards he sat in the office with his shirt pulled up around his face. This became a pattern for Michael over the next few weeks. Staff tried to support Michael by allowing him to leave class when he needed to, with a paraprofessional monitoring his location, but Michael would not communicate when he needed support and would often throw or slam things down instead. After Michael threw a notebook at a teacher, a staff meeting was held with his mother, and I was asked to initiate an anxiety coping program for him.

"I met with Michael in my office once per week for 30 minutes. The purpose of the sessions was for me to support Michael and enact behavioral strategies for keeping him in class without being disruptive. After each of our first five meetings, however, I felt frustrated. I tried to teach Michael about different emotions and body sensations connected to what he may be feeling but he didn't have much to say about any of that and didn't appear to want to learn anything. When I asked if he remembered what we had spoken about the previous week, he never did. I moved on to describing some skills that I thought could help Michael deal with his frustrations, but he didn't want to try any of them.

I was at a loss as to how to engage Michael. He acted like a much younger child. When he didn't want to do something, which was most of the time, he would stop talking and cover his face with his arm while slumped in his chair. Nothing I did got through to him.

"I talked about my frustrations with my supervisor, and we came up with a plan to challenge Michael more directly to participate in our meetings. So, at the time of our next meeting, I called Michael into the office as usual. He appeared to be unhappy. He mumbled when I said hello and quickly sat down. I began by asking if he remembered anything from the previous week. When he gave his stock answer, 'I don't know,' I pushed him to think. I told him he was smart and capable of remembering, and that I believed that he could come up with at least one thing he remembered. He was quiet for a moment, and then said that he remembered talking about 'feelings and stuff.' I felt good that he was able to come up with an answer and that I had decided to challenge him.

"As the session went on, I was surprised that Michael chose to participate in some of the relaxation skills I demonstrated. We practiced having a mindful body, sitting calmly, and breathing deeply. During this practice I joked with Michael, showing him different silly body postures and asking him if I looked like a mindful body. When he responded with laughter I became even more ridiculous with my 'posturing.' Michael appeared to enjoy the lighter tone of the session and sat up to pay more attention and try to imitate my gestures. Afterward, I told Michael that he had done a great job. He seemed embarrassed, looking down at the floor, and said that he hadn't, but he did smile. The smile was new; in fact, he had never displayed any positive feelings with me. I was encouraged by that smile. It felt like I had found a strategy for engaging Michael. When the session ended, he told me goodbye and left, still smiling.

"I know that a social worker's lack of confidence predicts a poor relationship. I struggled with my confidence in working with Michael during those early weeks. I had little experience in direct practice and felt unprepared to work with a child with such a young mindset. I felt stiff and formal. This probably made Michael feel as though he was being punished with these sessions. When I finally loosened up, Michael became more engaged.

"The personal and professional sides of a social worker blend to form a characteristic way of engaging with clients. I tried at the start of my work with Michael to adopt a formal manner, hoping that he would take our sessions seriously. All this accomplished was to make me feel unnatural and have Michael shut down. When I adopted a tone that better matched my personal style, the sessions flowed much better. I think that Michael felt more at ease *and less 'in trouble.' I was trying to strike a balance between building an alliance and providing a structure in which he seemed comfortable. At the end of this session, I felt hopeful. Michael's smile felt like an indication that this process was becoming positive. The session boosted my confidence."*

With the help of her supervisor Dorinda became aware of what she was doing wrong with her client. She was pushing Michael to talk prematurely, was purposely formal with him, and, partly as a result of that, talked to him with a "superior" air. He was not likely to respond to any of those behaviors. It is noteworthy that her engagement of Michael improved when she decided to be more "herself" with him. She became playful and more conversational. Even though she pushed Michael to respond to her she was complimentary in doing so, noting that he was bright and attentive. Dorinda became willing to customize her approach to meet his needs, and in doing so her attitude toward him became more positive. Still, she might have been more verbally validating of Michael's probable mixed feelings about his situation at the school, and more actively collaborative from the beginning, taking time to find out how he wanted to spend their time together.

Building Alliances with Adolescents

Relationship development with teens can be considered a two-step process, beginning with transforming their often-negative expectations into a believable promise of collaboration, and then carefully selecting intervention activities in which the teen can recognize potential benefits (Diamond, Liddle, Hogue, & Dakof, 1999). Practitioner behaviors associated with positive alliances have been identified through a variety of measures (Bachelor, 2013; Fjermestad et al., 2012; Quirk, Miller, Duncan, & Owen, 2013; Ribeiro, Ribeiro, Gonçalves, Horvath, & Stiles, 2013), some of which overlap with those that are appropriate for children. They include:

Validation of the adolescent's perspectives. Acknowledge that clients may be either ambivalent or unmotivated for intervention and invite them to share what they see as significant in their lives, including what they want (and don't want). The social worker cannot erase client mandates or other external pressures but by acknowledging them can demonstrate empathy and a realistic awareness of their situation. As a part of this perspective-developing process, the social worker should be open to learning in general about the client's life. The older the social worker, the less familiar he or she will be with the stresses involved in "current" adolescence.

Orient the adolescent to the collaborative nature of therapy. The social worker should inform the client at the beginning of the relationship, in as much detail as possible, what the intervention process will be like, highlighting opportunities for client choice. This includes being clear about boundaries on both sides and soliciting the client's help in articulating goals in a manner that makes them the client's own, and not those of a parent or other authority figure. In this way the social worker communicates to the client that he or she has real influence over the intervention process regarding agenda and goal setting, as well as (possibly) the frequency of meetings and type of intervention. Many adolescents feel as if they have no voice at all in the process, so confronting that assumption (with realistic attention to constraints) can help them to develop trust.

Present the self as an ally. The social worker should not come off as a source of criticism to the client but should demonstrate a preparation to advocate for the client's interests. At the same time, the social worker must not take sides between a client and caregiver. Also, addressing issues of trust, honesty, and confidentiality in the relationship, including the limits of the latter, can help the social worker avoid putting himself or herself into a position of perceived betrayal.

The following vignette comes from Rachel, a 24-year-old Hispanic single female social work student, who was aware of her adolescent client's sensitivity to the feelings of others and used that knowledge to help the client undertake a difficult transition, a process that enhanced their working relationship.

A Death in the Family

"Annie was a 15-year-old White female referred to the child advocacy center after reporting physical abuse by her mother's then boyfriend, now husband. Since then the stepfather had been in and out of jail, and Annie's mother lost shared custody of her. Annie missed them both and remained faithful to the

point of denying her experiences of abuse. After the abuse allegations, concerns had emerged about Annie's acting-out behaviors, isolation, and verbal aggression. She now lived with her biological father, stepmother, biological brother (also an agency client), half-sister, and paternal grandmother. This was a supportive and nurturing environment.

"More recently, Annie's grandmother, whom they called 'Grammie,' had entered hospice care for longstanding congestive heart failure with a life expectancy of two to three weeks. Grammie had lived with the children their entire lives. They had seen her admitted to the hospital on several occasions, visiting her each time and always seeing her pull through. Grammie had been a strong support for Annie and her siblings, and they had a close relationship. Dad expressed feelings of urgency in telling the children about their grandmother's imminent death. I spent time sharing ideas with dad about how to address this and assured him that both myself and his son's therapist would be there to provide support for the entire family. I worried that because Annie is observant, she and her siblings might sense a change in the family dynamic prior to the meeting.

"Annie and I had been a working together for six months. During that time, she had made large strides in feelings identification but continued to struggle with acknowledging her trauma. She enjoyed creative activities and instituting rules, desiring the control in sessions that she did not have in life. She had difficulty managing unstructured time as well as following directions, observing limits, and maintaining boundaries. I found myself having to reinstate limits on a regular basis with her. There were few instances where Annie leaned into her vulnerability and allowed me to address her feelings related to her current situation.

"As soon as I entered the waiting area that day and shared with Annie and her siblings that we would be meeting as a family, her affect changed. She looked curious and concerned, and hesitantly followed us back to the office area. We met in a different room as well, which was an additional tip-off to her that something unusual was about to happen. Both myself and the co-therapist, Audrey (the brother's therapist), tried to be warm and supportive. I opened the session by expressing that dad had something to share, and that this was a safe place to talk about how we were feeling. Dad said, 'You know Grammie has been sick for a long time. She's not doing well, and she won't be with us much longer.' There was silence. 'Grammie is doing to die soon,' he went on to say. Dad began to cry, and this gave the children permission to express their feelings. I permitted the ongoing silence to give the children time to process *what they had heard. Annie began to cry loudly, while her brother withdrew into himself, and their little sister innocently shared what she would miss most about Grammie. I was aware in this moment of my own feelings and experiences with grief and loss. After introducing time for any questions or shared feelings, to which the children didn't respond, we allowed the family time to grieve together.*

"Then, during the last half of the session, we took the three children to our play therapy room to paint pictures for Grammie and help them identify and express their emotions. We emphasized that while she was dying, she was still with them now, and they should cherish this time and use it to tell her how they felt. At the end of the session, I kept Annie back for a five-minute check-in: 'I just wanted to take a moment to touch base with you privately. I know that we didn't have our usual alone time this week, and that was a lot of information to take in. I'm wondering how you're feeling?' 'Good,' she said. 'You're saying you feel good. Sounds like spending some time making Grammie pictures helped you feel better. Is that right?' 'Yup. It did,' she responded. It was clear to me that she was not ready to talk, and as I knew, pushing promoted her further closing down. 'If you have any questions, or want to share how you're feeling,' I stated, 'this is a safe space and I am here to support you. You can tell me as much or as little as you want.' Annie nodded in agreement, and after a few moments of silence I asked, 'Would you like a hug?'

"Annie quickly stood up and held her arms out. I met her halfway, and we embraced. 'I haven't been honest with you,' she said. I reflected back this statement, to which she responded, 'I'm afraid to tell you how I'm feeling. I'm scared that you'll tell dad private things I tell you.' 'You're scared that I will share private information with your dad?' I said. 'Yes, because last time I was here I told my old worker a lot of things about my stepdad [the offender] and how I was feeling, and it was private, and she told my dad . . . so I've kept a lot from you, because I don't trust anyone here.'

"Many relationship issues emerged during that session. Most obviously was my role in facilitating the news of Grammie's imminent death. With no previous experience with grief, Annie would be mining new territory on feelings related to this anticipated loss in addition to her current struggles in acknowledging trauma. More surprising to me, however, were the issues that emerged about trust after our hug. Annie had been able to make room for trust. During my work with Annie we had experienced several decline and regrowth periods, so Annie's taking that moment to express feelings of mistrust and insecurity after receiving that contact spoke for itself. I was communicating *support, emphasizing the experience in the present moment. I knew, too, that I needed to stay mindful of our boundaries, given her history with physical abuse and vulnerability to trauma."*

Rachel was sensitive to Annie's emotional state, especially during this family crisis. It seems that they had already developed a good working relationship. Rachel implies that they had engaged in playful activities and enjoyed much general conversation, and that she exuded positivity in her approach to the client. Still, Rachel understood that Annie was holding back, keeping important thoughts and feelings to herself. During this family crisis, however, Rachel behaved in ways that drew Annie closer to her. Using nondirective person-centered therapy, she customized the session structure to focus on the recent family tragedy but was also collaborative in asking Rachel what she wanted to do during the second half. She validated Annie's feelings and demonstrated her caring and concern with the hug. She also had a new opportunity in this instance to present herself as an ally and attend to the client's emotional reactions. Following all this, the two of them could move past the barrier related to the client's issues with trust. We can't know how the rest of the intervention unfolded, and while it may have continued to be challenging, Rachel and Annie had reached a more authentic level of understanding.

Building Relationships with Parents and Caregivers

Working with children and adolescents usually involves working with their parents or primary caregivers as well. Developing alliances with these persons is sometimes difficult because they are often put in a position of being judged negatively as caregivers. Efforts to engage with parents can be effective, however. In a survey based on a national U.S. sample of families with a child receiving social services, it was found that effective working relationships were associated with the practitioner's efforts toward collaborative engagement, understood by these parents as being helped with service applications, making appointments, and following up after a service has begun (Cheng & Lo, 2016). With such an alliance parents are more likely to confide to their social workers about their family issues, make efforts to attend meetings, and take initiatives to contact the practitioner with their concerns (Lamers & Vermeiren, 2015). A large-scale study in Pennsylvania found that caregiver ratings of the therapeutic alliance were consistently high (84% of parents reported high and steady ratings over time) in a home- and school-based behavioral health service when the practitioners gave special attention to building alliances (Hutchison, Karpov, Crisan, Hulsey, & Dan, 2018). In a Southern California child care clinic study it was found that professionals tended to underestimate the extent to which families felt allied with them (Accurso & Garland, 2015). It appeared that practitioners were unaware of the quality of the alliance because they typically received little feedback about it.

The potential for a positive alliance with parents depends partly on environmental factors. In a study of a parent management training program at a prestigious eastern U.S. facility it was found that positive alliances with practitioners were associated with the pretreatment quality of the parents' interpersonal relationships and social functioning. The existence of material and lifestyle barriers to participating in an intervention predicted a poorer subsequent alliance (Kazdin & McWhinney, 2018).

An Australian study revealed that parents sometimes actively tested their social workers' trustworthiness and attempted to reduce the power inequities between them (Reimer, 2013). The parents' initial resistance to social workers' attempts to build relationships appeared to be a healthy protective response, as they were challenging the professionals' expectation that they would submissively work with strangers who wielded influence over their lives. In fact, the parents' attempts to test for the social workers' trustworthiness seemed fundamental to eventually reversing their reluctance to honestly discuss their child care concerns. This finding supports the notion that it is important for social workers to find a balance between professional restraint and empathic attention when working with parents in social welfare settings. The onus must be on the professional to ensure that the parents' and clients' experiences of the relationships are positive. Parent alliances are also enhanced when the practitioner asks evaluation questions of each family member at the end of each session (Barnard & Kuehl, 1995). This routine practice sets a tone of open exchange with parents and a more symmetrical relationship that advances their empowerment. Practitioner skills can be improved with this feedback as well.

Diamond, Diamond, and Liddle (2000) proposed five sequential steps of alliance building with parents and their children in family intervention:

- Reframe the goal of the intervention as being to improve family relationships rather than "fixing" the youth.
- Bond with the adolescent in individual sessions by exploring damaged parent–child trust issues and contracting with the youth to support discussions of these issues with the family.
- Build alliances with parents by spending time with them alone and exploring their stressors and parenting challenges. Emphasize that the focus of treatment is on relationship building and reattachments within the family.
- Maintain a focus on helping the youth and family discuss feelings and thoughts previously identified and impeding positive relations.
- As family tensions diminish, shift the focus to competence building for the youth in relation to peers and other social groups.

This final chapter vignette, intended to illustrate these points, comes from Chuck, a 33-year-old married White male who had initial difficulty engaging with the distrusting mother of his identified client, and Brenda, an adolescent who had recently given birth to a daughter and was being negligent in her parenting.

The New Mother

"Brenda Talley was a 16-year-old Black single mother of an eight-month old girl, Irene, both of whom lived with her 35-year-old divorced working mother, Doris. When Brenda got pregnant her longstanding problem with school truancy had worsened, which brought her to the attention of my children's services agency. Brenda eventually dropped out of school and lived at home during her pregnancy, but since the birth of the infant her mother had become exasperated with her lack of attention to the child. Doris, who worked as a beautician, said Brenda would not abide by basic household rules, had parties when her mother was away, lacked any sense of personal responsibility, and spent her time with a 'bad crowd.' She contacted us and I got involved with the family again.

"My assessment concurred that Brenda showed little concern about consistently meeting the child's basic needs. She expected her mother to take care of Irene while she pursued a social life. Doris had become so distressed about the

situation that she was put on probation at work due to excessive absenteeism and poor performance. She was concerned about the infant's welfare but said that she lacked the energy to provide proper care for her around the clock. Doris became so angry that she had thrown Brenda and the infant out of the house four times in the past two months. She believed that mothers needed to care for their young children, and she would not provide a setting where Brenda could avoid responsibility for her child. This was not as heartless as it might sound because there was an extended family in the neighborhood and Brenda and Irene stayed at the homes of her aunts, cousins, and friends for brief periods during those expulsions. Doris eventually allowed Brenda to return home, but the cycle continued.

"Doris was willing to participate in the interventions offered by my agency, but she did not seem enthusiastic about the possibility of change. She also didn't seem to trust me; maybe she thought I intended to take Irene away, which she did not want to happen. Brenda, for her part, seemed willing to participate in my interventions because she enjoyed the attention.

"Despite the high tension level in the household I enjoyed working with the Talleys. Brenda and I developed a good relationship quickly. She saw me as someone who would help get what her baby needed and would advise her mother to calm down about her behavior. This was naïve on Brenda's part, of course, and I did not encourage this line of thinking, but nevertheless it was a part of the reason she was always happy to see me. I implemented a behavioral program to help Brenda take steps to assume more responsibility for her child as well as her schooling, and Brenda participated gamely. She would not be expected to give up her friends and social activities but she did need to gradually spend more time with Irene and on her schoolwork. Brenda responded well to structure, a point I tried to emphasize with Doris.

"Doris had a realistic perspective on the challenges that lay ahead for herself and her daughter. She was an equal participant in the intervention, and I usually saw them together at the agency or their home. I liked Doris, and she was always pleasant, but for several months I felt that she was holding back information about herself and the family. She never said much about her personal life and was vague in her responses to my questions about her own activities. One day during a joint session, Brenda reacted to one of her mother's angry admonitions by saying, 'You just don't want to be interrupted when you're with your boyfriends doing drugs. I know you're out on the porch snorting that stuff.' Doris seemed stunned, as if her daughter had violated a family secret. She accepted the comment without a response, but after a few seconds she

CHILDREN AND ADOLESCENTS   147

became tearful and walked out of the room. I gathered that Brenda's comment was more or less accurate.

"Later that evening, I called Doris at home. She seemed surprised, and not happy, to hear from me. She said she was tired and didn't want to talk, but I asked her to listen to me for a minute. I said something like 'I know you love your daughter and do your best as a working single mother, and that this situation is hard on you. I get that. What is important here is how well your family and household can function with two dependent girls under your watch. I'm concerned about the welfare of all of you. I don't need to know everything about you, Doris, in order to work on stabilizing things at home. I'm not here to pry into your personal affairs or judge you. You have a right to a personal life and whatever you do there is of no concern to me as long as we can all work together on resolving the problems related to Brenda being a new mother. I hope you can believe that I am not to "catch" you in any questionable behaviors. You were a good mother before Irene came along and I believe you are still a good mother.' Doris didn't say much in response, but she did say thanks and that she would see me the next week.

"I meant what I said. I should have been concerned if Doris was using drugs, but if so it wasn't having a directly negative effect on her parenting. I needed her to participate with and trust me, and it wouldn't happen if I allowed our focus to get sidetracked. Doris gradually seemed to relax and show more motivation to particpate in our sessions. We were able to work on reinforcement strategies to improve her daughter's mothering skills and sense of responsibility. I tried to demonstrate my interest in Doris's position by talking with her in advance about all the ideas and resources I planned to share with Brenda."

Chuck understood that he had a reluctant parent in this situation and that he needed to reach out to help her understand that his intentions to help the entire family were sincere. He already had a good relationship with Brenda, but he needed a similar relationship with Doris, and his empathizing with her position helped this to come about. He emphasized that the family's welfare was his concern, encouraged Doris to be more honest with her feelings in family sessions, and kept the focus on building competencies among the two adults rather than trying to unearth new problem behaviors. Chuck also made a point of having as many one-on-one conversations with Doris as he did with Brenda. In retrospect, Chuck probably should have addressed with Doris his concerns about her "holding back" sooner, but fortunately her reasons for doing so eventually came up. It may also be questioned whether he minimized the seriousness of her drug use as it related to her relationship with Brenda.

Summary

Children and adolescents, because of their physical, cognitive, and emotional developmental levels, and their dependence on adult caregivers, can at times be challenging for social workers to engage in productive working relationships. Young people are slow to trust adults outside their family and peer groups, and authority figures in general. Understanding the developmental stages of middle childhood and adolescence can help social workers to devise engagement strategies that are likely to mesh with the life perspectives of these clients. Social workers must additionally take care to develop empathic relationships with caregivers, who often feel judged negatively because of their children's behaviors. This chapter has presented sets of engagement strategies for all three of those populations. The case vignettes served to illustrate the process of relationship development with children and adolescents in several types of problem situations.

8
Clients Toward Whom a Social Worker Feels Attraction

The broad nature of the social work profession offers opportunities for its practitioners to work with diverse clients in many settings. This variety of possible experiences is wonderful, but social workers tend to be drawn to some types of clients more than others, due in part to their abilities to connect with and enjoy them. A social worker's positive feelings about his or her clients is a good thing, but it is possible that at times he or she will experience a special fondness or attraction for a client, creating biases that get in the way of a constructive working relationship. The purposes of this chapter are to explore the circumstances in which positive feelings about clients develop and to suggest ways for social workers to manage those feelings in a way that keeps their focus on the client's welfare. The issue of negative feelings toward clients will be explored in the next chapter.

Attraction to Clients

People decide to become social workers for many reasons, one of which is that they care deeply about the welfare of others. It is this dedication that accounts for their persistence and effectiveness. Many people who come to the attention of social workers are dismissed or marginalized by other people in their lives; they may seem unlovable to many, but social workers are able to see qualities that help them form a connection. A social worker's positive feelings about clients can come from a variety of sources, including:

- Liking people in general and being naturally empathic
- Being drawn to certain types of client populations (for example, children, substance users, or older adults)
- Developing an admiration for the personal characteristics of a client

- Being favorably reminded of a person from the social worker's past whom the client resembles (countertransference)
- Developing physical attraction toward a client.

In this chapter reactions to clients based on any of the above sources will be termed "attraction" to distinguish them from the narrower concept of countertransference, which was described in Chapter 1 as a social worker's unconscious reaction to a client's attitudes toward him or her (Kachele, Erhardt, Seybert, & Buchholz, 2015). Countertransference is most closely identified with psychodynamic theories, although it has been adopted, usually in a broader form, by practitioners from other theoretical perspectives. For example, in a survey of 510 psychology practitioners, most of whom were either psychodynamic or cognitive-behavioral in orientation, all respondents endorsed the importance of monitoring and analyzing their emotional reactions to clients, whatever their source (Gordon et al., 2016). The psychodynamic practitioners, however, did so more extensively. The researchers concluded that such monitoring should always be a major component of direct practice regardless of the social worker's theoretical orientation.

Emotional reactions to clients can be positive or negative, but this chapter focuses on positive feelings that become strong enough to become problematic for the relationship. Common social worker behaviors that may be an indicator of problematic positive feelings toward a client include:

- Eagerly anticipating seeing a client
- Thinking excessively about a client during off-hours (except while adjusting to a new job, when doing so is common)
- Having trouble understanding a client's problems due to identifying closely with the person
- Being unduly impressed with a client
- Feeling hurt by a client's criticisms
- Doing things for a client that he or she is capable of (treating this client differently than others).

In some extreme circumstances, social workers may cross a boundary and try to form a friendship or romantic relationship with a client (Hepworth, Rooney, Rooney, & Stromm-Gottfried, 2017).

The social work profession's movement toward egalitarianism with clients increases the likelihood of mutual influence and the development of intense feelings by each person toward the other (Abbot, 2003). Further, the profession has moved from an assumption of practitioner objectivity to one that recognizes the human relationship at the core of intervention (Parth, Datz, Seidman, & Loffler-Stastka, 2017). The concept of intersubjectivity (Chapter 1) suggests that each person continuously reacts to the other on emotional levels and as such influences the other's perspectives on the relationship. There are certain challenges posed by this egalitarian spirit. Clients often want a personal relationship as well as a professional one, and they may come to mistake therapeutic positivity for friendship. Most practitioners accept that friendship with clients is never appropriate, and as much as social workers strive for a collaborative orientation, there is always a power differential in the relationship. Clients who expect reciprocity often feel betrayed when the worker needs to set limits on these expectations.

One may wonder if social workers can be said to love their clients, and if so, whether this is appropriate. The topic is not extensively discussed in the literature, possibly because practitioners believe that it is unprofessional to talk about love. It may help to acknowledge that love has many definitions, five of which may be pertinent to this discussion (Gelso, Rojas, & Marmarosh, 2013). Love can be understood as:

- Strong affection (feelings of liking and caring) for another person based on kinship or personal ties, as with friends and family members
- Affection based on admiration or having common interests, such as club members or professional colleagues
- A warm sense of attachment, enthusiasm, or devotion
- Altruistic or unselfish loyalty and benevolent concern for the good of another, which may apply to clients but also to social causes
- Attraction based on sexual desire.

Considering that practitioners may routinely experience the third and fourth definitions, it might indeed be said that social workers love many of their clients and that doing so is professionally appropriate.

Overly positive feelings about a client may, however, prevent a social worker from fully addressing the client's presenting problems. In one study 55 clinical psychology trainees from four university programs in Australia anonymously completed a questionnaire about their countertransference experiences, broadly defined (Cartwright, Rhodes, King, & Shires, 2014). Regarding their positive feelings, one major respondent theme was the desire to protect or take care of clients who were suffering. This sometimes led them to take more responsibility for the client's behavior and mental status than was warranted or to attempt to rescue the client from a negative situation. Another major theme was that of over-identifying with a client, which made it difficult for the practitioners to perceive the greater severity of the client's challenges. The trainees struggled at times to manage the strength of their emotions, and some noted that when they saw themselves as similar to a client they lost confidence in how to intervene.

The challenging effects on the relationship when strong positive feelings develop between the parties are illustrated in the following two vignettes. The first was written by Kailyn, a 30-year-old single Black social work student who worked with domestic violence survivors, a client population for whom she had great empathy and commitment. While she maintained good boundaries throughout the encounter, she was made uncomfortable by her client's expressions of a desire for a deeper relationship.

A Surprise Revelation

"Shayla was a 26-year-old White female who identified as lesbian and worked as a stock clerk in a retail store. She roomed with an elderly married couple. Shayla did not identify with a specific ethnicity, although in the past she identified as Arab. Two years ago, Shayla experienced multiple incidents of sexual violence perpetrated by her male roommate. She had experienced significant retraumatization while navigating related court proceedings, symptoms of which included flashbacks, panic attacks, and dissociation, which led her to seek services. Shayla's goals were to process her past trauma, decrease her anxiety, and develop distress tolerance skills. She had attended a counseling intake here two years ago but did not return because she was not comfortable with the practitioner and was not ready to deal with her emotions.

"At the time of this encounter, I had seen Shayla weekly for three months. When she came to the intake session her anxiety level was so high that her hands trembled and she experienced significant dissociation. Due her anxiety it was difficult for me to assess our rapport during the early sessions, but Shayla continued to attend and after a month she began to relax, coming prepared with topics to discuss. While most of our early work focused on her developing distress tolerance skills specific to court, Shayla's legal case had since concluded. Our recent sessions had focused on developing better communication skills

and confronting negative self-cognitions. I utilized psychodynamic and cognitive-behavioral therapy (CBT) interventions, as well as some narrative and somatic therapy techniques.

"The meeting before this one was our first teletherapy session, made necessary by restrictions due to the coronavirus pandemic, and I found it to be frustrating. Our internet connection was weak, and the stilted video, combined with Shayla's slow and deliberate communication style, made for an awkward interaction. My purpose for this session was for both of us to settle into this new therapeutic medium and to assess Shayla's anxiety levels related to the health crisis. On the day of our second telehealth encounter, I logged onto our session and found Shayla waiting for me. She had changed internet devices to improve our connection. I thanked her for her thoughtfulness and asked how she was doing. Shayla responded, without making eye contact, that it had been a long week. It appeared that she was fidgeting, so I commented on what I was seeing and asked how she was feeling. Shayla lifted her gaze abruptly and said, 'Well, I'm anxious.' I tried to normalize her experiencing that feeling but Shayla interrupted me, explaining she was also anxious about this session. She continued, 'I gave myself ten minutes before the session today to try to settle down, but it didn't help. I just sat here being anxious. I've been meeting with you for months now, and I'm still anxious every time.' I asked if her anxiety was any different than during our early sessions. She paused before responding, 'Now it's more like excitement. Like butterflies in my stomach. I . . . feel like I should apologize. I'm trying to remind myself that I'm your client, you're my therapist, and that's what this relationship is. It's not anything else. But I really like our time together. I wish we could see each other more often.' I paused and took a breath, wishing that this conversation wasn't occurring over video.

"Several important things had just happened. Shayla had been vulnerable and honest about struggling with her feelings about me and how to conceptualize our relationship. I began by thanking her for being vulnerable and sharing that, and I told her she did not have anything to apologize for. I said that the social worker/client relationship is unique, and boundaries can be challenging to maintain when you have a connection that in some ways is intimate and in other ways distant. I told Shayla that I, too, sometimes feel challenged to remember my role with clients because I care so much about them and their well-being. I said that I liked our time together as well, and that I was honored that she was so invested in our work. She smiled and nodded, and I turned the conversation back to the topic of her anxiety symptoms.

"I was quite anxious myself during that exchange, as I understood that Shayla had developed romantic feelings for me. Early in our work together, she said that she didn't feel safe in any area of her life. Shayla had experienced abuse by her mother, sister, foster family, and roommate and was still struggling with incidents of emotional abuse where she was living. I had initially taken a person-centered approach with her, demonstrating unconditional positive regard and expressions of benevolent curiosity. I tried to be both physically and energetically present in our sessions. Once our rapport developed we began to have rich conversations that I enjoyed very much. Shayla was an avid reader and interested in Eastern philosophy, as I was. We were able to discuss her trauma experiences by referring to the work of Viktor Frankl, with which we were both familiar. She practiced yoga, as I did, and I offered some related interventions for her anxiety management. In short, I came to like Shalya very much, and since one definition of love is 'a warm sense of attachment, enthusiasm, or devotion,' I can say that I loved her. As far as I could tell, few people in her life have loved her or believed that she was worthy of love. Because I had been demonstrating a depth of feeling for her over time, I should not have been surprised that a conversation like this would emerge.

"I know that the social worker/client relationship can sometimes lead to ambiguous, easily crossed boundaries. While I did not have feelings of sexual desire for Shayla and did not cross any professional boundaries with her, it was sometimes challenging for me to treat her the same as my other clients. I had to catch myself before offering to schedule a check-in call on a day I was not at my internship and to reflect when I found myself thinking excessively about her during off-hours and felt disappointed with myself when something I said did not 'land' with her. I had to think critically about my feelings toward Shayla and my role in her life. This involved considerable vulnerability in my supervision sessions.

"I think I handled my encounter with Shayla adequately, in that it didn't seem to adversely affect our future sessions, but I wish I had done more. I deflected the issue of her attraction after a few minutes rather than risk being vulnerable myself. I felt uncomfortable about how strongly I cared about Shayla and didn't feel confident navigating the conversation. The teletherapy medium made it even more uncomfortable for me, as I couldn't adequately assess her body language or read the emotional climate. When I discussed this later in supervision, I realized that I was almost intimidated by Shayla's disclosure. Because I had had similar feelings, my response was in part defensive to prevent me from having to disclose my own experience. I now regret not asking *her follow-up questions about what she wished our relationship looked like or how she envisioned it. Our relationship would not change, but it might have improved if we had talked the issue out."*

This vignette provides a good example of social worker's attraction to a client that was perhaps atypically strong but not inappropriate. The client exhibited several personality characteristics that were appealing to Kailyn, and while tempted to offer more of herself to this client than she did to others, she avoided doing so. Even when she learned of Shayla's feelings about her, Kailyn attempted to constructively address the situation and maintain their boundaries without making her client feel rejected. Kailyn admits that she could have been more thorough in processing their mutual feelings, but this was an unusual, awkward situation with which she had no prior experience. The social worker should be credited for processing the delicate session with her supervisor, and it appears that she was able to continue working effectively with the client afterward.

The next vignette was provided by Madeline, a 22-year-old single White female who was placed in an inpatient psychiatric facility. The outcome of her attraction to one client, which was more romantic in nature than that of Kailyn, almost compromised her position as a social worker and put her on the witness stand during the client's subsequent court hearing.

Going Out of My Way

"Michael was a 19-year-old single Hispanic male who was admitted to the psychiatric hospital for 'treatment of an incompetent defendant.' He had pending charges of malicious wounding. Prior to admission he had been demonstrating aggressive and even psychotic behavior in the jail, at one time running out of the showers naked and tackling a corrections officer. At his admission, though, Michael presented as withdrawn and quiet. When engaged by staff he either did not respond or used one or two words and spoke about topics that were unrelated to the conversation. After a few days Michael began to talk coherently and quickly returned to a normal functioning level. He did not take medication.

"As one of the student social workers I completed Michael's assessment and participated in developing his treatment plan. He was also in one of the legal education groups I was facilitating. Prior to the interaction described here, he

and I had been building rapport through art activities. Twice a week I brought supplies onto the ward and spend time drawing with him. We had casual conversations about our hobbies and interests, and over time he was able to have honest discussions with me. Michael was thinking clearly and said that his psychosis was probably due to bad drugs he got in jail. We built a friendly rapport and I found myself looking forward to spending time with him on the ward. He often shared things about his family, his treatment, and his interests. I found him to be a good guy but was not aware at the time that my working relationship with him was bordering on me wanting to call him a friend.

"One day I brought Michael into the treatment team room for a meeting. He displayed a bright affect and said he was happy to see me. He began talking about some events that had happened on the ward and then described his life before he was incarcerated and the events leading up to his arrest. Because I was feeling so comfortable with Michael I decided to ask some questions regarding his personal life and the arrest that were not necessary to my work. He was happy to oblige, and I was so interested in his story that I asked many details about his criminal actions. He responded willingly, but suddenly I realized that I had crossed a boundary and I told him to stop. If it was discovered that I had information relevant to his crimes I could get subpoenaed for his court hearing.

"Drawing this line felt awkward to me as our interactions up to then had been more casual than professional, and working with him felt like catching up with a friend. Michael was someone I would like to have spent time with outside of work, and it was at this point, finally realizing that I was attracted to him, that I knew I had to start putting stricter boundaries on our relationship. He stopped talking about the events surrounding his crime and thanked me for reminding him about where that could lead. He then started discussing his tumultuous family relationships, and I couldn't resist disclosing information about my family as well, which is something I rarely do. I liked Michael and told him more about my personal life than I should have. Clearly I was still having trouble with boundaries. Our relationship continued along those lines and I had to constantly remind myself of my role with him as a professional during the three weeks he was at the hospital.

"I realized that I was giving Michael preferential treatment over other clients. He may have concluded that my behavior was the norm for social workers and become confused when others on the staff did not provide this kind of reciprocity. Also, my treating him as a friend may have resulted in him not taking me seriously as a professional. If I had to confront him or implement a structured intervention, he may not have felt compelled to make the effort. I was concerned that my positive feelings for Michael may have blinded me to his flaws and rendered me incapable of suggesting corrective actions.

"I did not behave appropriately with this client. There is no excuse for that, but Michael had many qualities of the people I am friends with. He was laidback, intelligent, and humorous. He was close to my age and I could relate to some of the struggles he was facing with friends and family. It's possible that Michael's positive feelings toward me could have been helpful to his progress, as he was eager to process his thoughts and feelings with me. I tried to be honest with myself about how my feelings for Michael affected my role, but I kept fooling myself that our visits were for his benefit and not mine.

"Looking back on this relationship, I should not have questioned Michael about the events leading up to his arrest. I also should not have self-disclosed so much personal information. We connected, but in the end, I really did not know him well and had no idea what he might do with the information I was providing. I should have been more professional and limited the information we shared. In doing so I would have been respecting our boundaries and not opened him up to possible legal ramifications. My efforts helped Michael to come out of his shell, but ultimately I am afraid that he did not take me seriously as a professional."

While Madeline's roles in this setting were primarily those of assessment, supportive counseling, and discharge planning, she seems to have taken on a reflective theoretical approach with Michael, encouraging him to broadly explore the influences of past personal and family events on his current problem situation. Unfortunately, she failed to fully consider how that process can stir up strong feelings in the provider as well as the client. Madeline had developed romantic feelings about this client but did not admit this to herself until far along in his hospital stay. After the fact she was able to identify some of the sources of her feelings, but it does not appear that she ever processed them with a supervisor or peer. Madeline's engagement in mutual reflection was also dangerous in that it paradoxically put her at risk of having to provide negative testimony about Michael in court (although this did not happen). What sets this vignette apart from the first one is that the social worker's behaviors could have put her in a compromising situation, providing damaging evidence about the client to whom she felt favoritism.

The occasional experience of feeling sexual attraction for a client is common but not often discussed in the literature, which is why the topic is addressed in the next section.

Romantic Attraction to Clients

It is widely acknowledged that romantic and sexual attraction to and by clients happens at least occasionally to most direct practitioners (Kirby, 2019). This may be unavoidable because "unconscious" selves are never in exclusive relationships. That is, despite their efforts to uphold boundaries, social workers will at times develop some level of attraction to some of their clients. The nature of direct social work practice, in which clients' personal lives may be highly exposed, puts both parties at risk for these feelings. Intensive intervention, more common in longer-term work, can be an emotionally arousing process for both parties. Some practitioners normalize the occurrence of sexual attraction while others are distressed by it. Few social workers contemplate actual sexual involvement with their clients, but in every case it is something to be managed. Social workers should accept that romantic feelings may occur and seek to understand their sources and implications. When expressed by a client, the social worker should treat those feelings with the same respect as any others, although it is rarely advisable to share one's own romantic attraction with a client. Doing so places a special and needless burden on him or her.

In research studies practitioners report that their romantic feelings toward clients can have positive or negative effects on the quality of the intervention (Hayes, 2014). On the positive side it may increase their understanding of the working relationship, the client's relational patterns, and the worker's vulnerabilities. On the negative side sexual attraction may inhibit the practitioner's interventions and lead to actions based on poor judgment. The practitioner may become detached, seductive, aggressive, or dominant or actively pursue sexual involvement, always with damaging effects. While it is possible that these feelings may reflect a genuine loving bond, it is more often an indicator of the social worker's unresolved attachment needs or current experience of emotional deprivation (Gelso et al., 2013). The practitioner must always take responsibility for resolving the situation, preferably with a supervisor or trusted peer.

Studies conducted over at least the past 40 years yield consistent results about the frequency and effects of practitioners' attraction to clients. In a national survey a majority of social workers admitted to experiencing sexual attraction to clients at times (Bernsen, Tabachnick, & Pope, 1994). Among the 453 respondents (229 men and 224 women) 81.3% had been attracted to clients, with 90% of males and 70% of females admitting such attraction. Further, 19% of the males and 6% of the females who experienced attraction had considered sexual involvement with a client, with 7% of men ($n = 8$) and 1.5% of women ($n = 1$) having acted on those feelings. Over half (57%) reported that their attraction had ultimately been helpful to the intervention process and 63% said it had not been harmful. Further, half said that their feelings of attraction had not made them feel uncomfortable, guilty, or anxious. Eighty-five percent of respondents said that their clients were probably not aware of the attraction, and 61% sought supervision to deal with the issue. Significantly, 76% of respondents admitted that they had received little or no training on the topic.

Other studies report similar findings. In a survey of 122 members of the British Psychological Society, 87% reported experiencing sexual feelings toward clients at times (Giovazolias & Davis, 2001). More males than females admitted to occasional attraction (59% vs. 41%), but almost half of the total (45%) assessed those feelings as normal. Their common reactions to the experience included surprise, guilt, and anxiety about their unresolved personal issues; fears of losing control or being criticized by those who might learn of their attraction; frustration about their reluctance to speak openly about it to supervisors; and confusion about boundaries and appropriate actions to take. Fortunately, 82.6% discussed their attraction with another professional (48% with a supervisor). Half of the respondents (50.5%) felt that the attraction had a positive impact on therapy, even though they rarely admitted to their feelings with the client. Only 6.3% saw the attraction as having a negative impact on the intervention, while 43.2% believed it to be a neutral issue.

In a more recent study, 138 marital and family therapy students and their faculty supervisors responded to a national survey that included questions specific to treating couples (Harris & Harringer, 2009). Interestingly, 50% of students reported not having been sexually attracted to a client, but only 6% of their faculty agreed. The researchers surmised that the supervisors were more alert to signs of attraction than their supervisees. Fifty-three percent of the practitioners stated that when one member of a couple expressed attraction to them, they would process the issue with both parties, and more than 70% reported that they would meet with either the attracted or non-attracted partner to process the issue. If the attraction was reciprocated by the practitioner, 47% of respondents were not sure if being honest about their feelings would hurt the couple, while 53% said that reacting openly to the couple's disclosure might derail their interventions.

A group of researchers in the United Kingdom assessed the experiences of direct practitioners regarding sexual attraction to clients through interviews with 13 volunteers (seven men and six women) (Martin, Godfrey, Meekums, & Madill, 2011). It was again found that sexual attraction to clients is common and not necessarily harmful. The practitioners noted that there was an unavoidable tension in their efforts with clients to balance intimacy and closeness with distance and objectivity. They admitted that they were especially vulnerable to desires for romantic intimacy during times of their own personal stress, such as when they were experiencing conflicts with significant others or feeling emotionally deprived. The researchers in this study observed four problematic practitioner reactions to the experience of attraction: a self-protective/defensive reaction (strict reinforcement of boundaries), a moralizing/omnipotent stance (the worker taking on the role of the superior ethical party), overprotective anxiety (offering additional supports to the client to avoid the appearance of rejection, which was more common among newer therapists), and neediness/over-identification (pursuing a relationship and crossing boundaries).

Some scholars have wondered if sexual acting out by practitioners might be more common with certain types of clients. In a Swiss study 57 women who had been sexually assaulted by their practitioners were interviewed along with a control group of 43 women who had not experienced such an assault to determine if there were any common personality factors, personal background factors, or personal circumstances that put them at risk for assault (Moggi, Brodbeck, & Hirsbrunner, 2000). No such factors emerged, which led the researchers to conclude that therapist factors more likely contributed to these episodes, possibly involving the practitioner's narcissistic needs and an absence of intimate relationships outside of the therapist's professional work. Not surprisingly, the abused women had poorer intervention outcomes than those in the control group.

A literature review focused on the reactions of practitioners whose clients expressed attraction for them (Sonne & Jochai, 2013). The authors noted that when this happens, some providers become uncomfortable and worry that the event may negatively influence the intervention. The practitioners might develop their own sexual feelings in response to the client. Few clients report an awareness of this attraction because practitioners rarely bring the issue up, although men do so more often than women. Therapists disagree whether it interferes with their work, and they admit that their willingness to process the issue with another person depends on their relationship with that person, their perception of the ethicality of their behavior, and their degree of training. A minority of professionals rate their training as adequate for managing instances of client attraction.

Recommendations for Managing Attraction

Several authors in this chapter offer recommendations, based on their research or practice backgrounds, to help practitioners effectively process romantic or sexual feelings toward clients (Gelso et al., 2013; Giovazolias & Davis, 2001; Martin et al., 2011; Sonne & Jochai, 2013). These include:

Accept that having romantic and sexual feelings about clients is normal. They do not represent a mark of weakness or lack of professionalism and should not be considered a secret to be kept from peers or supervisors.

Maintain explicit boundaries with clients. Boundary crossing is often an appropriate strategy during an intervention, and with a clear base one can be more confident that when he or she decides to cross a boundary it is for the client's benefit, rather than a means for the social worker to meet his or her personal needs.

Take care to get personal needs met outside of work, so that they will less likely become a major feature of the professional relationship.

Recognize vulnerabilities. The social worker should try to develop an understanding of the kinds of clients, situations, or personal circumstances that put him or her at risk of strong attraction. In this way the social worker can predict when it might occur and prevent those feelings from becoming problematic.

Notice when it happens. Many practitioners tend to minimize or deny their feelings of attraction, which puts them at risk of remaining unaware of how those feelings may affect their work with a client.

Accept the need to take measures to resolve the issue. It is always the social worker's responsibility to ensure that the relationship remains professional, and it is usually best not to involve the client in processing issues related to attraction, unless the client admits such feelings first, as in Kailyn's experience.

Be proactive in consulting with supervisees and peers. Like any other challenging issue that arises in practice, attraction to a client can be constructively processed if social workers feel able to take others into their confidence without a fear of being somehow reprimanded.

Reflect on the experience between sessions to understand its sources. This should be done independently or with a trusted other.

Formulate a solution and continue to work for the client's therapeutic benefit. In some cases the client will need to be transferred if the practitioner's feelings cannot be adequately managed, but this is generally not indicated. With time and support the social worker will in most cases be able to devise a strategy for resolving the feelings and continue to work productively with the client.

Get training in the issue. Many practitioners do not get education or continuing education on this sensitive topic, which is consistently noted as a problem for the profession and a reason why some practitioners are at risk for mismanaging the issue.

The following vignette comes from Amber, a 24-year-old White single female who developed intense positive feelings for a client based on identifying strongly with her. Fortunately, Amber recognized what was happening and was able to take measures to keep her feelings from contaminating the intervention.

Over-identification

"Morgan was a 23-year-old Hispanic female who was working on a graduate degree in occupational therapy. She had been in an abusive heterosexual relationship for six years, being subject to continuous body shaming. She sought services at my agency to help her cope with these traumas. Morgan had been experiencing severe anxiety related to her trauma as well as post-traumatic symptoms, including panic attacks, flashbacks, and nightmares. With the help of medication there had been improvement in her panic symptoms, but the

other anxiety symptoms were still present. Despite all the trauma she had experienced, Morgan was a kindhearted and hardworking individual.

"I had been working with Morgan since she ended the relationship with her abuser. When we first met I felt great compassion for her, as she expressed such a negative self-image. In the first session her body physically shook the entire time, but over the coming weeks I also found Morgan to be highly engaging. We were similar in age and worked in a similar field. I was impressed with her dedication to her professional field. Additionally, Morgan identified as bisexual, as I did. I always tended to be more comfortable around people like me who identified as queer. All these things led to my becoming particularly fond of this client.

"Our work together had been productive, although Morgan continued to struggle with anxiety and had trouble focusing on school assignments, sleeping, eating, and getting up in the morning. Her abuser was continuing to pester her. He would come to her apartment and bang on the door and leave. His behaviors made Morgan feel unsafe in her own home. When she went to get a protective order, she was refused. Together, we had worked on safety and sleep planning, coping skills for anxiety, and trauma education.

"This session began with my inquiring how Morgan was feeling and what had gone on over a longer break between our sessions than usual. She smiled weakly and said that her break had been good but she had a difficult night the evening before. She had a panic attack that was triggered by a phone conversation with her sister about dieting and losing weight. Her abuser had often made fun of Morgan's body, criticized her weight and appearance, and terrorized her into not eating in front of him. She had once recounted a story where they were attending a social event together. She fasted the day before to 'look pretty' but had ended up fainting at the event and her abuser berated her for fainting.

"As Morgan continued talking and crying though her description of the previous night, she disclosed that she had been binging and purging every day for the past few weeks. When she said this, I felt my stomach drop. I knew that Morgan had difficulties with body image and eating but I had not realized that she was struggling with bulimia. I had always struggled with body issues and bulimia myself. I felt a stronger wave of affection for my client and wanted desperately to comfort and support her, to validate her pain as well as inquire further about the binging and purging behaviors.

"Morgan explained that she did not like eating in front of people and would not eat anything at school except for coffee or a portable vegetable. Lately, she had been losing control of herself, prompting binging and purging episodes. When she had gone home for spring break, her mother, too, had been hard on her because of her weight. She tearfully explained that she was now feeling shame, guilt, and disgust with her binging and purging behaviors. She said she knew she was not a bad person but could not help but feel that she was disgusting anyway. My heart was breaking for her. I knew that feeling as well.

"I had started to cry and needed to say something. I stated that I knew how she feels because I had struggled with bulimia as well. I told her that she was not a bad person; she had been through so much and was fighting to overcome it. I said I was proud of her for being able to tell me and that I felt she had come a long way, pointing out how her panic attacks had almost disappeared. I suddenly worried, too, that I had said the wrong thing by disclosing my own eating disorder history, but I hoped it would help normalize her feelings. Morgan looked at me and smiled tearfully. She thanked me for sharing with her because she knew it was hard to do so. I became concerned that she might feel like she had to comfort me, so I quickly reminded her that I was there for her. She smiled again and said she knew that. I changed the subject by asking her if she thought it would be helpful to make art related to body image issues, since she was a creative person in the past, and she agreed. I suggested doing a 'happy place' body scan before she left, which seemed to help her.

"Strong feelings can get in the way of the intervention process, muddying the relationship between client and social worker. This was a clear case of over-identification on my part. I had my own unresolved feelings around my body and eating habits that had affected my behavior toward Morgan. When I shared my eating issues, I wanted her to know that she was not alone, but I could have caused harm by validating the binging and purging behaviors. I hoped that this was not the case.

"When Morgan disclosed her struggle, I felt a surge of emotion that I later recognized as a desire to protect her. It was important for me to later address those feelings and identify where they were coming from. I had always been fond of this client, and when she shared her bulimia, it took me to another emotional level because I could so perfectly identify with her. Even before, when she would tell me about the horrible things her abuser did to her related to body shaming, I felt uncomfortable and didn't know how to respond because I had also been bullied for my appearance. I could see myself in her and I longed to care and protect her from all the hurt she experienced, the same way I wanted someone to do this for me.

"Self-disclosure should always be used purposefully, and I think I failed in this regard because my sharing was a result of feeling happy to find another person like myself to talk with. I saw her as a peer because of our closeness in age, experiences, and career fields. I may have shared more than I should have. I was able to support the client but she may have also felt burdened with this information. If I could relive this session I would not share as much about myself. Our subsequent sessions seemed to unfold appropriately, with the focus always being on Morgan, although I still wondered if she might feel the need to take care of me."

Amber appears to have recovered from her mistake of excessive self-disclosure that resulted from having strong positive feelings about Morgan. Immediately after the problematic session she attended to some of the recommendations presented earlier in this chapter about managing romantic feelings toward clients, but she could have gone farther. To her credit, Amber seemed to accept her feelings of love and attraction as normal and recognized her vulnerabilities as being based on unresolved issues from her own past. She noticed when the boundary-crossing incident occurred, accepted the need to take measures to resolve it, and reflected extensively on the experience. On the other hand, Amber did cross a boundary when in her vulnerable state and did not consult with anyone later about the issue. Amber could also have made a point of getting additional training about the matter and, as part of her reflections, made sure that she was getting her own needs met outside this relationship.

Things can go very wrong when a practitioner gives in to his or her romantic feelings for a client. This final vignette was provided by Jordan, a 30-year-old White divorced social worker with no children who, to his later regret, committed a major boundary violation by entering into a romantic relationship with a client.

A Chance at Intimacy

"I am a clinical social worker and have been in private practice since receiving my license many years ago. I consider myself to be an effective professional and have enjoyed a long career working with individuals and couples. I have made mistakes and used poor judgment with clients at times, like anyone else. The worst mistake I ever made had to do with a female client with whom

I developed a romantic relationship. At the time I thought my judgment was good, but in retrospect I know that it was terrible. Fortunately, I never repeated the mistake. I learned the hard way to better manage sexual feelings toward clients.

"I always had an active dating life, although during my three-year marriage I learned it was difficult for me to maintain emotional intimacy over time, to responsibly handle the bad times as well as the good times. After my divorce I resumed seeing women and enjoying their company, but it bothered me that I was apparently not good at emotional intimacy and that I tended to have romantic relationships that were rather superficial.

"At about this time a colleague referred a client to me named Lisa. She was in her late twenties and was seeking help for chronic depression. She had been depressed since her adolescence, and despite one short-term hospitalization in her teens she functioned well socially and vocationally. Her depression manifested as a pessimistic attitude about relationships and a general fatalism about her chances of ever being happy. Lisa was moody, appearing pleasant and composed at times but other times seeming sullen. She worked successfully as an office manager at a large craft store and lived alone in an apartment. She had female friends and dated men from time to time, although not for long, and she tended to obsess about her difficulties building trust and feeling comfortable with men. She wanted to develop a stronger sense of individuality. I should add that Lisa was also physically striking to me, very attractive. She was also intelligent. We connected well from the beginning.

"The intervention went well for the first eight weeks. I was a cognitive-behavioral practitioner and we focused on identifying her core beliefs, analyzing how her self-statements intruded negatively into challenging social situations, developing a behavioral chain analysis to account for her mood states, and examining her assumptions about relationships, including her anxieties about sex. I was always aware that I found Lisa to be attractive and that fact might have worked positively in her case for a while, as I always felt energized and attentive to her. On the other hand, as Lisa explored her social history, I became aware of her desire for intimacy coupled with attachment fears, and the sadness that resulted from her disappointments. All of that struck a chord with me, as I was experiencing the same issues. I felt even then that this was a woman I would enjoy being with, and that we might be able to experience emotional intimacy together. I knew then that my attraction was getting out of hand, but still, no thoughts of acting on that impulse occurred to me. Of

course, one of the lessons I learned afterward is that a social worker might minimize the significance of his romantic feelings about a client.

"We continued our work together, which we had estimated might require three or four months. I didn't have a supervisor at the time and chose not to discuss my attraction issues with anyone else for fear of being negatively judged. Instead I started feeling more sexual with her and recognized that I wanted to comfort her whenever she described her ongoing loneliness. I was on the brink of crossing a boundary and considered offering her a hug at the end of one session, but I continued to resist. I should say that I never suspected that Lisa was being manipulative with me. She was always presenting authentically. She was supposed to be open with me; I was her therapist. I was relieved when it came time for my vacation, so I could get away for a while and process my feelings.

"A few male friends and I went to the Caribbean for two weeks and had a marvelous time on the beach. I did think about Lisa, but I was able to live in the moment and enjoy the time with my friends. I felt much better when I returned, but it was during my first session with Lisa that our relationship took a drastic turn. When I asked how she had been doing she said something like, 'I have to admit I spent most of my time these last two weeks thinking about you, and wondering what you were doing, and how I missed you. To tell you the truth, I think I'm falling in love with you.' This stunned me. In retrospect I had obviously been vulnerable to her attractiveness. Instead of addressing it openly with her, or with anyone else, and processing its source, and perhaps helping her recognize her feelings as a manifestation of a problematic pattern, I responded, 'Well, I feel the same way, Lisa. I think about you, too, and sometimes wish I could be with you socially. But I can't work with you under these circumstances. It wouldn't be ethical. So, the first thing we must do is decide whether to stop seeing each other as therapist and client.' I was surprised and secretly gratified when Lisa agreed with me and said that we should end our current relationship. After a short, awkward conversation that I can't even recall, she said 'So now what? Can we see each other socially?' I responded, 'I think we need to take some time. Let's both think about this. I'll get in touch with you within the week. We need to be careful to not get involved in something we may regret.' She agreed.

"Her admission of attraction to me was powerful, and given my reciprocal feelings I felt that I had acted professionally about ending our therapy. I suppose that gave me a rationale for doing what I did next, which was to call her a few days later and ask to see her for lunch. That was the beginning of a dating relationship that went on for two months. We did what all new couples do: went out on the town, shared a lot of meals, stayed at each other's apartments, and had sex. It was all quite wonderful at first, and I remember being amazed that I would find my soulmate as a therapy client. I knew that entering such a relationship would normally be questionable, but it had all worked out and had been worth the risk.

"Then it all fell apart. Over time we started presenting our less attractive selves to each other, and arguing, and I felt especially stung one day when Lisa said to me, 'You're not behaving at all like the man I knew as a therapist. What happened to that guy?' Now, one reason for never dating a client is that they are accustomed to seeing the therapist in his most positive, compassionate light. There's no way that a real partner can measure up to that for long. Lisa seemed to get depressed again, and she broke up with me a few unhappy weeks later, saying that she was sorry our romance had ever started. I returned to my old life feeling that I had broken a cardinal ethical rule and damaged a client. It was awful. I never heard from or about Lisa after that. I suspect she continued to have the same sorts of problems that brought her to me, and it was my fault.

"Not right away but about a year later, I got into therapy to explore the reasons for my vulnerabilities to certain kinds of clients. I don't want to get into my personal issues here, but I do want to say that I became much more aware that when it comes to sexual attraction, one's judgment often suffers, and so one must always have a trusted colleague to talk with about it."

Jordan acknowledged that his judgment was severely compromised by the reciprocal romantic feelings between himself and Lisa, but he also stated that at the time he felt his judgment was sound. He felt that he was behaving responsibly by terminating the therapy relationship when those feelings were openly exposed and doing so made their new relationship justifiable. Of course, the romance was short-lived and ended in disaster. But his decisions went against the social work code of ethics, which states that romantic relationships with current or former clients are never appropriate. Further, his decision to end therapy rather than process the client's feelings toward him prevented him from helping her interrupt a problematic relationship pattern and even made it worse by facilitating her continued reliance on it. Lisa might have benefited from processing the issue in therapy, and Jordan may have kept his own feelings in check while doing so with the help of a supervisor. But that didn't happen.

Notice that Jordan did recognize his vulnerabilities, knew that his romantic feelings were developing, accepted them as normal, reflected on the situation (briefly), and accepted the need to take measures. However, the measures he took were inappropriate and damaging to his client. This is because he did not consult with a trusted other and consider that his personal needs should be met outside of his work.

Summary

Having positive feelings for, and enjoying relationships with, clients is an indicator of a social worker's humanitarianism and dedication to the profession. The material in this chapter is not meant to imply that such feelings are inappropriate. At times, however, strong feelings of liking and attraction to a client can compromise the social worker's judgment and result in a lesser quality of care, as the practitioner may begin to attend to his or her needs as much as the client's. In rare cases those feelings can result in damaging acting-out behaviors. For that reason, it is important for social workers not only to be aware of the normalcy of occasionally developing strong feelings of attraction toward clients but also to implement corrective strategies learned in advance so that they can manage them proactively and avoid the possibility of doing harm to a client.

9
Managing Negative Feelings About Clients

You are in a first meeting with a 35-year-old single mother of two children, ages six and four. The children have been removed from the home by the local children's services agency because of maternal neglect. The unemployed client, who is required to see you as a condition of regaining custody of her children, seems more focused on getting her social needs met. She had been in the habit of leaving the kids home alone for hours while running errands and visiting with friends, and when at home she often kept them locked in a bedroom as she watched television and talked on the phone. The client has a boyfriend and doesn't want to give him the impression that the children will be her priority. During your assessment she complains about mistreatment at the hands of the social services system and says there is nothing you could possibly know about the challenges she faces living in an oppressive society.

Another client is a 40-year-old married male who experiences chronic depression. You meet with him weekly for psychosocial counseling as he wants to overcome his lack of energy and motivation and get a paying job. His wife, who works full time and is supportive, does not seem to mind that her husband is "stuck" because her own career and social life is full. The client, who has not been active outside the house for two years, tends to complain in sessions about how nothing goes well for him and none of his treatments seem to be working. He wonders at times if seeing you is worthwhile, as you do not seem to be helpful.

A third client, a 12-year-old boy with conduct disorder, has a history of bullying and fighting with his peers and does not see his behavior as a problem, even though it gets him suspended from school regularly. He shows you little respect and sometimes talks of "needing

> *to take care of myself by attacking" people who "hassle" him. He becomes angry with you sometimes and you can imagine that he might act out toward you in some way.*

All three of these clients might be difficult for a social worker to like, or feel comfortable with, for different reasons. The first client is engaging in behaviors (child neglect) that would be offensive to most people. The second client might be difficult for some social workers to like due to his lack of evident effort to change, even in the context of his depression. The third client might feel physically threatening to a social worker, which could make him or her reluctant to enforce an intervention plan. In all three examples the social worker might transcend his or her initial negative reactions, but not easily.

Social workers are like anyone else in that there are people to whom they are drawn and others who repel them. Some clients have engaged in behaviors so repulsive that almost anyone would feel uncomfortable in their presence, but there are others who simply "push the buttons" of social workers in ways that are unique to each of them. The purposes of this chapter are to recognize that social workers may have difficulty experiencing empathy for some clients and to consider how they can transcend that barrier to develop positive working relationships with them. Three sources of negative feelings will be considered: client rejection of the social worker, client violation of social norms, and unconscious practitioner reactions.

The term *reactance* is used here to characterize a social worker's negative reactions to clients rather than the classical term of countertransference because, while related, the former term does not assume a particular theoretical perspective (Hepworth, Rooney, Rooney, & Stromm-Gottfried, 2017). Social workers should assess and monitor their negative reactions when they occur in any practice encounter regarding how they influence the relationship. Many such negative reactions can be evidenced by:

- Dreading an upcoming session with a client
- Feeling intimidated by a client
- Being bored with a client
- Feeling angry with a client for nonspecific reasons
- Feeling hurt by a client's criticisms
- Feeling uncomfortable discussing certain topics (Hepworth et al., 2017).

These reactions become problematic when they cause the social worker's interventions to be based on his or her own feelings rather than the client's needs.

The first source of negative reactions, a client's rejection of the social worker, is described next.

Recognition Theory

Recognition theory asserts that constructive relationships with clients (and all people) include the three conditions of recognition, respect, and reciprocity (Turney, 2012). The first condition refers to the importance of being "recognized" by another person, or being seen, considered, and taken to be significant, as a way to get one's needs for affirmation met. As a result of being recognized as significant, the person perceives the self as worthy of concern and interest. Second, respect is the condition of being treated as an end in oneself, not merely as a means to an end. For example, clients feel that they are being treated with respect when they perceive that the social worker is according them innate worth as human beings, not only because they are means to a paycheck or an object of curiosity. There are many ways that a social worker shows respect to a client, including being explicit about concerns and requirements for change, being clear about the limits and range of services, and adhering responsibly to the structure of the intervention. Finally, reciprocity is the perceived opportunity in a relationship to give and to receive. Through this process both parties have a shared sense of egalitarianism rather than one feeling subservient to or "less than" the other. Social workers can achieve some level of reciprocity with their clients through collaboration and accepting the client's input into all intervention decisions.

Regarding its role in reactance, social workers can be negatively affected by a refusal or failure of recognition from their clients. One (but not the only) reason that people become social workers is to develop and sustain a sense of self-worth by helping others. Toward this end they try to provide their clients with secure holding environments that, when accepted by clients, serve to hold the practitioner as well (Green, 2006). The rejecting client, however, deprives the social worker of recognition and precipitates reactions of anxiety and anger. The social worker gives and the client receives, or refuses to receive, without any indication of appreciation. The social worker's resulting negative reactions are normal and should not be denied. In fact, the negative feelings related to the absence of recognition from clients have been described in the object relations literature as "hate" (Winnicott, 1949). While owning this term may be hard for many social workers, doing so enables it to be worked through, potentially resulting in a better practice relationship.

When a social worker is in a state of frustrated need (recognition), his or her task is to find a way back to recognizing the client as a person who is not responsible for meeting the social worker's personal needs. When the social worker becomes aware of the anger or hate (the term "frustration" can be substituted here), he or she can learn to control it rather than be controlled by it. The experience of anger can be empowering, as the social worker can say (internally) to the client, "I don't need to rely on you to recognize me; I am freeing myself from my need for affirmation from you." The social worker can use his or her aggression constructively in this self-delineating way, and the client can then be recognized more clearly as a separate subject. In other words, using aggression in the service of appropriate separation can be a forerunner to greater comfort with the relationship.

This theme of reactance due to a failure of recognition is illustrated in this case description by Amber, a 25-year-old single White female.

Leave Me Alone

"Jack was a 17-year-old White male who grew up in a small town with three younger siblings. When Jack was six years old, his father died by suicide. When he was 14 years old, Jack took it upon himself to take his younger siblings and leave his mom, who was addicted to heroin and would not care for the kids. Jack and his younger siblings lived in abandoned houses most of the time and Jack would steal food and water to take care of them. Jack was also selling cocaine and heroin on the street. Jack and his siblings lived with their maternal grandmother for a time until she kicked them out for being too difficult to handle.

"Jack was caught selling heroin when he was 16 years old and spent a few months in jail until he was sent to a residential drug treatment facility. His siblings were taken in by his maternal aunt, who said she had known nothing about the children's prior living arrangements. Jack was later referred to the Independent Living Program (ILP) at my agency and came here four months ago. He was 17 years old at the time. It was assumed that he was no longer

using drugs; he came to the ILP to learn more functional independent living skills so that he might live successfully in the community.

"Jack had a diagnosis of attention-deficit/hyperactivity disorder and had a prescription for Adderall, which he took when he "felt like it." Staff suspected that Jack was selling his medication, as sometimes his entire supply would be gone within days of refilling it. When asked about this, Jack would say he flushed them because he changed his mind about taking medication.

"While at our agency Jack worked five days per week at a restaurant and spent the rest of his time creating music or practicing tattoos on himself or his friends. I was assigned to work with Jack along with a caseworker, as our supervisors thought he would need two staff to support him. I worked from a cognitive-behavioral theoretical approach. I tried teaching him skills such as making and going to doctors' appointments, obtaining proper identification from the Department of Motor Vehicles, grocery shopping, and applying for jobs. Jack was completely resistant to receiving any kind of help, though. He would usually shut down when working with me, refusing to talk. Most of the time he would glare at me and ask, 'What is the point of this crap?'

"I tried my best, for a while, to build a positive relationship with Jack, but he was always nasty with me. Sometimes, if I smiled too much, he would tell me to stop smiling. If I went to his apartment, even for a scheduled visit, he would curse at me to leave. I would often find him smoking cigarettes, which was against the rules, and when I asked him to put them out, he would say no, and talk about how ignorant I was. After about four months the agency no longer saw him fit for the program as he was disrespecting all other staff as well, breaking the rules, and damaging his apartment. Jack put out cigarettes in the carpet and there were tattoo ink stains all over. He was discharged into the care of the Department of Social Services, where he was placed in another apartment. I wasn't sorry to see him go. In fact, I had come to dread seeing Jack, and for the last month he was there I was just going through the motions with him. I did feel guilty about that, but I told myself that Jack was hopeless.

"A few weeks later, during winter break when students had time off from their internships, the agency hired me to work part time in the ILP, as they needed additional help over the holidays. One of my duties was to get ready for Christmas. Part of that project involved getting gifts for the clients in the program. Our budget was roughly $150 per youth. The director assigned me to collect Jack's gifts, since he had just left the program, as well as those of another youth. I had enjoyed working with the other client, so I enjoyed shopping for him. As for Jack, not so much. The director's idea was to purchase tattoo *ink for Jack, as he dreamed of being a tattoo artist. This was also to ensure his safety, as he had been using pen ink, which can be dangerous. The only place I could find that sold tattoo ink was a one-hour drive away, and the director assigned me to go there. I understood the importance of treating all youth equally and not letting personal opinions get in one's way, but the last thing I wanted to do was travel for two hours to buy a Christmas present for a youth who had been nothing but harsh to me. I was somehow able to push my feelings about Jack aside and make the trip to get his gift, but it was a challenge.*

"I later realized that I developed negative feelings toward Jack at least in part due to his not according me any significance and making me feel worthless. He did not show me recognition, respect, or a desire for reciprocity while I was putting effort into his treatment. I know that when social workers have negative feelings toward clients, they sometimes externalize the issue by choosing specific things about the client that are unlikeable. With Jack, I blamed my dislike on his inability to accept help and his rudeness to my colleagues and myself. I struggled with my confidence as a social worker, too, and not being able to get through to Jack made me feel that I did not have strong social work skills. I admit that I wanted to look good at my internship and be the intern who was able to get through to Jack when others could not. I believe I am a pretty dedicated person, so I took on this task with all my effort. I reached out to Jack every day and gave him the space he needed when he seemed to be overwhelmed. My desire to 'prove myself' to the director kept me going with Jack but made his rejection of me more painful.

"The only thing I would do differently in working with Jack would be to utilize my field instructor more. When I was feeling such strong dislike toward Jack I should have consulted with her. I might have been able to better identify the reasons for my feelings toward Jack and brainstorm ways to push past them. I worried, though, that admitting to my feeling might be seen as immature, so I chose not to do so."

Amber's negative feelings about Jack were based in his consistent refusal to recognize her, which left her own needs for affirmation unfilled, as well as making her feel inadequate as a social worker. Neither did the client show her any respect, and there was certainly no reciprocity in their interactions. Jack's behavior indicated that he felt Amber had nothing to offer him, and he was certainly not about to share anything of himself with her. Amber understood that as a professional she needed to treat Jack as a person with dignity, although her insecurity kept her from processing the issue with her supervisor.

Coming to see Jack's behaviors as representing learned survival skills might have helped her to see some of his strengths, but her labeling the client as "hopeless" was extreme, and her "going through the motions" was unfortunate. Amber's sole reliance on cognitive-behavioral intervention strategies may have been premature as it kept her at an emotional distance from Jack when spending more time on nondirective, relationship-based conversations might have helped her to understand his nature more thoroughly.

Working Through Negative Reactance

What follows is a series of steps intended to help social workers think proactively about their negative reactance to clients and take measures to ensure that it does not interfere with their ability to engage in constructive relationship development (Friedrich & Leiper, 2006; Goodman, 2005; Linn-Walton & Pardasani, 2014; Tishby & Wiseman, 2014). These incorporate the other two sources of negative feelings that will be discussed later in the chapter.

Reflect on the origins of the negative reactance. Be open to exploring the values, interpersonal patterns, and areas of unresolved conflict in one's life from which negative reactions may stem. Such self-examination is always helpful to social workers in any practice relationship and should be a career project.

Identify triggers. Be alert to practice-related events that seem to touch on the emergence of negative reactance, including general client behaviors, the client's feelings and behaviors toward the social worker, content areas raised by the client, and current circumstances in the social worker's own life.

Monitor its manifestations. Attend to the affective, cognitive, behavioral, and visceral reactions experienced with the client that signal that a significantly negative reaction is developing.

Note the effects of the reactance on the intervention. Reflect on the consequences of these reactions for the nature and quality of the intervention process.

Manage the reactance. Having considered the above processes, develop strategies to minimize the negative impacts of reactance (for example, how one deals with related anger or anxiety in sessions). This can be done in two general ways. First, developing empathy and understanding with all clients, regardless of their off-putting presentations, can serve as a buffer. It can help the social worker to find the client's constructive yearnings that underlie many of his or her off-putting behaviors. Second, ongoing supervision is critical in developing the ability to deal with negative reactance if the social worker experiences a supportive professional environment where honest reactions can be shared without fear of negative repercussions. Peer supervision can also be useful in this regard.

Clients Who Violate Basic Social Norms

Some clients present with behaviors that would be offensive to most other persons because they violate fundamental social norms and harm other people. Examples include persons who commit the crimes of child abuse, robbery, murder, and assault, including rape. The social work code of ethics emphasizes the dignity of the individual, indicating that all people, regardless of their behaviors, are worthy of respect and care, but this value is sometimes difficult to sustain. How can a social worker engage with such clients?

This is a common challenge for practitioners. In one qualitative study in the United Kingdom, nine practitioners read transcripts of recorded interventions in which an adult male client had committed incest, and they were subsequently interviewed about their reactions to the perpetrator (Friedrich & Leiper, 2006). The researchers wanted to discover how the practitioners would feel about working with such a client. An analysis of their responses produced three themes. First, all of the practitioners expressed negative reactions to the client, including feelings of anger, hostility, criticism, and disgust. They were ambivalent about their willingness to work with the person, and some even reported that an absence of feeling might provide a defense against their disgust. Others said that their personal lives would be negatively affected by involving themselves with the client. Second, most of the practitioners expected that such a client would attempt to control or deceive them in therapy, making the intervention process frustrating. Third, several practitioners indicated that they would probably have trouble ever being able to develop a therapeutic relationship with the client.

The results of the study indicate that practitioners, like all persons in a society, live by powerful social rules about sexual assault and the treatment of children. The researchers stated that social workers might best become able to provide assistance to clients who violate those norms by, first, recognizing and acknowledging their negative feelings rather than suppressing or denying them, because in doing so those feelings might come out in subtle ways that would be detrimental to the intervention. Practitioners should not share their negative reactance with the client unless they determine that the client might benefit from such a reality check (for example, by becoming more aware of how his or her behavior is perceived by others and causes interpersonal problems). Second, practitioners can attempt to develop empathy with these clients by recognizing and building on any positive qualities that they observe and by understanding that the client has likely been a victim of adversity in his or her own past. This might serve to humanize the client.

The next vignette, provided by Imani, a 24-year-old Black female, illustrates these themes.

The Brawler

"I can vividly recall the client whom I have disliked more than any other in the past 10 years. His name was Thomas, and he was a 29-year-old White male who was referred to my agency for counseling as part of his sentencing after being convicted of domestic assault. He had beaten up his girlfriend after breaking a restraining order and having a violent argument with her that turned into a fight, in which he broke several of her ribs. She filed charges and won.

"Thomas had been married and divorced twice, with no kids. He always had girlfriends, none of whom lasted for very long. He was a good-looking, well-dressed, physically fit man with a great deal of energy, and he was quite talkative, which might explain his intermittent success in working as a salesman for several local companies. Those jobs did not last long, however, because of his habit of getting into conflicts with supervisors about his attitude and his adversarial behavior with clients. He was between jobs when we began meeting.

"Regarding his background, I learned that Thomas had been given up for adoption by his single unmarried mother before his first birthday, and that, unusually, he had been raised by a mixed-race couple featuring a Black mother and White father. The father was away working much of the time and the family had been poor. Living in a rough urban neighborhood without siblings or other extended family supports, Thomas had become an 'angry brawler' at a young age, learning to take care of himself with his fists. He was

a poor student and was often in trouble at school for disruptive, aggressive behaviors. His only notable strength at the time was being a member of the high school's wrestling team. He was a star, but the team did not do well. Thomas said proudly that he became interested in girls in middle school and was always sexually involved with one or more at a time. It was hard for me to listen when he described his 'sexual conquests' and what appeared to me to be a clear lack of respect for women. I thought he was trying to intimidate me with those comments. The other difficulty I had was hearing the client talk about his being 'White through and through' even though his adoptive mother was Black. It seemed that he was embarrassed about his parentage and wanted to distance himself from his mother, the only person who had cared for him consistently over the years, because of her race. As a Black woman this was offensive to hear and was made even worse so when he said from time to time, 'I don't have anything against Blacks, but I don't hang with them. But you're fine.'

"If these behaviors weren't hard enough for me to have to manage, Thomas was also an ambivalent client who often no-showed for appointments and rarely followed through with the therapy tasks we had agreed to. These involved his practicing more adaptive coping skills rather than aggression. (I utilized a cognitive-behavioral skill-building approach with him.) He was a good talker, of course, always having excuses for why things didn't go his way or why he failed at certain things, and I could see that he was in the habit of talking himself out of trouble. The last bothersome observation I made about Thomas is that he never seemed to look me in the eye or share any feelings with me besides anger. As a social worker I know that all clients deserve dignity, and that we sometimes must work with clients who anger us, but this case was particularly difficult for me.

"I saw Thomas about 10 times before he found a new job and dropped out of therapy, but there was one session where my efforts to be professional failed me. He had started seeing another woman and was bragging about how beautiful she was. This upset me because once again he was being superficial and entering a relationship that I felt was probably going to end badly. I asked how he might try to avoid his relationship patterns of the past and, after assuring me that he was a changed man, he went on to say that, 'But you know how most women are: They really like the excitement of a fight. They have a way of baiting a guy into an argument. They keep it up so he has a hard time controlling himself, and then when the pushing and shoving starts, they seems to enjoy the whole scene. I'm not saying you're like that, but a lot of women are.'

"I lost my cool for just a minute, but it was long enough to sharply criticize his attitude, saying, 'I think you're looking for excuses to behave badly when you want to, and I can't see that you've yet learned to have any respect at all for women.' Thomas shrugged and didn't say anything. He didn't seem to take my comment seriously. When I watched the tape later it was clear to me and my supervisor that I was angry, because I had raised my voice and was shaking a finger at him. I also appeared to be irritated with him from the beginning of the session. It wasn't my finest moment. I didn't like the guy, but it wasn't helpful of me to do what I did. I couldn't help it at the time. I have never been abused myself but so many of my friends have been, and their lives have been ruined by guys like him."

This client was unapologetic about engaging in behaviors that would offend almost anyone, and Imani was a Black woman, representing two types of people for whom her client expressed disdain. While it might be assumed that men like Thomas are not uncommon, many of them would temper their communications to a social worker in an effort to be perceived as socially appropriate. This would not make their behaviors any more acceptable, but Imani in this case suffered the indignity of her client's open display of prejudices.

Regarding how she might manage her negative feelings in light of the practice principles described earlier in the chapter, Imani could easily identify their origins (her own history of living in a society that was oppressive to both women and minority groups), its triggers (witnessing its open expression), and its manifestations (her anger and feelings of hate toward the client). The client's behavior clearly was inhibiting Imani's potential to be a resource for the client, and he dropped out before she had resolved how to respond in a manner that might be constructive for him. Still, it is evident that she put some effort into understanding Thomas's attitudes and behavior in its context (his history of abandonment, lack of supports, and poverty), hoping that this would help her feel some empathy for him. It can't be known if she would have learned to contain her reactions or been able to work productively with the client, but perhaps Imani would have had more success if, rather than initiating structured interventions, she had openly shared her personal as well as professional discomfort with him as a means of helping him understand the impression he made on others. If that wasn't effective with the client, a transfer may have ultimately been indicated.

Unconscious Reactions

Many reactions that social workers experience about clients emerge outside of their awareness. That is, a client may be viewed positively or negatively based not on the current presentation but because he or she subconsciously reminds the practitioner of a significant other from earlier life who was loved or hated. This type of reactance resembles countertransference in its original analytic form (Schamess & Shilkret, 2016). All people are subject to these processes, but they can be constructively managed if the social worker is alert to their possibility and guards against their influence, most effectively with help from a supervisor or peer.

The dangers of unchecked countertransference have been borne out many studies, one of which was conducted by Linn-Walton and Pardasani (2014), who interviewed five practitioners from three disciplines in the New York City area about their related experiences. The researchers learned thorough open-ended interviews that the practitioners were often unable to identify their negative feelings about clients as coming from within themselves. Instead, they externalized the issue by pointing to specific attributes and behaviors of clients as the causes of their dislike. This can be the actual source of one's feelings at times, but the researchers speculated that the practitioners were using the defense mechanism of projection to avoid assuming responsibility for their feelings. Interestingly, some of the reasons for their dislike appeared to pertain to their feelings of professional inadequacy in a challenging situation rather than the client's presentation. It appeared that their frustrations with clients who were resistant to change or difficult to engage in treatment may have reflected the clinicians' own insecurity. A related theme was echoed by Goodman (2005), who noted that young practitioners are often negatively influenced by their clients' projections of anxiety onto them because they are already having difficulty managing their own anxieties as new practitioners and erroneously conclude that an anxious client is being uncooperative.

A survey of 560 practitioners in New York state found that participants tended to have negative reactance to members of certain diagnostic groups, including those with borderline personality, conduct disorder, and persistent major depression (Liebman & Burnette, 2013). Practitioners tended to experience less empathy with clients who exhibited characteristic patterns of interpersonal conflict. Many of the client behaviors were attributed by their practitioners to willful manipulation rather than a mental disturbance.

Practitioners with more experience treating persons with these disorders endorsed more positive reactions and feelings of competence with the same clients.

One's feelings about a client can certainly change during an intervention. A study including 42 clients seen over a period of 16 months by 11 therapists from one agency in Norway concluded that practitioners were most easily able to manage their negative reactance at the beginning of intervention, regardless of the client's symptom presentation (which in this study included anger, hostility, depression, and borderline personality disorder) (Rossberg, Karterud, Pedersen, & Friis, 2010). If the client's disturbing symptoms persisted during the intervention, however, the practitioner's negative reactions tended to intensify, as their attitudes changed from initial confidence to feelings of inadequacy, being overwhelmed, or experiencing rejection.

The adverse effects of unchecked negative reactance on the quality of intervention has been supported in other studies. A group of Danish researchers randomly assigned 112 clients to experimental and control conditions over a multiyear period to five psychotherapists to determine if negative reactance affected their ability to successfully provide "depth" interventions (focused on exploring and correcting the clients' interpersonal patterns) (Dahl et al., 2017). The results indicated that negative reactance, when uncorrected, led to feelings of disengagement among the practitioners from their clients, which could have adverse effects on their work. For clients with a history of reciprocal, sound relationships, such disengagement had a minimal adverse effect, but for those with a history of poor, non-mutual, conflicted relationships, even a slight elevation in the therapist's feelings of disengagement over the course of the intervention adversely influenced aspects of interpersonal depth work.

A similar study in the eastern United States investigated how reactance might influence a practitioner's ability to engage in depth therapy with a client over the course of an intervention. The relationships between client and therapist reactance and therapist emotional expression were examined regarding how they affected session quality in the beginning, middle, and end phases of supportive-expressive therapy (intended to help clients identify their maladaptive central relationship themes and learn how those tendencies are related to their problem symptoms) (Markin, McCarthy, & Barber, 2013). Five independent raters reviewed the work of four practitioners and 44 clients seen for 15 sessions or more, using a variety of quantitative and qualitative measures of transference, therapist emotional expression, countertransference, and session quality.

The findings indicate that the course of an intervention is indeed influenced in complex ways by the interactions of the client and worker's reactance. Negative reactance from a client predicted a difficult session, while positive client reactance predicted a deep session. Practitioner expressions of positive reactance and affect combined with negative client reactance predicted comfortable but superficial sessions, and those sessions became even more superficial over time. It appeared that the practitioners who were overly supportive did not connect well with clients who did not share their positive feelings. The hypotheses that positive client reactions would relate to positive therapist emotional expression and reactance behaviors were not supported, however, as the client's behavior evoked positive reactance in some practitioners but not others. The hypotheses that negative client reactance would predict therapist negative emotional expression and reactance behaviors were only partially supported. Shared positive practitioner and client reactance predicted a smooth session, but smoothness was negatively correlated with productivity, possibly because the combination stifled constructive differences in perspectives about important topics from surfacing. Interestingly, positive client reactance and a lower level of positive therapist reactance were associated with a deeper session. Perhaps the positive client reactance helped him or her to trust the practitioner to dig a bit deeper. It was difficult to draw any firm conclusions from this study, but it did indicate that the ability of a practitioner and client to develop a positive relationship is based on their mutual perspectives on the process rather than only one or the other's feelings.

Some themes in practitioners' subconscious negative reactance have been suggested. Tishby and Wiseman (2014) conducted a study of session transcripts generated by five therapists and 12 clients for up to 32 weeks using the Core Conflicted Relationship Theme method of identifying negative reactance patterns in the beginning, middle, and ending stages of intervention. The purpose of the study, based on interpersonal theory, was to identify specific provider negative reactance patters that emerged in the work, and why. The results produced the following five themes:

> *A wish from the parent is transferred to the client.* The practitioner's wish that her parents had behaved in certain ways toward her was repeated with clients. For example, the therapist's unfulfilled wish from her

parents was to be soothed, so she tended to look to her clients to serve this function. Such a tendency had occasional negative consequences for her work, as the practitioner developed negative feelings toward clients who did not behave warmly toward her.

The projection of a parent's typical responses onto the client. The therapist perceived the client's responses to him at times to be similar to how his parents responded to him. For example, the practitioner perceived his father as a reticent man with difficulty expressing feelings, and as a result he concluded that clients were cold and emotionally distant when they behaved in this way, an assumption that might be erroneous.

Repetition of the response of the self to parent behaviors. The practitioner replayed her own habitual responses to clients whose behaviors reminded her of a parent. For example, the therapist always felt misunderstood by her parents and believed that they were unaccepting of her. Consequently, she spent so much time explaining the reasons for her feedback to clients that they became confused at times by the unnecessary repetitions.

Repeating the negative parent response. The therapist's response to the client was the same as his parents' negative response to him. For example, the therapist's father tended to worry a great deal, and he described how, as a boy, he was overwhelmed by his father's worries and felt a need to soothe his anxieties. His first instinct with clients in distress was above all else to soothe them.

Repairing the negative parent response. The therapist's response to the client appeared to be an attempt to correct his own parents' negative responses to him. For example, the therapist perceived her parents as controlling, not attuned to her emotional needs, and angry when her emotional needs conflicted with their life routines. She thus got sidetracked whenever a client did not seem to understand her, losing some of her focus on the client in the process. She devoted time to educating the client about her own emotional processes when the client appeared to be unaccepting of her.

The purpose of this study was not to portray these practitioners as incompetent or damaged, and it was based on one theoretical perspective, but it describes the types of ingrained and unconscious interpersonal patters that can surface in the course of a practitioner's work. Coming to understand these themes through self-examination and supervision is important so that social workers can confront and give up some of their automatic tendencies and address the client as a unique person.

The following vignette touches on many of the points just described. Regarding the emergence of strong negative reactance, initially from an unknown internal source, it illustrates the difficult experience of Ashley, a 25-year-old single Black female who worked with a client for whom she developed a quite visceral negative reaction.

Little Miss Sunshine

"Rita was a 37-year-old Black female receiving services at our crisis stabilization unit to obtain housing and employment. She was single and had two sons. Thomas, 18, lived in Utah and was not on speaking terms with her. Dave, age 20, was currently in a correctional center and seldom spoke to his mother. Rita had no contact with her sons' father. She claimed to have no one in her support system. In addition to her housing and employment needs, Rita wanted help overcoming her depression, for which she took medication. She was once an executive chef at a hotel but had a mental breakdown two years ago that caused her to lose both her job and her home. Since then, she had enlisted in various housing programs, but none of her efforts had been successful.

"The crisis stabilization unit worked with clients for 15 to 30 days at a former hotel. The crisis specialists helped clients to pursue their housing and employment goals and conducted daily counseling sessions with them. As a student my role was to provide case management services to clients, which involved much contact with them but not primary responsibility for their goal achievement. That is, we supported their development of a nurturing environment. The first time I met Rita, the specialists and I were accompanying her to a psychiatry appointment. I was nervous about meeting her because the staff who knew her told me, 'She is going to be a handful.' I was apprehensive but sat in the van next to her and introduced myself. She looked at me suspiciously and did not respond. This made me more uncomfortable and I did not feel optimistic about our relationship moving forward. To my surprise, though, as we continued to drive, she began talking. She told me how great it was that I was in school and talked about her own college days. She had graduated high school early and went on to receive a master's degree in food sciences. I was fascinated and began to feel optimistic about our relationship.

"The next day, things took a different turn for me and Rita. Again, the specialists and I were accompanying Rita to an appointment. This time, we were joined by a second client, Tina, who we needed to drop off for a court hearing. I stayed with Tina at court while the specialists took Rita to her appointment. They would pick us up afterwards. Tina's time at the court was shorter than we expected, so we sat outside to wait for the van. We talked, and Tina made a few phone calls. At one point, a man looking to borrow a lighter for his cigarette approached us. Tina offered hers and he stayed to speak with her for a few minutes. Soon the van arrived.

"Once Tina and I got back inside, the specialists asked how everything went. Tina described how court went and then began to talk about how she had to 'save' me from a man we met outside—the man who had borrowed her lighter. It was clear that Tina was joking harmlessly, but Rita said, 'Little Miss Sunshine couldn't possibly survive downtown. With her timid self . . .' and she began to mock my voice and body gestures. I was stunned by her cruel statement and actions. Everyone else in the van began to laugh, but I was holding back tears. At the time I had no idea why I was reacting this way.

"Once we got back to the hotel, Rita followed us to the office, casually chatting about different things. I was not paying much attention, as I was still trying to get a handle on my bad feelings about what happened in the van. Then, Rita looked into the office sink and said, 'Who left noodles in the sink?' Before anyone had a chance to respond, Rita continued, 'Little Miss Sunshine probably did it. Only a little girl with no manners would do something like that.' I felt myself becoming angry, and this intensified the longer she stayed in the room. I had to excuse myself in order to calm down.

"Due to this encounter, I developed strong feelings of dislike toward Rita. Later, when she would come into the office to speak with the staff, I had a hard time looking at her, let alone speaking. I avoided accompanying her to appointments and counted down the days until she would be discharged. Of course, this kept me from building any rapport with her. She continued making snide comments about me to the specialists within my earshot. They seemed to find these comments to be harmless, so they never confronted her about them.

"The more time that passed, the more dislike I developed toward Rita. It got to a point where I ignored her whenever she was in the office. I know that *this was unprofessional, but I was able to get away with it because students were not obligated to work with clients individually. We worked as a team to manage the caseload. One day, though, Rita came to the office when the specialists were away getting lunch and I had stayed behind. Somehow, I was able to suppress my feelings and politely answer her questions, which only pertained to getting some supplies. Still, this did not change the way I felt about her.*

"As I mentioned, I was not sure at the time why I reacted so negatively to Rita's comments, especially her first one. Now I realize that negative reactance was taking place. I was reacting to Rita's tendency to belittle and mock me for reasons pertaining to my quiet personality and protective background. From Rita's perspective, her actions may have been based on my young age and quiet, reserved persona. Maybe she was even envious of me. I was never good with confrontation, so I shied away from bringing up my concerns with her. Fortunately, at those few times when I was the only staff person available at the front desk, I was able to help her, although without enthusiasm. It would be unethical for me to ignore a client's need for help. Besides, she never teased me when we were alone.

"Reflecting on my encounters with Rita now, I recognize that I am especially sensitive to people who make fun of my timid and quiet nature. These are lifelong insecurities, likely due to negative experiences I had with my older siblings and the older kids in the neighborhood. People who 'pick on' me make me feel weak and incompetent. Rita reminded me of those people. I believe now that I could have handled some things differently to create a more positive outcome in this case. I should have confronted Rita the first time she made a negative comment about me. This would have been a way for me to set boundaries with her and contradict her view of me as a timid 'little girl.' It may have been a simple exchange, and she may have stopped making those types of comments about me. In return, I would have interacted with her more, possibly helping us to build a good relationship. Even if Rita would have reacted negatively to my confronting her, I would have felt at peace with at least putting the issues out in the open. Either way, it have helped me feel better about working with her."

Ashley had been aware that she might have difficulty with "rude" clients because she felt apprehensive about Rita before they met after hearing that she would be a "handful." Ashley later wrote that she knew the origins of her sensitivity lay with her early family and neighborhood relationships.

She was able to identify her triggers as any overtly critical or teasing behavior directed at her by any client whom she did not know well enough to understand. In this case, Rita engaged in many sarcastic and appropriate communications with others, but Ashley did not know her well enough to understand why she made such comments, and she became immediately intimidated. Had they come from a client Ashley knew well enough to have some positive feelings for, she may not have become so upset, but she was highly sensitive to Rita's perceived bullying behavior.

The manifestations of Ashley's negative feelings were clear as well: She tried to avoid the client entirely. This would not have been possible if she had been Rita's primary social worker. Ashley knew she had to maintain ethical behaviors with all the clients at her agency, and it is hoped that being Rita's primary worker might have prompted her to deal directly with the situation. Clearly, her avoidant behaviors and physical symptoms would have had a negative effect on the intervention if they were working together. How she would have addressed the issue is unknown. She would have benefited from supervisory assistance in fully grasping the sources of her feelings and developing a strategy for resolving the issue in a constructive manner.

It may have helped Ashley to understand that Rita's behaviors toward her may have been based on a "survival attitude," a need to threaten and dominate others in order to feel safe. Learning about the limitations of this coping style may have helped Rita to grow psychologically. It should be mentioned, too, that Ashley's coworkers were complicit in reinforcing Rita's sarcasm, and this was a serious problem. As Ashley mentioned, their tolerance of the behavior may have been due to an agency culture that accepted this kind of worker/client bantering, but this case shows that their encouraging attitudes lacked a degree of professionalism as well.

Summary

All social workers will provide services at times to clients whom they have difficulty liking or accepting. The reasons for such negative reactions may include the here-and-now characteristics of the participants that clash, the social worker's professional and personal values, and the social worker's countertransference patters. While social workers may perceive it as a personal weakness when they fail to empathize with a client for any of these reasons, their related feelings are normal and can usually be successfully managed if they are identified and accepted rather than denied or minimized. In this chapter strategies for managing negative reactance have been described. One theme common to them all is that a trusted peer, hopefully a supervisor, will be invited to help the social worker work through and resolve those feelings.

10
Relationship Development with Psychotic Clients

What follows is an example of psychotic communication from Elliot, a 28-year-old man with schizoaffective disorder:

> *"I'm the type of person who, when I have a problem, it all comes undone. So, if I have a small problem it's like waiting for the sun to go down, like it's gonna just explode, and come undone, and there are parts I just have to clean up in the morning. A lot of people my age, they're waiting for the sun . . . it's like Japan, land of the rising sun, it's like they've been out for so long they're just waiting for a new day to dawn. I'm not like that, people are not like that, some of them don't know it's a fantasy. Sometimes I don't know, or I forget whether I should talk about my friends who have screwed up, if it's important to go over those things, or if I should focus on happier things. It can be important . . . I have a lot of issues."*

It is often difficult for social workers to develop positive relationships with psychotic clients because their language and perceptions can be difficult to comprehend. Much of the practice literature is focused on what social workers can achieve with psychotic clients *after* they have stabilized, often with the assistance of medication, and they can communicate in more conventional ways. Yet it is important to be able to engage psychotic clients in working relationships even when their active symptoms are prominent, as they may retain or experience recurrences of them throughout their intervention. The purposes of this chapter are to examine the relationship capacities of clients who are psychotic and to present strategies for social workers to engage with them.

The responsiveness of psychosis to medication has increased professionals' emphasis on *biology* and detracted from their attention to clients' *existential issues* that go beyond mere symptom rehabilitation. A social worker who is sensitive to a psychotic client's life challenges, acknowledges his or her personhood, and supports a self-determined approach to life can generate positive relational responses from the client and help to alleviate much of his or her emotional burden. In the context of psychosis these behaviors can be understood as *empathic attunement*, in which the social worker's primary role is to offer a steadfast, positive emotional presence. In the context of such a relationship, the client can become aware that the social worker appreciates the threads of meaning in his or her fragmentary statements, and the gradual trusting response facilitates the client's movement toward personal integration.

Theories of Relationship Development with Psychotic Clients

There is a rich history in the psychotherapy literature on the importance of relationship development with clients who have psychotic disorders. Frieda Fromm-Reichmann (1952) was among the first analysts to determine that a strong relationship can be established between a client with schizophrenia and the practitioner, even though the client will likely continue to prefer limited social interactions in everyday life. Elvin Semrad (1955) demonstrated through his charismatic use of self that empathic connection with psychotic clients is critical for their improvement. He asserted that psychotic symptoms were in part defenses against feelings of loss or failure and that a shared emotional connection can help to reduce the client's need for such defenses. Rather than being preoccupied with treating symptoms, practitioners should help clients tolerate what has previously been unbearable and then find ways to help solve their life dilemmas. Sullivan (1947) wrote that a lengthy interpersonal relationship may be required to shed light on the psychotic client's difficulties in living, because it takes time for a practitioner to become able to understand the meanings of the client's communications.

A bit more recently, Weiden and Havens (1994) wrote that elements of a strong relationship include empathizing with the mistrust of paranoid clients, making affirming statements to demoralized clients, normalizing the experiences of stigmatized clients, and providing clients with alternative points of view about their life situations. Havens (1996) characterized the worker/client relationship as a sanctuary that attempts to hold in a nurturing balance the client's conflicting desires for solitude and society. Finally, a meta-analysis of studies on the significance of the therapeutic relationship with clients who have schizophrenia concluded that clients who experience an empathic, positive, and facilitative relationship have better overall treatment outcomes (Hewitt & Coffey, 2005).

The positive potential of a strong worker/client relationship is perhaps most evident in the Recovery perspective on mental illness (Walsh, 2013). First promoted by clients and later incorporated by many professionals, Recovery does not imply "cure" or even "control" of a mental disorder. It is a broader process of personal transformation in which the psychotic disorder becomes less central in a client's life as he or she seeks activities that foster personal meaning and life satisfaction. While the professional concept of rehabilitation focuses on the achievement of tangible goals, Recovery is an internal, subjective, nonlinear process of personal growth that may or may not include the elimination of symptoms as a primary goal. Client preferences in the Recovery process exist on a continuum ranging from conventional medical-model interventions to a rejection of the professional mental health system. In every case there is a need for a collaborative relationship between a social worker and client in which the client's perspectives are given priority.

Understanding Psychosis

There is no single definition of psychosis, but it can be understood as a mental state in which external reality has a diminished meaning for a person or is perceived in a distorted way (Campbell, 2009). The *core* of psychosis is characterized by cognitive deficits such as thought blocking, thought deprivation, poverty of thought, and loose associations. The violation of internal versus external boundary conditions is also a feature of psychosis, as the distinction between reality and fantasy, or the self and world, becomes blurred. The *periphery* of psychosis, or the ways in which the core disorder is manifested, may include hallucinations (auditory, visual, tactile, olfactory, somatic), affective impairments (flat, blunted, social withdrawal, non-communication, anhedonia, passivity, ambivalence), delusions (persecution, thought broadcasting, thought insertion, thought withdrawal, being controlled, being the focus of external events, somatic distortions, grandiosity), and loose speech (tangential responses, circumstantiality, loss of a goal, or seemingly purposeless and illogical associations) (American Psychiatric Association, 2012).

Psychotic ideation is evident in many disorders, both medical and psychiatric, including schizophrenia, schizoaffective disorder, delusional disorder (thought disorders), major depression, and bipolar disorder (mood disorders), among others. Psychosis is not "rational," defined as thinking that is based on accurate perceptions of external evidence, is life preserving, and keeps one directed toward personal goals (Corcoran, 2014). In psychosis the person makes some rational observations and choices, but it is the relative absence of such thinking, and the social worker's inability to comprehend the client's communications, that can make relationship development difficult.

Thought Disorders

The thinking and perceptual distortions in psychosis result from neurological changes, the origins of which are not clear. These include disruptions in the person's short-term memory and information-processing capacity, which are in turn related to impairments in the ability to filter sensory stimulation (Moritz et al., 2017; Strik, Stegmayer, Walther, & Dierks, 2018). That is, an overload of normally screened externally and internally generated stimuli leads to the person's misinterpretations of words and events. There is also impairment in executive functions, which normally allow a person to plan, organize, follow sequences, and think abstractly. Emotionally charged topics intensify the level of disorganization in psychotic thought and communication, further inhibiting the person's ability to reason or channel emotions (Lincoln, Hartmann, Kother, & Moritz, 2015). The ways in which these deficits become evident are described next.

The perceptual field in persons with schizophrenia features a loosening of the "common sense" visual context (Uhlhaas & Mishara, 2007). Whereas a person's normal visual field is characterized by coherence, with objects perceived in meaningful relationship to one another, the psychotic person's uncontrollable loosening of perceptual schema separates fragments from the larger context. The individual perceives partial elements of a scene without grasping their natural relationships to each other, and therefore the scene's overall meaning. Still, the person always tries to make sense of what he or she is perceiving, so the emergent delusion consists of the person's elaboration of a new context for the otherwise unexplainable perceptual fragments.

There is an ongoing mutual reinforcement between the presence of delusions and the person's subsequent social isolation. The person loses the ability to connect with others, and in circular fashion the self-imposed isolation reinforces misperceptions of the internal lives of others (Keefe & Krauss,

2012). Auditory hallucinations are in turn the result of mental processes that are experienced as detached from their internal source (Henriksen, Raballo, & Parnas, 2015). Abnormal speech patterns are also associated with psychosis and include poverty of content, derailment (poor connection and tangential responses to questions), circumstantiality (wandering and over-detailed messages), and loss of goal (the original point is lost).

An example may illustrate these processes. A socially isolated client with schizophrenia named Daryl lost himself in religious fantasies, based on fragmented perceptions experienced in the contexts of his actual family and cultural religious background. Without the ability to attend to, sort out, and evaluate the many internal and external factors that contributed to these perceptions, and in the context of his loneliness and anxiety, Daryl constructed a "sensible" story that he had been sent to earth by God, doomed to suffer in isolation for the betterment of mankind. He had the "gift" of being able to interpret evil messages hidden in popular music (a topic of interest to a segment of his peer group) and took on as his mission the warning of others that they were being brainwashed by Satan.

Mood Disorders

In major depression and bipolar disorder, a person's thinking style and language is at the mercy of his or her uncontrollable moods (Piguet et al., 2010; Stanghellini & Raballo, 2015). When depressed, the client's thinking is slower than normal and lacking in focus, which may lead to erroneous or delusional beliefs. During the experiences of hypomania and mania, the person's elation brings on an overwhelming influx of ideas, perceptions, and verbal tendencies. In hypomania, a moderate amount of elation may sharpen one's cognitive abilities, but speech and thought begin to degenerate into psychosis during mania. Manic persons cannot complete thoughts because the affective rush propels them in different directions, as evidenced in the following example from Sara, a client who was expressing resentment of her successful younger brother, a computer engineer:

> "They're making computer chips out of sand from the beach. That's two huge work issues, organic versus sustainable. Like, you can't rip down the rainforest, but you can extract plants from it. Well, why are you allowed to go in if you aren't allowed to touch anything? But organic, a lot of people argue,

'What is inorganic?' A problem to a psychologist is some idiot did heroin and fused both halves of his brain together; how do you get them apart? You can't open it up. It's like a person, you can't open him up."

Unfortunately for the social worker, efforts at verbal intervention make little impression on an actively manic client. Setting appropriate behavioral limits is required to keep the client and others "safe," and only when the manic episode remits can the social worker engage the client in a working relationship (Fava, Ruini, & Rafanelli, 2005). Still, as a mood episode stabilizes, remnants of disordered thinking may persist. Over the course of bipolar disorder, a person may develop mild to moderate problems with attention, learning, memory, and executive function (Burdick, Braga, Goldberg, & Malhorta, 2007).

The Experience of Psychosis

Clearly, the experience of psychosis is terrifying to a client, especially at its onset. In addition to the bizarre symptoms, the client suffers from being marginalized and discounted by others due to his or her preoccupation with strange ideas and accompanying behaviors. The client experiences an overwhelming sense of loss as his or her social circles contract, vocational choices narrow, and past accomplishments fade from significance. The former sense of identity becomes confused. Still, while the presentation of psychosis presents challenges for the social worker, it also provides opportunities for developing a relationship. What the client lacks in verbal ability may be compensated for in part by sensitivity to the emotional responses of others. The client feels rejected by most other people, so any sustained attempts by another person to show genuine acceptance will be perceived and eventually welcomed. Further, even when overwhelmed by bizarre ideas and associations the client does not completely lose an understanding of social conventions.

One can accept the neurological basis of psychosis but value the relationship as a means of helping clients develop improved attachments toward others, which can lead to a more rational awareness of social contexts that can facilitate their goal attainment. In a comfortable working relationship, the social worker can help the client place his or her perceptual fragments into a wider, more cohesive context. The social worker can help the client explore his or her biography in a way that incorporates more "factual" perceptions into the delusions. The prognosis for improvement in fact depends on the presence or absence of a nucleus of purpose around which the client can develop a cohesive sense of self.

The following vignettes provide illustrations of how two social workers successfully engaged with clients who experienced schizophrenia and bipolar disorder, respectively. The first case provides a wonderful example of how a relatively inexperienced social work student, a 24-year-old Asian American female named Iris, was able to be helpful to a client with schizophrenia purely because of her natural welcoming attitude.

The Irritant

"I had a field placement in a psychiatric hospital where patients, as they were called, were admitted for stabilization of their symptoms of mental illness. The patients were usually only there for a week or so, and the main intervention was medication adjustments. The social workers put a lot of effort into family contact and discharge planning so that the patients could move into a stable environment when they left the hospital. There certainly wasn't much talk therapy going on. Because of that I wasn't sure about my role there. I sat in on team meetings, which were informative, and was encouraged to spend time with the patients to help them feel comfortable and see how they were doing.

"Kate, a 40-year-old single White female with schizophrenia, was one of our patients. She was paranoid and had many delusions. She thought everyone on the unit was plotting against her, poisoning her food, and causing her aches and pains with telepathic assaults. She was also loud and talked all the time, even though no one wanted to listen. She seemed to annoy most of the staff and other patients because she always wanted to talk but never made any sense. I think the staff was frustrated with Kate, too, because she wasn't medication compliant and had been there for three weeks, far beyond what was typical. She was supposed to be moving into a shared apartment after her discharge, but she didn't have any family available to help with this task or visit her.

"I was kind of afraid of Kate because she never made any sense, so for a few weeks I avoided her. But since I had a lot of free time I decided one day to try to talk to her. I guess I was feeling adventurous that day. I sat down next to Kate in the living room area and asked how she was doing. At first she seemed annoyed with me and started rambling incoherently about all kinds

of delusional ideas, jumping from topic to topic, and I couldn't follow her at all. But I thought for the first time that her bizarre talk was fascinating, so I kept listening, even though I said very little. I guess she wasn't used to anyone sitting with her as long as I did because she calmed down after a while. At the beginning I had the impression that Kate wasn't aware of me at all (I could have been anyone), but this changed, too, and she started looking me in the eye. I got concerned at one point because Kate asked me to promise not to tell the staff certain things she was sharing (I didn't respond to that request), and then she talked about sexual abuse in her past, which I wasn't sure was true because she described it in such bizarre terms. I was surprised, though, when eventually Kate became more coherent, talking about what I considered to be 'real' issues, like not having any friends, so I started asking her questions about her life and what she thought about being in the hospital. She answered my questions in ways that made sense. We finished our conversation when a nurse said it was time for lunch. I felt good about the conversation and hoped that I had acquired some useful information for the other members of the team to use in her planning.

"I'm not sure what I did to help the conversation become civil other than show interest in Kate and be patient with her. In truth I found her to be relatable after a while and not annoying. She never became fully rational but was much easier to follow. I guess I was empathic with her, and she responded to that. I don't know if the conversation was therapeutic as far as helping to improve her mental status. We had a few more pleasant conversations after that, although she was discharged a few weeks later. I was sorry to see her go."

Iris had indeed behaved in a therapeutic manner, because she had utilized the engagement principles of presenting with a calm, patient stance; not exhibiting too much emotion (which can be overwhelming to a psychotic client); not trying to interpret Kate's psychotic ideas; and accepting her as she was. The client appeared to alienate other staff and patients with her intrusive behaviors and strange ideas, and in the context of a busy inpatient unit this may have been inevitable. Iris's actions showed, however, that Kate had the potential to make a connection in a calmer environment with the sustained attention of a practitioner. If Iris has been able to work longer with Kate she might have been able to help her set some "reasonable" goals and implement behavioral strategies toward her gradual functional improvement. The process would likely be slow, however, as Kate may have experienced high levels of anxiety when attempting to make these changes. Iris's ongoing empathic attunement would be needed to support the client's tentative efforts.

The next vignette features Iyana, a 27-year-old single Black female, and her client Terri, a 30-year-old single White bisexual female who was recovering from a manic phase of bipolar disorder. Terri's psychotic ideation was transient, and during the period of these sessions she was fairly stable but still troubled by her recent experiences with delusional thoughts.

The Family Next Door

"I completed my second MSW field placement at a regional community services board, which offered follow-up mental health services to persons discharged from area hospitals. That's where I met Terri. She was a college graduate in sociology and was working full time at a mail-order goods warehouse when she experienced her first manic episode. Earlier in her life Terri had experienced occasional problems with bulimia and depression, but she had never seen a counselor and experienced what appeared to be a secure upbringing. An older brother was married and living on his own. Terri had been living with her parents since finishing college and was comfortable with the situation. She tended to stay home during the week after working but had some contact with friends on weekends.

"For years Terri's family had been close with the family next door, the Wilsons, who had watched a young Terri and her brother often when their parents were working. The Wilsons had children of their own who were Terri's playmates. It had been more than 15 years since the Wilsons provided childcare for Terri and her brother, but the families remained in regular contact. Six months ago, however, Terri had become 'hyperactive' for a period of weeks and began to think (without evident reason) that Mrs. Wilson, who was 25 years older, wanted to have a romantic relationship with her. Terri was interested in such a relationship, too, and began visiting Mrs. Wilson most evenings, asking if they could spend time together and be 'special friends.' Mrs. Wilson was confused and eventually upset about these strange overtures and talked to Terri's parents about them, who admitted that their daughter's 'odd' behavior was becoming a problem at home as well. Shortly afterward they facilitated Terri's admission to the psychiatric unit of a local hospital. She was diagnosed with bipolar I disorder, manic type, and stabilized on medications within a few weeks. When we met Terri was in remission.

"We seemed to get along well from the start because Terri was naturally friendly. She was initially guarded in her responses to personal questions but soon relaxed with me. I was alert to her mental status and medication responses but mostly focused in our first few sessions on earning Terri's trust, being a confidante who would not judge her thoughts and feelings. Terri seemed to appreciate this and soon began talking about her fears. What struck me most was Terri's ambivalence about her delusion. At first she said that even though she no longer had feelings about her older neighbor, they might recur, and she also worried that her parents would never again treat her like a responsible adult. Later, as she started trusting me more, she admitted that at times she still wondered if Mrs. Wilson had romantic feelings about her, even though she knew that didn't make sense. Terri was frightened by her state of confusion and had lost confidence in her ability to lead a 'normal' life. In summary, the manic episode had frightened her deeply and left her wondering about her identity and the stability of her perceptions.

"Terri's mental status had improved greatly since the hospitalization, and she appeared to be functioning fairly well at home and on the job, but internally she was terrified about what had happened and the troublesome thoughts that lingered from the manic episode. I had worked with several clients who had bipolar disorder before, and while all clients are different, I knew that they benefited from reassurance that they would likely return to their previous level of stability with the support of family and friends and carefully monitored medications. There was a good chance that they would experience a recurrence of their mania, hopefully not for a long while, but if so quick intervention would likely bring them back into remission.

"Thus, in addition to providing empathic attunement and validation, I was providing Terri with education about her disorder. When a person with bipolar disorder experiences psychosis, he or she is usually able to discuss the experience 'rationally' after those symptoms subside, unlike some persons with chronic psychosis. Over time, with my support and validation, Terri's delusion remitted further; she became more comfortable with herself and was able to develop a more optimistic perspective about her disorder. Eventually I began exploring the stressors in Terri's life that might have contributed to the onset of her mania, but it was in these early sessions, when I was providing consistent, nonjudgmental support and encouragement, that she became able to overcome her fears regarding being able to resume a normal life. I was in no hurry to move her beyond that stage into other reflective and cognitive-behavioral interventions, although I did so when she gained strength."

Iyana's efforts to develop a relationship with her client were in some ways less difficult that those facing Iris because Terri had experienced a transient psychosis and was in partial remission. Her delusion had not disappeared completely, but Terri had regained most of her rational thinking capacity and was able to reflect constructively on her situation. Notice, however, that Terri was not able to admit to the persistence of her unrealistic thoughts until she trusted that Iyana would not judge or negatively label her. Persons with bipolar disorder carry a great fear that their symptoms might recur and may feel an ongoing isolation due to their concerns that their significant others may perceive them as being fundamentally unstable. Iyana was able to convey to Terri that she accepted her despite her fragile mental status.

Fortunately, Iyana had previous experience with clients who had bipolar disorder and was able to provide Terri with reassuring education about the anticipated course of the disorder, instilling in her client a confidence that she would be able to control its course. This process is called psychoeducation (Walsh, 2010) and is usually a key part of intervention with all currently or formerly psychotic clients who are aware that their symptoms are not reflective of the external world. When engaged in psychoeducation a social worker explains in simple terms to a client how a disorder manifests itself and how the client can take steps to minimize its negative impact on his or her life. It was also significant to the relationship that Iyana was patient with her client, holding off on providing other interventions until their it was secure.

The following three guidelines are offered for social workers who must develop and maintain relationships with psychotic clients, with examples.

Relationship Development Guidelines for Use with Psychotic Clients

Sustainment

The social worker/client relationship is the sustaining link between the psychotic client and the external world and provides the client with an environment of safety. The social worker "sustains" and enhances the client's sense of self through verbal and nonverbal interventions that feature (Goldstein, 1995):

- Listening actively and sympathetically
- Conveying a continuing attitude of good will
- Expressing confidence and esteem
- Realistically reassuring the client about the potential for goal achievement
- Offering environmental support resources.

Through these behaviors the social worker promotes a confiding relationship and instills in the client a sense of the worker's competence and caring. The social worker's presence becomes an antidote to the client's alienation, enhances morale, inspires the expectation of help, and creates a setting where constructive confrontation can eventually take place. Within the relationship the client comes to appreciate the significance of internal and external limits in pursuing goals, improves reality testing, and experiences learning and enhanced self-esteem.

In a systematic review of 26 studies it was found that a practitioner's use of sustainment-related interventions resulted in a facilitative working alliance that predicted positive outcomes for clients with psychotic disorders (Shattock, Berry, Degnan, & Edge, 2018). Interestingly, when there was a difference in perception of the alliance, it was the practitioners who tended to underestimate its strength. When clients exhibited "negative" symptoms (flat affect, poverty of thought, slow speech, withdrawal), practitioners especially rated the alliance as weak, while the clients often rated it as stronger. An important point here is that clients who lack a capacity for nonverbal expressions of feeling may develop an attachment even though it may not be evident to the practitioner.

In the following statement, Elliot (quoted earlier) expresses faith in his relationship with the social worker in an indirect way:

"Does counseling help? Not in the sense of my daily life. But it helps with my routine. If I have a problem I know I'll have an answer when I'm here, so I can make a note, a mental note, so if I have some work to get done, if I have something to say, and it's intense, I can say it in a scientific manner, and use my psychology, I trust that this is a real outlet. I've learned from experience that a degree is useful to have, and it reinforces that there is an answer. Where science is cold, a scientific person will not be offended by a scientific answer."

The social worker may not initially comprehend what a psychotic client is saying, and any quick attempts at interpretation should be avoided as they may amount to nothing more than the practitioner's free association. The sustaining social worker does not rush to interpret the client's comments but accepts them with curiosity. This acceptance allows for the development of empathy and a valuing of the relationship over intellectual comprehension. Even if the client becomes confused trying to understand what the social worker means, the perception of the worker's positive regard will encourage his or her trust.

The social worker regulates the emotional pace of their interactions by structuring conversations to minimize the possibility that the client will become overwhelmed by negative feelings. A low-key behavioral presentation can be effective in this process. With the social worker's acceptance and support, the client can stand back from distressing experiences, memories, or concerns so that he or she is no longer overwhelmed by emotion when speaking about them. When the client's distress is modulated, he or she can participate in more intense discussions.

It must be acknowledged that working with clients who have psychotic disorders can be stressful. The social worker is entering an ambivalent client's world and must be prepared for initial mistrust. The pace of change for these clients is usually slow, which can be frustrating and perhaps cause one to doubt one's professional competence. Social workers should look beyond the stereotypes of people with psychotic disorders and see the person behind the symptoms who desires connection. Also, the patience required for sustainment may work against agency policies that encourage the early use of active interventions. The social worker may feel pressured to be "productive" in terms of establishing concrete goals and objectives with the client. As public funding for mental health interventions is always limited, administrative structures tend to enforce more rapid movement through the care system than is practical for many clients with psychotic disorders (Mechanic, 2008). Yet, the possibility of eventual success may be diminished by quick interventions, as the client may fail to engage in a process that feels abrupt and impersonal.

The next two guidelines, adapted from Dilks, Tasker, and Wren (2008) and Spaulding and Nolting (2006), follow directly from sustainment to further promote the psychotic client's recovery.

Encourage the Client's Expression of All Thoughts and Feelings

In the context of a positive relationship, the social worker can gradually come to understand the meaning of the client's bizarre statements, at least tentatively. The practitioner becomes aware of themes being expressed in the client's private symbols. In a calm atmosphere, with a stance of curiosity, the social worker can encourage the client to elaborate on his or her areas of concern, regardless of their coherence. The quiet client may be encouraged to speak more openly, and the easily overwhelmed client might be encouraged to slow down. The social worker can attend to the emotional context of the client's statements, which helps to reveal the anxieties present in his or her inner world. In this spirit the social worker should not argue against the reality of a client's hallucinations or delusions but rather explore the feelings behind them. That is, the social worker should never openly agree or disagree with the client's delusions, and if asked for his or her opinion should provide the affirming but neutral response that these beliefs are certainly real to the client but outside the social worker's experience.

As an example of this process, here is a statement by Elliot:

Eye color... when I was in college eye color got really important, I can talk about it. Apparently in adolescence your eye color can change, but it doesn't permanently change. My eyes look green sometimes when they were brown my whole life. And some people are overly intense with eye color, in college, and eye contact is intense, so when you start making eye contact... I'm comfortable with you, but some teachers are big on it. It's not like high school where you can really get out of order, and I really have a bad reaction to staring. And I can be intimidating because I'm an athlete. My personality is, I'm the kind of person who can bring up an eye contact discussion. But you can't do that every day in class.

The social worker responded that Elliott appeared to be expressing the difficulty he experienced being around other people, especially strangers, whose gazes were threatening and exacerbated his fears. When they looked him in the eye, they were intruding into his space, and when they tried to get physically close to him, or talk to him, he became uncomfortable. The social worker speculated that this was an issue the client wished to process and see if he can move past. Elliott agreed with this feedback. (It is important to emphasize that the social worker was only able to formulate his hypothesis [anxiety about being scrutinized by others] after spending five sessions getting to know him.)

Encourage the Client to Consider Alternative Meanings

The sharing of feedback about beliefs between a trusted social worker and client can move the client toward considering alternative conclusions regarding his or her psychotic perceptions. The social worker's tentative filling in of perceptual gaps can make available to the client new possibilities for assessing and managing his or her major concerns. A paranoid client, for example, who often sees certain physical movements of others (including those of the social worker) as malevolent threats of harm may learn to consider that at least some of those behaviors have nothing to do with him. A client with schizoaffective disorder, whose impulsive decisions include buying a gun and taking up shooting as a hobby, may trust the social worker's judgment that he consider how such an activity might affect his ability to get custody of his daughter from the county children's services agency. This process is founded on the worker's repeatedly observing and empathizing with the client's experiences. If the client trusts the social worker as a concerned listener and "reality tester," he or she will consider this input and reconsider the nature of his or her priorities, opening up possibilities for behaving differently in the social world.

The next vignette features Maggie, a 23-year-old White social worker who was not sure what to make of her client's bizarre pronouncements, but even before completing a full assessment provided her client with an empathic, supportive presence.

The Frantic Survivor

"Sonja was a 73-year-old Black female, divorced and living alone. She sought services from our agency because of a domestic violence situation that involved her ex-husband, Daniel. Sonja was concerned that Daniel was breaking into her house and destroying her property to continue his longstanding harassment of her. She had received a protective order against him a year ago, but it

had expired. Sonja wanted someone to listen to her because she had run out of people to ask for help. She said that everyone in her life, including her family, the police, and her neighbors, thought she was 'crazy' and was fabricating all of her complaints against Daniel. Sonja had done everything in her power to stop the threatening situation by changing the locks on her doors five times, repeatedly calling the police, putting up cameras in her home, and hiring a private detective. None of these strategies had produced evidence that convinced anyone else that harassment was taking place. Sonja had been encouraged by her family to get a full psychological assessment but she refused, maintaining that there was nothing wrong with her.

"*I had only seen Sonja three times over two months prior to the meeting I describe here. She often cancelled appointments with various excuses, such as having knee pain, being concerned about the rain, or having to watch a friend's child. In our previous meetings Sonja had presented the same way: being concerned about her belongings, her house, and her safety. She was always able to speak clearly, but the more she talked the less sense she made. My fourth session with Sonja began like the others, with her updating me about what Daniel had done since we last met. She said he had been poking holes in her underwear, unraveling her robe, and scratching the woodwork in her house. For the first time, though, Sonja exhibited the extreme torment that Daniel was causing her with his harassment. I could tell that she was in great pain and struggling.*

"*Sonya described how her ex-husband had in the past gone onto her roof and taken off tiles, gone onto her porch and scraped off the paint, gone into the bathroom and rearranged the tiles so the pattern was ugly, punched a hole in the wall and then repaired it, removed the wood bar in her closet and replaced it with a metal one, dyed her bedspread so the colors were wrong, moved her medications, eaten her food, stolen her neck brace, taken objects from the home and returned them weeks later, and other far-fetched actions. I felt conflicted because Sonja needed help but her story seemed unbelievable. Everything Sonja expressed seemed like a symptom of paranoia and perhaps memory problems. Practitioners at my agency always come from a place of 'believing' abuse survivors but I had a hard time believing Sonya, and that made me feel sad. When I asked about the last time she and her ex-husband talked she said it was a month ago, when she called and screamed at him to stop his harassing behaviors. He responded that he was not doing anything to her.*

"Sonja had told me that she and her ex-husband had been married for 20 years until she found out he was cheating, after which time they got divorced. They had been separated for 30 years but reconnected and resumed a close relationship one year ago. Sonja soon realized, however, that he had not changed and was still up to his old ways, so she stopped seeing him again. At that point, the harassment began and she got a protective order against Daniel. This was interesting to me because I doubt that the court would have issued a protective order without some evidence to its merit. Some of what she had described may have been based in fact, at least at one time.

"Sonja said that she wanted to move into a retirement community but could not afford it. I felt sad for her again, realizing that she had no one to turn to and that being elderly made things even more difficult. I validated her feeling, saying that it must be difficult for her and that she was being very strong despite the situation. The session ended with Sonya saying that she liked coming to talk to me because it felt good to be believed. Her comment made me feel awful, knowing that I did not completely believe her, but I wanted desperately to help her. She was reporting many things that are unlikely to have happened, but her feelings were quite real, and she needed help.

"Sonja trusted me, and I wanted to enhance her willingness to confide in me. It seemed that confronting her about her possible delusions was not an appropriate way to proceed, especially so early in the relationship. I wanted to show Sonja that I was there to provide her with support and any other help for which she might qualify. Psychosis does represent a client's reality, and Sonja's reality was that she was being tormented by her ex-husband. I wanted to provide her with empathic witnessing, to sit with her in those feelings and offer a steady emotional presence. That is what I tried to do. I did not question Sonja's delusions, but instead commented on and empathized with her feelings. I decided that I could continue building this relationship by doing a better job of listening rather than trying to help her come up with ideas to keep Daniel away. I also needed to be calmer with Sonja, not get worked up worrying about her and trying to decide if her stories are real. This would give me more room in the session to build the relationship so that when I suggested a full evaluation, something she had thus far refused, she might eventually consider it."

Maggie did a nice job of evolving from a position of being a problem-solver to one of providing sustainment to a psychotic client. Having little prior experience with psychosis, Maggie became confused and didn't know what to make of Sonja's bizarre presentation. Because of her high level of empathy Maggie eventually realized that even though Sonja's stories might be mostly or entirely false, her client was in great emotional pain, and it was that pain on which her attention should be focused. Most of Sonja's significant others had apparently given up on her, so she had been alone with her distress. Maggie responded empathically and listened without judgment, validated her client as a person of worth, and presented as an ally. Maggie had realized that she could do more for her client, at least in the short term, by backing off and demonstrating more calmness in her demeanor, to offset her client's high anxiety. Maggie certainly wanted to go beyond sustainment to help the client get a proper assessment, which would likely be followed by other interventions, but she had the wisdom to know that she needed to focus on developing the supportive relationship for now. It isn't known whether Sonja eventually found her way into a more peaceful lifestyle, or whether she developed any healthy support symptoms.

This final vignette provides an example of the application of all three relationship-development strategies with a client who had a marginal ability to communicate verbally. The social worker, a 40-year-old White male named Jacob, cared deeply about this client and it appears that she responded well to his efforts even though she never overtly acknowledged them.

The Quiet One

"Claire was a 25-year-old single Italian American woman whose schizophrenia featured extreme social withdrawal and auditory hallucinations. She was referred to my agency by the hospital from which she had recently been discharged. Her psychotic break had occurred five years ago, and she had been marginally functional ever since. Her lack of social skills, lack of awareness of many basic social conventions, and extremely preoccupied behavior made me think that Claire would have spent much more time in hospitals if her father hadn't provided her with an apartment and an allowance. She didn't bathe or do laundry regularly, her diet was poor, she rarely went outdoors, and she never interacted with people outside her family. Her father was quite involved in her life; he was a good man who tried hard to motivate Claire to take better care of herself, but she always seemed lost in her thoughts.

"As someone who loved working with people who have schizophrenia, I liked this innocent-looking woman immediately. I was fascinated by her constant spaciness. She seemed oblivious to her surroundings all the time, and because

she often mumbled to herself I believed that she was experiencing auditory hallucinations, although she denied doing so and never shared her thoughts. She was rather mechanical in her short, polite responses to my questions, never elaborating on a comment. I hoped that with a positive relationship and appropriate medications she might become better oriented to her surroundings and develop some social skills. She stated vaguely that she would like to have friends, but she didn't want to 'work on that right now.' In fact, she was always polite but adamantly uninterested in any kind of structured intervention. She didn't want to come to the agency more than once per month, which I thought was too seldom, so as a way to engage with her I negotiated a plan of biweekly sessions whereby we would trade off meeting at my agency and her home. We could talk about whatever she wanted. She agreed to that, although without any enthusiasm.

"As the months went by Claire continued to say little and seemed preoccupied. We got along well, however, in our quiet way. Claire always thanked me for my time at the end of our visits, however stiffly. At my suggestion we always took long walks through her neighborhood during my home visits, which she seemed to enjoy, although she never initiated conversation. Those visits always lasted for an hour, but in my office Claire always excused herself after about 20 minutes, making sure that we scheduled a meeting for the following week before saying, 'Thank you for your time.'

"Over time I continued to enjoy my 'work' with Claire, although it was limited to our structured series of visits with little conversation. I continued to have strong positive feelings toward her; I'm not sure why, but I always enjoyed being with her. I always tried to engage with her verbally, but eventually I decided that, for the time being, I would be satisfied that Claire always showed up for our meetings and avoided re-hospitalization. That is, I knew Claire was functioning better than she had been in the past, as minimally as it may seem, because she was never back in the hospital. I often talked with her about how I was feeling (in general; nothing personal) on the days we met, as a way of trying to get her to comment about feelings in general, and maybe talk about herself, but that didn't go very far. I did pick up from her occasional comments that she felt threatened by other women, but that's as far as my 'interpretations' ever got.

"I eventually expanded the routine of our walks in that I would often ask Claire if we could stop by a shop or market so that I could purchase a few items for myself. I really did this on her account, hoping that she would show some interest in shopping for her own needs. Occasionally we ate lunch at fast food *restaurants. About once per month her father called to ask why Claire wasn't progressing more quickly and I tried to help him understand that Claire was severely impaired by the mental disorder of schizophrenia and was managing herself as best she could. He often asked me questions about the disorder and I did my best to provide him with practical information and assure him that her condition was not his fault.*

"After about six months Claire surprised me by agreeing to take a small amount of medication to 'calm' herself. I had brought up the idea several times before but had been careful not to push it, because whenever feeling pressed to do anything she became angry, and I knew from her history that this often resulted in her dropping out of treatment. To this day I don't know what went into her decision to take medication, because we hadn't addressed it for months. Before her medication appointment (for which I was present) I met with and 'coached' the agency psychiatrist on the proper way to engage with the fragile, withdrawn client. He was agreeable to my plan and it was successful. Claire took the medicine regularly, and while it didn't bring about any dramatic changes she said she was sleeping better and taking better care of her apartment. Her hygiene improved, although modestly.

"Claire and I worked together for one year, until I left my position at the agency. I felt sad to leave her and was careful to select another social worker who I thought would be patient and empathic with her. I had wanted desperately to 'get through' to Claire, but I had learned that if pushed she would withdraw even further. I patiently offered positive regard and consistent interest and hoped that in time she might become better oriented to her social environment and capable of more social interactions. My interventions were not dramatic by any means, and there was marginal evidence of her growth, but I had learned what kind of relationship Claire could tolerate and modified my approach to respect her needs. I was happy to learn a few months after I left the agency for another job that Claire was still coming to the agency, taking her medications, and living outside the hospital. There is nothing I would have done differently in this case."

Claire was a challenging client, due to her extreme detachment from the external world, but Jacob was able to help her, perhaps not dramatically, by utilizing all three relationship-development strategies. He presented himself to Claire as someone who was interested in her preferences and would listen to her, even though she said so little. His sustainment, which featured patient refusal to push her to talk more, and mild encouragement about her efforts to care for herself, probably helped Claire relax in his presence and tolerate his company. Jacob was always pleasant with the client and showed her respect. While she usually refused the supports he offered, Jacob continued to make them available, until she finally decided to agree to one of them, the medication evaluation. Jacob also helped his client's father through providing psychoeducation, which helped him overcome some of his guilt about her.

Jacob encouraged Claire to express herself, without judgment, and while his knowledge of her inner life never reached a point that he could interpret any of her ideas, he tried to validate her feelings whenever she expressed them. Further, by taking Claire along as he "ran errands," he exposed her to tasks of daily living that she had been avoiding for years. It cannot be said what Claire thought about their relationship, but based on her behavior she seemed to value it. It is likely, too, that a more aggressive approach from Jacob would have alienated her. The strength of their relationship also helped her to tolerate a transfer when Jacob left the agency one year later, and fortunately, because he had choices, Jacob was able to successfully match Claire with another practitioner whose approach resembled his.

Summary

Psychotic symptoms, which are significant features of several mental disorders, can severely compromise a client's ability to engage in successful personal and vocational relationships. Clients may experience those symptoms to greater or lesser degrees, but while it is always difficult to predict recovery outcomes, psychosocial interventions as well as medications are usually required to maximize a client's growth potential. All interventions depend on a practitioner's ability to establish a positive relationship with a client, but this can be especially difficult with psychotic persons due to their irrational perceptions of the world. Still, it is important to realize that these clients want to experience interpersonal connections even as they are often fearful of risking them. Only by developing an appreciation for the lived experience of psychotic clients can social workers maximize their potential to develop a relationship of trust through the interventions of sustainment, encouraging the expression of thoughts and feelings, and encouraging clients' consideration of alternative meanings of their perceptions. Sustainment is the most important of these because it results in the client's trust that the practitioner will be affirming and will keep the client out of danger as he or she attempts to make any changes.

11
Physical Contact in Relationships

Relationship encounters are characterized by both verbal and nonverbal behaviors. One of those nonverbal behaviors is physical touch between the parties, which can communicate a variety of feelings, both positive and negative, depending on the type of touch and how it is delivered. Other than simple handshakes (perhaps), touch is considered in Western society to be a relatively intimate form of emotional expression and as such tends to be used with caution, especially in formal relationships. This includes professional relationships.

The potential benefits and dangers of non-erotic physical contact between social workers and their clients, including handshakes, hugs, holding hands, patting, and stroking, have been debated for decades. Some theorists and practitioners assert that touch, when done with discretion and consent, may promote a client's positive change, while others caution that such contact, regardless of intent, risks being disruptive to the relationship and harmful to clients. Those who endorse the use of physical touch see the act as a supportive technique when requested by the client or offered by the social worker during moments of extreme emotional distress. The National Association of Social Workers' Code of Ethics (2017) urges caution on this issue, however, stating that "social workers should not engage in physical contact with clients when there is a possibility of psychological harm to the client as a result of the contact (such as cradling or caressing clients). Social workers who engage in appropriate physical contact with clients are responsible for setting clear, appropriate, and culturally sensitive boundaries that govern such physical contact." The purposes of this chapter are to review the literature on the effects of physical contact between clients and practitioners on their working relationship and to provide recommendations for social workers who choose to engage in such contact.

Physical Touch in Human Development

The significance of physical touch in early life and the role it plays in forging healthy interpersonal attachments is undisputed. Studies consistently attest to the importance of maternal or caregiver tactile stimulation for the positive physical, emotional, and social development of infants (Woody & Hutchison, 2019). Caregiver stroking, cuddling and soothing help the infant to build a healthy body image and promote relationship capacity by cementing the child/caregiver bond. Through touch the infant also develops a conception of what exists inside and outside the self, which gives rise to a sense of identity and appropriate connection to the environment (Diamond & Fagundes, 2010). The absence of adequate physical contact in infancy gives rise to serious developmental problems, including attachment deficits (Marrone, 2014). Children may become uncomfortable with their bodies and construct exaggerated physical distances between themselves and others (Toronto, 2002). They may react peculiarly to being held, be unable to cuddle, deny the need for closeness, or avoid touch altogether.

In addition to the developmental importance of touch, those behaviors are an important part of interpersonal communication for many people throughout life (Thompson & Hampton, 2011). Physical contact is a means of communicating acceptance, support, empathy, and caring and giving sexual pleasure. Extending these points to the realm of direct practice, it seems that clients who have experienced tactile deprivation, or are experiencing significant emotional and relational problems, may benefit at times from the social worker's therapeutic use of touch, and learn to incorporate them into their own lives. Still, there is disagreement among professionals about whether, how, and when a social worker should provide such contact, and how it might affect the practice relationship.

The Therapeutic Potential of Touch

The Benefits

One group of clinical researchers takes issue with practitioners who are cautious about physical contact, calling the "touch taboo" an irrational product of Western value biases (Swade, Bayne, & Horton, 2006). It is also noted that a bias against touch largely represents a male perspective in the practice literature, given that women are more prone to engage in physical contact as a means of communication (Lawson, 2015). These authors emphasize that touch can help clients access, release, and clarify their emotions, make pain more bearable, and heal damaged self-esteem. Such contact can demonstrate a social worker's affective attunement, or ability to be emotionally present with a distressed client. Touch represents a powerful means of communicating empathy and helping a client to learn about the significance of tactile experience.

Many others agree that supportive physical contact should be utilized in direct practice when appropriate. Willison and Masson (1986) assert that touch can be effective for increasing a client's self-disclosure and ability to focus and can add emphasis to a point being made by a practitioner. Strozier, Krizek, and Sale (2003) emphasize that touch can convey acceptance, strengthen a client's sense of reality contact, and serve as a natural expression of the practitioner's empathy. The 91 respondents in their national survey, 40% of whom utilized touch routinely, reported that the practice was helpful when a client was entering the office (handshakes); was silent, crying, or in crisis; when the practitioner was encouraging self-disclosure; or when the client asked for such an action and the practitioner deemed it appropriate. They acknowledged using touch more often with children and older adults than with clients from other age groups, implying that there may be higher risks for boundary violations with certain types of clients.

Eyckmans (2009) writes that touch can provide clients with a sense of safety and support when discussing difficult issues, help isolated clients feel interpersonally connected, and restore or develop a client's awareness of touch as a positive experience in relationships. Calmes, Piazza, and Laux (2013) write that touch can create a sense of closeness and caring, communicate acceptance, model a new way of relating, and give clients a feeling of strength, comfort, and healing. Hunter and Struve (1998) argue for the use of touch in work with sex addicts, stating that the source of those clients' compulsions is often a desire to make up for a lack of physical contact in infancy, and that learning appropriate touch practices should be a fundamental intervention goal. In a qualitative study in Wales, a convenience sample of six experienced practitioners from one agency independently agreed that they occasionally used touch to help promote client goal attainment, and their decisions to do so tended to be instinctive rather than planned (Harrison, Jones, & Huws, 2012). Such behavior may indicate a lack of attention to the practice in education. In the Strozier et al. (2003) study, 82% of respondents admitted that the use of touch was not addressed at all in their graduate programs.

In a different sense, practitioners note that touch is sometimes required to keep a client, provider, or others safe in situations where there is a risk of harm to self or others (Piper, Powell, & Smith, 2006). Those who work with children may be especially subject to aggressive acting out during professional contacts, although all practitioners should be educated and trained in appropriate methods of restraint.

What follows in an example of the positive use of physical touch between Ken, a 41-year-old Latino male social worker, and his elderly female client.

A Steadying Hand

"Barbara was a 77-year-old White female hospice patient residing in an assisted living facility. She had diagnoses of Parkinson's disease and Parkinson's-related dementia. Barbara was widowed with one daughter, Debbie, and one son. Her son did not visit and her daughter had ceased regular visits one year ago, reporting that it was too emotionally difficult for her because her mother became so upset each time she had to leave the facility. Barbara could no longer walk and while she was often verbally communicative most of her words did not make sense.

"Barbara and I had been meeting weekly for six months, most often in her room but at times in other areas of the facility. When awake, Barbara was almost always talkative, although little of what she said was intelligible. She did, however, have pronounced facial expressions that seemed to communicate her feelings. It was usually not difficult to tell when she was happy, annoyed, calm, frustrated, or afraid. I found that Barbara responded well to having conversations, even though her comments might not make logical sense. She also responded well to tactile interventions, which included giving her fabric or stuffed animals to play with, or by holding her hands in mine, which I did frequently. No one saw this as a problem.

"One day my supervisor was at the facility, meeting with Barbara and her daughter. Debbie was moving to another state and wasn't sure if it would be best to let her mother remain in this familiar environment or move her closer to the new home. Debbie expressed sadness and guilt over the fact that her mother was in an assisted living facility. She eventually became overcome

with her feelings of sadness and left the room, saying she did not want to upset her mother anymore. I took Barbara back to her own room for my regular visit with her while my supervisor continued to support Debbie.

"Once Barbara and I arrived at her room, she became more agitated than I had ever seen her. She was visibly upset and tried to get out of her wheelchair. It was clear to me that Debbie's description of her interactions when attempting to leave her mother were accurate. I wanted to do what I could to help Barbara calm down, so I stayed with her, holding her hand and speaking to her in a soothing voice. Eventually she returned to a less agitated state. Our session ended when it was time for Barbara's lunch, but I chose to take her to the lunchroom to provide a few more minutes of contact.

"During my work with Barbara I had become comfortable having conversations with her, knowing that she could understand some of what I was saying even though I could not understand most of what she said. I also used therapeutic touch with what would seem to be success. I always rely on conversations to build relationships with clients, but in the hospice setting I found myself making use of touch more often than I might have in a different agency. Touch came naturally to me in my personal life, but translating that to a professional setting required more intentional thinking on my part. My use of touch with Barbara allowed me to help her through what was clearly a difficult emotional experience. I can also say that I was more comfortable using touch with Barbara because I had been meeting with her for months and we had an established relationship. I likely would not have chosen that course of action during our early meetings. But by touching Barbara I was showing her that I was present and attentive. This was important to the client, as she felt confused much of the time and, I am sure, isolated. Holding her hand provided her with reassurance that she was being thoughtfully attended to.

"Another important consideration related to my interactions with Barbara is that due to her physical limitations and dementia she was a vulnerable adult. It is my opinion that touch should always be used with caution as one does not want to unintentionally be seen by the client or others as using it to exploit or cause them harm. Taking this caution into account, I believe that there is value in the use of touch with clients like Barbara for communication and reducing their feelings of isolation."

Clearly, verbal interventions with clients who experience major cognitive deficits have limited impact, and thus supportive and behavioral strategies tend to be used most often. Ken's rationale for using touch with his client

Barbara appears to be appropriate. Because of the insidious development of her disorders Barbara was feeling increasingly cut off from her social surroundings, which would be a horrifying experience for many people. The consistent use of touch, and the way it was done (holding hands while looking her in the face), provided her with the sense of connection she sought. It was a comforting act with no evident negative potential. Ken's approach also included a type of patient person-centered support that was highly effective in calming his client.

The Risks

Other writers emphasize the risks of physical contact. Alyn (1988) notes that a practitioner's use of touch cannot be separated from cultural norms of intimacy and power, keeping the client in a vulnerable position in the relationship. That is, despite the professional value of empowerment, in the Western world clients may not feel able to honestly refuse a practitioner's offer of physical contact. She further argues that the distinction between what is erotic and non-erotic is subjective and client interpretations of touch are difficult to gauge. Alyn makes another interesting point—that it is possible to engage in gender bias when using touch. In other words, if a heterosexual male practitioner is more apt to offer supportive hugs to females than males, this may indicate a bias against males or perhaps associate an element of sexual attraction to the client. In a study by Dorros, Hanzal, and Segrin (2008), practitioners admitted that any form of touch might feel coercive to a client and that the action may possibly create sexual feelings in the client or practitioner (or both). Further, it may create in the client a felt obligation to continue the practice and thus, contrary to its intent, disrupt the relationship. Another study of 67 social workers in a metropolitan area found that clients and social workers tended to agree on the relative benefits or detriments of various forms of physical contact, except that clients rated the behavior of being held by the practitioner as more detrimental than did the counselors (Ramsdell & Ramsdell, 1994). Harrison et al. (2012) note that the use of touch can cause emotional dependency in clients and prevent them from developing their own self-soothing practices. Eyckmans (2009) adds that touch may be counter-therapeutic with clients who are paranoid, violent, seductive, or working on sexual issues (although this final point would be disputed by Hunter and Struve [1998]). Dorros et al. acknowledge that touch can be counter-therapeutic when it is so gratifying to a client that it alters his or her choices of what to present to the practitioner (more negative and fewer positive self-evaluations) or when it represents a repetition of the client's problematic relationship dynamics.

Next is an example of a situation where the use of touch was deemed counter-therapeutic for the client of Kat, a 26-year-old White female social worker, even though the practitioner struggled with her decision to forbid the practice.

A Too-Quick Connection

"Amy was a 21-year-old part-white, part–Native American woman whose presenting problems were depression and overspending. Her father left the family when Amy was two years old, and she had to sacrifice her own childhood to help raise her two younger brothers. When she was 10, she was raped by a family friend, an event that further stunted her emotional development. Following high school graduation, Amy continued to live with her mother, her mother's physically abusive boyfriend, and her 10-year-old brother. She held a series of jobs, working as a child care assistant and a restaurant server. After accumulating over $2,000 in credit card debt, she realized that her spending was out of control. She wanted help in controlling her spending and reducing her depression, which had been present for as long as she could remember. I had been working with Amy on a weekly basis for three months and found it easy to establish rapport with her, as she was pleasant and forthcoming. Nevertheless, I experienced some anxiety about the survival of our relationship when I had to confront her about hugging me.

"The issue emerged after our second session, when Amy surprised me by initiating a goodbye hug that qualified as an 'A-frame,' meaning we had our arms around each other face to face without making significant abdominal contact. I wasn't sure what to make of the event, so I talked with my supervisor about it. We agreed that it was an action to be discouraged because the client had a history of poor boundaries that led to her being taken advantage of sexually. For Amy, a reciprocated hug was evidence that the other person liked her, but to the other person it may have presented a sign of the client's vulnerability and put her at risk of sexual exploitation. I asked my supervisor how to discourage Amy's hugging without hurting her feelings, and she recommended that I introduce the idea of a 'verbal hug' in which I would describe,

as a send-off, how she had shown progress during the session. During the third session, while I was describing what a verbal hug was, Amy reached out and hugged me goodbye again. I was again surprised by her action, this time because I had been talking with her about why it might not be appropriate. My supervisor later suggested that I confront the practice more sternly and explain why I wanted to limit our physical contact to handshakes, which we agreed would be acceptable. But when Amy arrived for her fourth session, she greeted me with a hug, which caught me off guard. I decided to say nothing at the moment but wait until near the end of the session as planned, since I always invite my clients to present their agendas at the beginning of a session.

"Shortly before the session ended I said to Amy, 'Because part of our work includes identifying and protecting your boundaries, I think it is important to limit our physical contact to handshakes.' I was nervous about broaching the topic, and as I talked further it was difficult for me to look in Amy's eyes because I was afraid that I might see hurt or anger. Nevertheless, I hoped to convey that I had her best interests at heart, and I believe there was warmth in my voice. Amy responded in what seemed to be an understanding tone, 'Okay, I understand.' Still seeing out of an anxious haze, I talked about the progress she had made that session (the verbal hug). My demeanor during this exchange was bright, but it felt like overcompensation for my fear about the possible disconnect I had created with her. We stood up and both reached out our hands for a handshake and wished each other a good week. Our remaining sessions ended the same way.

"A major relationship issue that emerged for me in this encounter was the appropriate use of physical touch. In considering how to handle the issue, I weighed the risks and benefits with my supervisor. A theme in the client's life had been her vacillation between isolation and connection with others, and she tended to settle for isolation, which then made her unhappy. A possible benefit to accepting her hugs was that it may have encouraged her toward appropriate social connection. On the other hand, the client lacked clear boundaries in many of her relationships, and the practice of hugging me may have contributed to a lack of clarity about the nature of our relationship and by extension her relationships with other people. It seemed that she could only experience a sense of attachment through physical contact. Though there were some potential benefits to accepting her hugs, I agreed with my supervisor that the least harmful option would be to limit our physical touch practice. As our positive relationship continued, she might learn that there were other ways of developing secure attachments with others.

"One reason it was so important to be careful in this case is that the client had a history of sexual abuse. Her movements toward connection seemed delicate and fragile, something to be approached gradually. To use hugging as a means of encouraging connection seemed too risky a strategy. My personal relationship with touch also had bearing on our interaction. My familial culture featured little physical contact, so I was always reserved in my use of touch. It made me wonder if my own discomfort with touch would deprive Amy of something that might contribute to her healing. Touch can be healing or traumatic, and I chose to avoid the possibility of maintaining her risk of traumatization. As a practitioner, I want to model for clients how to establish boundaries around appropriate physical touch, and if I can learn to do so in a comfortable manner myself, I may be able to demonstrate for them how to navigate the use of physical touch in their other relationships."

With the assistance of her supervisor, Kat became aware that her client had an attachment deficit that prompted her to use physical contact as a means of feeling connected with others. Kat hoped that Amy would learn that while physical contact is a healthy practice, it needed to be considered more carefully in personal relationships. The sources of Amy's deficit were not yet clear to the social worker, and while it is hoped that Kat later explored the sources of Amy's relationship anxieties, it was good that she began the process of re-education by setting a limit on the nature of their own interactions. It is also good that Kat was aware of her own "touch" practices and could admit that her own reservations might get in the way at times of constructive work with her clients.

Guidelines for Using Touch with Clients

Clearly, there are pros and cons to the intentional use of physical contact with clients. Given the complexity of the issue, the following guidelines for the use of touch are provided, based on the work of Eyckmans (2009), Harrison et al. (2012), Hunter and Struve (1998), Lynch and Garrett (2010), McNeil-Haber (2004), Orbach (2003), Strozier et al. (2003), and Swade et al. (2006).

Establish clear boundaries at the beginning of a relationship. This should of course occur in every practice situation. As described in Chapter 2, firm boundaries add structure and predictability to the client's intervention experience and promote a sense of safety. This provides both parties with a basis for eventual adjustments of boundaries, perhaps including offers of physical contact if appropriate.

This next vignette, written by Gina, a 24-year-old Latina woman, describes an agency that used physical contact as a matter of routine with its clients, but the nature of that contact and its rationale were clearly spelled out during client assessments.

Handle with Care

"My internship offered many services for children, including Applied Behavioral Analysis Therapy (ABA) for persons with autism spectrum disorder (ASD). The nature of ABA is highly structured and intended to teach clients how to develop appropriate personal and social behaviors through new reinforcement systems. Due to the complex nature of ABA, I was not permitted to intervene directly with clients, but through shadowing I was able to observe another practitioner's work. I reported to our treatment observation room two days per week in order to view the sessions conducted by Patricia, my assigned social worker.

"One of the clients I saw had a continuous need for physical intervention. Angie was an 11-year-old Black female with diagnoses of both ASD and attention-deficit/hyperactivity disorder. She lacked self-control and demonstrated severe aggressive behaviors when frustrated, including biting, spitting, hitting, punching, throwing objects, and kicking. During the first session I observed Angie would often strike at the social worker with her fists and Patricia would block those hits with her arms. Angie would also take whatever toy she saw available and throw it at the ceiling so hard that tiles would pop off. Each time, the social worker took the toy and placed it out of reach. Although doing so was an attempt to decrease the negative behavior, it did not immediately show results. I understand that change can be slow in ABA work. At another time during the session Patricia used physical contact to promote the value of client dignity. Angie was unaware of certain social decencies; in this case, her jeans kept sinking down, exposing part of her rear. The social worker appropriately helped her pull them up every now and then.

"It was clear to me that Patricia's blocking in order to deflect the client's hits was an appropriate and necessary use of physical contact. The rates of injury and physical assault are high among professionals who work with this client population. All agency staff were trained in a defensive, non-harming manner *to preserve their own and their clients' physical safety when working with them. Many of children diagnosed with ASD who came to our clinic exhibited self-injurious and aggressive behaviors that could be threatening to the well-being of their families, so those persons were also taught the blocking techniques. All clients and their caregivers were informed of this practice during the initial assessment and agreed to its use.*

"Throughout that session Patricia continued to use physical touch in the form of blocking punches but also to lead the client to a small trampoline and bouncing on it with her. This tactic was a means of distraction or disruption of the negative cognitive processes Angie seemed to be experiencing. Showing positive regard while also implementing ABA and physical care techniques is a complex balancing act. I was impressed at how patient the social worker was with this client who was striking out at her, and how she was teaching Angie more appropriate behaviors, for which the client was always rewarded with praise and snack foods. While Angie became angry at times she also laughed, and it seemed that overall she felt comfortable working with Patricia."

What is impressive about the above situation is that the need for physical contact to set limits with clients experiencing ASD was accepted by all staff and clients (or their caregivers) and formal protocols were in place to ensure that the practice was carried out in a thoughtful, consistent manner. It was probably also a great help to the caregivers that they were taught the same safety-preserving strategies for use at home. It was a disciplined use of behavioral intervention, highly appropriate to the client population. It seems that developing positive relationships with these clients would require much specialized training so that the social workers would be able to provide as many reward reinforcements as negative ones.

Be alert to any changes in the social worker/client relationship. Boundaries provide a context for relationship development, but the evolving perceptions of the relationship by each party represent a different matter. Clients and social workers may have different ideas about how relationships should develop, so it is useful for the social worker to review its nature with the client every few sessions (Norcross & Wampold, 2011). Theoretical perspectives also differ in their views of the appropriate nature of the relationship (formal vs. informal, structured vs. spontaneous, etc.) (Walsh, 2016). A social worker is more likely to be successful in a boundary-crossing activity, which may include physical contact, when both parties understand the existing limits. Further, a client is likely to be forgiving of any perceived boundary violations, including unwelcome physical contact, if they are both free to discuss their evolving relationship.

Receive client consent for the action. While there may be circumstances where informed consent is not practical, including the use of touch as a physical safety measure or when the client is emotionally overwhelmed, verbal consent should be acquired whenever possible. Acquiring consent is essential to ethical practice and gives both parties an opportunity to address the action both before and after it occurs. For example, a social worker should offer a hug before giving one.

The following vignette illustrates the importance of the previous two guidelines. It was written by Blake, a social worker who mistakenly crossed a relationship boundary and hugged his client in a well-meaning effort to provide her with support to during a difficult emotional moment.

A Holiday Hug

"I was a 33-year-old married White heterosexual male and had been working with Josie, a 24-year-old single White heterosexual female, weekly for a year when I gave her a full-body hug that I later regretted. I was a clinical social worker at an outpatient agency where Josie had come for counseling to get help with recurrent interpersonal problems that left her feeling rejected, isolated, and incapable of good judgment in relationships with both women and men. I utilized an object relations perspective to help Josie come to understand and adjust her interpersonal patterns. I believe we had been working well together, and Josie agreed during our occasional reviews of her intervention plan. I admit that I found her to be physically attractive, but I did not perceive this as an issue of concern in our work together. In fact, I think that my being a slightly older (and thus safer) male helped Josie develop confidence in her ability to connect with men.

"One November evening Josie was particularly upset. The Thanksgiving holidays were approaching, and she was estranged from her family with nowhere to go for companionship. Her birthday was the following week, and she had no one with whom to celebrate that event either. It was late in the session when she broke down crying about her loneliness. It was unusual for her to express her pain so vividly, and I felt terribly sorry for her, aware that in contrast to her I was going to be welcoming several family members into town for the holiday. The session came to an end, and as she stood up to gather her purse

and keys, I said something like, 'You are a good person, Josie' and took a step forward and hugged her for about five seconds. She hugged me back, said 'Thanks' without making eye contact, and then left the agency.

"At first, I was pleased to have reached out to my client in that supportive way, but as the days went by I became concerned about the effects of my action. Had it been a boundary violation? How had she interpreted my hug? Should I have asked permission? Was I reacting purely to feeling sorry for her, which might not have been professional? Should I have touched her reassuringly in another way, or not at all? I decided that I would ask Josie for her reaction when she came in the following week. I knew that she would give me an honest answer.

"During that session things got under way as usual, with Josie taking the lead. I was not going to raise the issue of the hug until after we had processed her presenting concerns. When a chance finally arose, I said, 'Josie, I gave you a hug last week because I wanted to remind you of my caring for you, and your worth as a person, when you were feeling so badly. But I thought afterward that it might not have been appropriate for me to do that. What do you think?' I felt badly about my action when she responded that the hug had surprised her, because it was unlike me. She said that it had momentarily confused her but added that she wasn't troubled by the act. We only discussed it for a few minutes, and I concluded by saying, 'I always want you to know that I think you are a good person, with much to offer others, but I won't surprise you again like that.' She seemed fine with how we addressed the issue, and I felt relieved that there was apparently no harm done. Still, the fact that she said little about my action made me suspect that she had been at least a bit unhappy about it. I wish she would have said that the show of affection helped her through the tough week, but she didn't say anything along those lines.

"I am a physical person by nature. I'm not averse to touching my friends and family members to express affection, using hugs and pats on the back and so forth. It was always done in my family. But I need to remember that it's hard to know how others perceive physical contact. I was more likely to offer hugs to clients in my earlier years, but I don't do it much anymore, since I've separated my personal style with friends and family from my professional style. I still think touch can sometimes be helpful, but I tend to think now that there are other ways to get the message across. And I always ask for permission first."

Blake's act was well-meaning and rather impulsive, but it was seemingly prompted by his awareness of the sad contrast between his full holiday plans and Josie's lack of any plans. His empathy for his client was sincere, although it is possible that his action was partly encouraged by his admitted physical attraction to Josie. The fact that she responded differently than he expected indicates that they did not see their relationship in precisely the same way, which supports the principle of asking permission in advance. It is good that Blake raised the issue with Josie at their next session and they were able to resume their work without adverse consequences, but such an action can damage a relationship if the client feels violated.

Consider the client's symptoms as they may influence receptivity to touch. The social worker must continuously monitor the client's symptom status in considering the impact of any intervention that might be perceived as intrusive. For example, a young adolescent who is distraught over his parents' breakup may benefit from a reassuring pat on the shoulder at the end of a session, but he may not benefit from, or even desire, such contact once he has adjusted emotionally to the family crisis. As another example, a person with psychosis who has a distorted sense of interpersonal boundaries may be traumatized by something so seemingly small as a social worker's handshake, but following the client's stabilization he may benefit from the same act as a step toward learning to connect with others.

Consider the client's established interpersonal patterns. It is important for the social worker to assess a client's interpersonal patterns for clues as to what kinds of interaction to promote, avoid, or adjust. As described in Chapter 1, interpersonal patterns are largely determined by a person's attachment styles. Avoidant or dismissing attachment patterns develop when a person's basic emotional needs are not met and he or she tends to dismiss the importance of emotion in relationships. That person has difficulty identifying and expressing feelings, and the social worker must respect the client's need for emotional distance and move slowly when addressing that issue. A vignette presented earlier in this chapter ("A Too-Quick Connection") provides an example of the importance of this guideline. The client had developed a pattern of becoming too familiar with others too quickly in those relationships (offering hugs) that put her at risk of being exploited.

Be clear about one's own, and the client's, general attitudes about touch. Beyond what may be helpful for a client, it is important that the social worker have self-awareness about his or her own comfort with physical contact. Eyckmans (2009) found that a general openness to touch is dependent in part on one's personality type. In his study, those who scored high on the Myers/Briggs agreeableness and openness to experience scales were more comfortable with touch. If a social worker denies a request for physical contact by a client because of natural discomfort with the practice, he or she should acknowledge this in some way so that the client does not interpret the refusal as a rejection. The social worker should assess this same tendency in clients, keeping in mind, as acknowledged by McDaniel and Anderson (1998), that attitudes toward touch are often related to one's cultural background.

Make sure that the type of touch used is authentic to the client's need. When a social worker believes that physical contact may be helpful to a client, he or she should consider the type of contact that will serve that purpose. If a client asks for a hug and gets a handshake, the client may be distressed by the social worker's apparently dismissive action unless the reason for that action is shared. If the client seems able to respond positively to a supportive touch on the shoulder, a hug may not be called for. The nature of the touch offered should be appropriate in the context of the social worker's assessment of the situation and the history of their relationship.

In the following vignette, Stacey, a 27-year-old White female, determined that her client, Monique, might respond well to a simple touch of reassurance, as the client was feeling badly about herself for, in fact, being a victim.

"I Believe You"

"Monique was a 20-year-old, Black, heterosexual female who had been transferred from another local hospital to the emergency department at my medical center following a sexual assault. Monique was accompanied by her mother but was alone for a while after she arrived in the ambulance while her mother made some phone calls. When I met Monica, she appeared to be frightened and uncertain of what to expect. I introduced myself and asked if she would like to move to another room that was quieter and more calming. Once we got there, I explained my role as an advocate, that I was there to provide support and resources to help her recover from her traumatic experience.

"At that time Monique's mother returned from the lobby and joined us. They appeared to be close and her mother seemed to be a great source of support. I learned that my client had a close extended family as well. Throughout the day several family members called her mother to check on Monique's condition. While this demonstration of concern might have been comforting to

Monique, it instead appeared to agitate her after a while, and she requested that her mother not disclose to the callers any details about her condition.

"As Monique relaxed I took the opportunity to discuss with her the recommended full forensic exam and the procedures it entailed, as well as well as other care options. This thorough, multi-stage exam was lengthy and I wanted Monique to know that she didn't have to undergo it until she felt comfortable enough, if at all. Monique needed time to process all of this, but I became concerned that her mother was pressuring her to follow through with the forensic exam when Monique was still ambivalent. Monique eventually decided that she wanted the full forensic exam. In that field placement I was privileged to be able to spend much time with clients who presented for sexual assault while the forensic exam was conducted, which could take five or more hours. The exam included a client's providing a detailed account of the events of the incident, which could be retraumatizing. Monique's experience was no different. She explained that she was at a party on campus the previous night. She was able to recall that she had two shots of whiskey and one malt liquor drink but initially could not remember any of the events that followed. Later she was able to remember bits and pieces of what happened, which made her more upset.

"While sitting with Monique during the forensic process, I struggled to convince her that she had done nothing wrong and that what had happened the prior night was not her fault. Her mother, however, while being supportive, made comments that could be interpreted as blaming her daughter, such as, 'It's okay, you can learn from this mistake.' 'I know you won't do something like this again.' 'Now you know what happens when you drink too much.' Hearing her mother make these statements was frustrating for me. It was important that Monique understood that nothing she did the previous night caused what happened to her. Her mother, perhaps unknowingly, was saying the opposite. I discussed with Monique that what she was feeling was a normal reaction to what happened and used the time to provide education about sexual violence to normalize her feelings and concerns.

"When Monique asked her mother to leave the room for the physical part of the examination, I remained in a chair close by her bedside. She looked at me and asked if I really believed that she did nothing wrong. While looking at her directly, I reached out and put my hand on her forearm to emphasize the fact that I absolutely did not think she did anything wrong. I kept my hand there for the next five minutes and gently stroked her arm with my fingers while I talked. Monique seemed comforted by my action. From that point she *seemed to gain more confidence and appeared willing to take control of the situation. My decision to use touch with Monique was based on my belief that it would not cause her any harm and that it might provide the emphasis that I wanted when conveying my point as well as my caring.*

"Responding to clients who have been sexually assaulted can be complicated. I have always been open with patients I see who have experienced sexual assault. I sometimes use self-disclosure to normalize their feelings of guilt after being taken advantage of and use touch when I feel it will benefit them. In this situation I used touch to emphasize that Monique was not at fault and did nothing to deserve what had happened to her. I believe that my use of touch was important for both ensuring that Monique understood my point and tapping into some of her resilience. I realize that some clients may not react as well to touch and that one must be cautious about using it with this population. In this case, my use of touch appeared to be comforting and to achieve the intended result."

Stacey considered that her use of touch, putting her hand on and stroking Monique's forearm, was a way of providing empathy as well as making sure the client understood a critical point she was trying to make. It may have served two other constructive purposes as well, although Stacey may not have consciously considered these. The intensity of the contact, as welcome as it was, may have helped Stacey's message take precedence over her mother's words, which were critical and might leave a lasting impression on the client. Further, the gentle intimacy of the act may have eventually helped Monique remember that physical contact can be a soothing experience, although it may be a long time before she could confront that issue in her personal life.

Be clear about whose needs are being met by the action. Physical touch should always be provided for the client's benefit. If a practitioner offers a hug to a client based on his or her own need for physical contact, the act may well be intrusive and damaging to the client. Social workers should be careful to get their own needs for affection and intimacy met elsewhere. Another concern relevant to this point is the "equality of use" of physical contact. That is, social workers should be alert to the possibility that they are more or less willing to use touch with some types of clients, such as men versus women, children versus older adults, and those who are more attractive versus those who are less attractive. Any bias shown in this regard may reflect a social worker's preferences rather than client need.

Be aware of power dynamics that may be played out with the action. This reflects the concern that, despite the professional values of egalitarianism and empowerment, the worker/client relationship is never equal in terms of power, and a social worker may unwittingly take advantage of his or her situation by assuming that a client is free to accept or reject a touch action (Turner & Maschi, 2015). Clients may be particularly vulnerable to the power dynamic when they have many rehabilitative needs and rely on the social worker and perhaps other professionals for a range of services.

Be aware of cautions regarding physical contact delineated in professional codes of ethics and the possibility of legal problems that may ensue if clients feel that their personal integrity has been violated. All state licensing bodies are intent on protecting the consumers of social work services, and they can file formal complaints to those boards if they feel they have been mistreated (Association of Social Work Boards, 2018). Unfortunately, such complaints are sometimes based on clients' perceptions of inappropriate behavior on the part of social workers. While codes of ethics acknowledge that physical contact may be appropriate, social workers should always err on the side of caution when making such decisions.

The following vignette illustrates each of the three preceding points. It concerns a social worker who, without acknowledging or even being aware of it, was getting many of her personal needs met through her client interactions. Because the clients were adolescents, they may have been particularly uncomfortable expressing their objections, if they had any.

I'm On Your Side

"I once worked with a colleague, a 30-year-old single White female named Sandy, who got into trouble at our agency because she was in the habit of being too 'chummy' with her adolescent clients and sometimes showing them affection inappropriately. This was a shame because Sandy was a fine clinical social worker who did good work with her kids. But she had boundary problems that featured frequently mussing her clients' hair, patting them on the back, and giving them shoulder hugs while making encouraging comments like 'I'm on your side, don't forget that!' Sometimes she even did this in the hallway walking to or from her office. She was also chatty with her clients about their personal lives, a practice that some of them seemed to like but others thought was too 'pushy' (as she later learned).

"As Sandy and I became friends I learned that as devoted as she was to her clients, she was getting too many of her own needs met through them. You see, Sandy was lonely. She had always wanted a life partner and children, but it wasn't happening for her. She didn't have any family nearby, either, and I think she had little to do when she wasn't at work. The reasons for her life disappointments are not important to explore here, and we all have our personal baggage, but the point was, she didn't or wouldn't realize how her clients were fulfilling her personal needs. In my opinion she developed a kind of 'parental' persona with them, which included the physical actions I mentioned. Once I told her that some of her adolescents might not like the touches and hugs she gave them. She replied rather defensively that none of her clients had ever expressed discomfort with her behavior. I responded that they might not say anything because of her position as a therapist, an adult, and an authority figure. Sandy disagreed, saying she had good relationships with her clients and they would feel free to comment on her actions. She said that she sometimes asked if she could hug clients, but I pointed out again that they might not have felt free to refuse. This conversation didn't help our relationship, but we continued to get along well in general.

"Eventually a client's parent complained to our clinical director that Sandy had been giving hugs to her 14-year-old son and that her son had admitted he didn't like it. He also was upset that Sandy often talked to him about his friends, and what they did together, in too much detail. Our clinical director spoke with Sandy about her practices and after several meetings that involved the client's parents she wound up being put on probation. No charges were filed with the licensing board, but Sandy felt humiliated, and this became a blemish on her reputation. She seemed to change her behavior after that, which was good, but it's unfortunate that it took a formal complaint for her to recognize that she was in a power position that put her at risk for violating client boundaries in those ways."

In spite of her known tendencies to get too familiar with her clients, Sandy was considered by her coworkers to be an effective social worker, and she was more devoted to working with adolescents than anyone else at the agency. Her supervisor had been working with Sandy on developing stricter boundaries with clients, but unfortunately she was not fully forthcoming with the supervisor in this regard or aware of how her behaviors could be perceived as transgressions. This appeared to be a blind spot in her otherwise helpful disposition. Sandy's example provides a good example of the need to be extremely cautious and reflective when engaging in physical contact with clients. While the parents of Sandy's client did not file any charges against her with the licensing board, they could have done so, and Sandy's future as a social worker may have been jeopardized.

Summary

Physical contact as an expression of caring has clear developmental and interpersonal benefits for people throughout the lifespan, and as such may have a place in direct social work practice. Still, clients differ in their understandings of touch and its meanings. Physical touch in practice may never be necessary, except as a safety measure, but it may at times be a constructive part of a social worker's intervention if it serves to effectively communicate his or her caring, support, and encouragement of an anxious, isolated, or distressed client to stay focused on goal attainment. It can also help an insecure client with attachment deficits learn about the appropriate and inappropriate uses of touch in their personal relationships. It is clear that there are risks with this practice, as some clients may experience such contact as invasive, threatening, and possibly re-traumatizing. Social workers must always be cautious when initiating such contact, taking into account the client's presenting problem, personal history, and cultural understanding of such contact and the worker/client power differential. Ten guidelines regarding the use of touch in practice were provided in this chapter. Practitioners should further engage in personal reflection and ongoing client assessment and accept supervisory input to ensure that such actions are client centered rather than somehow intrusive or self-serving.

12
Using Humor in Practice Relationships

People communicate their thoughts and feelings in many ways, one of which is through humor. It was argued in Chapter 3 that social workers should engage in the *use of self* in their practices, capitalizing on their personal strengths in conducting their work, and for some practitioners a sense of humor is such a strength. Humor can be defined as a feature of any interaction that is intended to be amusing (Rutherford, 1994), and the desired result is a positive shared emotional experience that builds feelings of affinity. Shared humor is a form of communication and as such can affect the quality of a relationship. While a social worker's sense of humor might be considered an asset for connecting with clients, the kinds of issues social workers deal with are quite serious, and using humor in those contexts might be perceived as insensitive. The purpose of this chapter is to consider the benefits and risks of using humor as a means of positively advancing relationships with clients. The chapter also examines social workers' use of gallows (or "backstage") humor as a means of coping with their job-related stress.

Understanding Humor

Humor refers to anything that people say or do that is considered funny and tends to make others laugh, as well as the cognitive processes that go into creating and perceiving such material (Vrticka, Black, & Reiss, 2013). The experience of humor activates a set of brain areas serving cognitive, emotional, and social functions, which accounts for its range of benefits (Sultanoff, 2013). Psychologically it reduces stress, helps a person to relax, boosts mood, and enhances emotional communication. Physically it relaxes muscles, stimulates circulation and the immune system, produces endorphins, and reduces the pulse rate, blood pressure, and stress hormones. Socially humor contributes to emotional bonding and can even allow people to express disagreeable feelings in an acceptable manner.

Two dimensions of humor are humor *generation* and humor *appreciation*. The personality trait *sense of humor*, indicating the ability to perceive things as funny and say and do funny things, includes both (Srivastava & Maurya, 2014). A "successfully" funny person must be able to use humor that is appropriately attuned to the audience, which is assumed to be able to understand that something is intended to be humorous and then "get it." Some people are naturally better at doing this than others, which is why it is more difficult to help people improve their ability to create humor than to help them use the humor they already have in a more functional way (Jordan, 2017).

There are several theories of humor, only one of which is described in detail here. This cognitive perspective explains humor detection as a two-step process based on *incongruity resolution theory* (Vrticka et al., 2013). This holds that, first, an incongruity created by the simultaneous presence of two normally incompatible elements produces an unexpected violation of convention, creating cognitive arousal. Next, the incongruity is resolved, accompanied by amusement about the process. Put another way, when facing any situation, a schema is invoked that enables a person to make sense of the incoming information. (The question "Why did the chicken cross the road?" implies that some type of elaborate pun is forthcoming.) The response ("To get to the other side") invokes a schema that is incompatible with the first one, and the subverted schematic perspective results in a delightful release of cognitive tension.

Humor serves many functions (Gibson & Tantam, 2017). The *relief* function is experienced when one's nervous energy is released and physically expressed in laughter, and the recipient feels calmer afterward. The *play* function enables people to develop a relationship when engaged in some activity characterized by cheerful interaction. Humor may also have a *superiority* function, where it allows one to receive malicious enjoyment from another's misfortune. This clearly has no use in social work practice, although it is quite evident in society at large.

Humor can also be divided into four types (Martin & Kuiper, 2016). *Affiliative* humor includes non-hostile jokes, witty comments, and lighthearted banter that is intended to boost relationships, reduce tension, and increase group cohesion and morale. *Self-enhancing* humor is a coping strategy used to buffer the self against stress and regulate negative emotions, but not at the expense of others. *Aggressive* humor, on the other hand, is intended to put others down—in other words, to denigrate another person as a means of bolstering one's own sense of prestige. *Self-defeating* humor is used when a person tries to gain the approval of others by using ingratiating and self-degrading comments. These comments serve to hide negative feelings about the self and avoid dealing with emotional needs. The first two types of humor are constructive and adaptive while the latter two are damaging to oneself or to the group being denigrated.

Humor in Direct Practice

Therapeutic humor is the purposeful use of humor by a practitioner to activate a positive alliance with a client or to help a client progress more comfortably through an intervention (Sultanoff, 2013). It is best used in specific practice situations where it might have a positive effect rather than as a general strategy. Related to this point, there is some literature that advocates training practitioners to use humor as an organizing strategy for intervention. Such interventions as provocative therapy (Kemp, 2011) and natural high therapy (O'Connell, 1985) are not consistent with the themes developed in this chapter.

The use of humor, and the observation of humor in a client, also has assessment value. Laughter triggered in clients is sometimes seen as progress; that they can joke about their behavior shows a playful side and an ability to distance themselves from their problems in a healthy way. When appropriately used, humor can also stimulate a client's discovery, expression, or appreciation of an incongruity in a significant life situation, which can lead to greater self-awareness (Franzini, 2001).

Both humorous and non-humorous interventions reflect in part the personality of the practitioner, so it is contraindicated for a social worker to "force" humor. There is certainly no need for a practitioner to be humorous. Further, humor can be offensive to a client if not received as intended. It can potentially damage the worker/client relationship and thus must be used carefully. Not all social workers should, or even can, integrate humor into their practices. The social worker may or may not be a naturally funny person, and the client may have a limited appreciation of humor or be too depressed, anxious, or tense to tolerate it (Saper, 1987).

When considering how humor might be used with clients, the social worker should first consider how he or she uses it in everyday life. For example, a social worker can use humor as a means of engaging with others, promoting a sense of fun, and putting others at ease. These are all constructive functions that can generalize to one's professional practice. A person can also use humor to deflect pain, keep people at a distance, and disguise anxiety, which are purposes that, while functional at times, are not always constructive toward a client's achievement of goals. How a social worker uses humor in general may characterize how he or she uses it with clients, and any of its negative functions should not be promoted.

The following vignette includes an example of how humor can be used in practice as well as its complexity. It was provided by a 24-year-old White male.

Fingerprints

"One of my clients, an anxious 30-year-old college graduate with a poor work history, was intent on returning to the workforce. After attending a comprehensive and stressful job orientation, she remarked in weariness to me during one session, "And then, at the end of it all, I had to get my fingerprints taken!" I replied, "You'll have be really careful the next time you commit a murder." The client laughed heartily. This was an effective intervention, as it cut through my client's anxiety about a difficult experience that she had in fact weathered. It also helped her realize that her complaint was relatively insignificant in the context of her larger task achievement.

"In a different context my comment might have been disastrous. The client was diagnosed with a personality disorder and had mild paranoid delusions. She did not have a criminal record. She was fearful of taking risks but when calm had the ability to step back and observe herself with rational detachment. She had previously demonstrated a sense of humor to me and sometimes made amusing and harmless self-deprecating comments to work off her anxiety. Understanding this, I rather spontaneously (the pun occurred to me immediately but I waited a few seconds before deciding to share it) gave a response that put her concern into a lighter perspective. My client was able to see that she was overreacting to a situation that was constructive, and she further perceived my caring because she knew I only made joking comments when I had faith in her ability to manage the issue of concern. They were intended to be affirming. If the client had been more paranoid, had a felony record or tendency toward violence, or did not have a sense of humor, she may have perceived the same comment as sarcastic."

An implication to be drawn from the above example is that social workers should use humor only when confident that it is appropriate to the context.

There is still no guarantee that it will accomplish its intention, however. It is always risky. What follows are some guidelines for social workers to consider when injecting humor into a practice situation.

Guidelines for Using Humor in Direct Practice

The use of humor requires a competent, caring practitioner, first and foremost. Social workers who consider using humor should know themselves and their clients well. The humor should fit the client, the social worker, and the situation. The appropriateness of therapeutic humor can be determined by the following principles:

- There is already a comfortable worker/client relationship in place. An exception to this principle might be when working with children, for whom humor might be used to break through resistance or shyness.
- The practitioner has some skill as a humorist.
- It is relevant to the specific situation.
- It is used episodically rather than continuously.
- The social worker knows the client well enough to believe that the humor will be comprehensible and received as intended.
- The client's current mental status is respected despite his or her history with humor.
- It is consistent with the overall intervention process.
- Any social worker comments featuring sarcasm should be aimed at himself or herself, not at the client or anyone else.
- And finally, half of wit is knowing when to keep quiet. That is, the social worker should refrain from using humor when he or she suspects that it might not be received as intended.

The Pros and Cons of Using Humor in Direct Practice

Following up on the point that despite the best of intentions, a social worker's effort at humor may not be effective, and might even be harmful to the relationship, the potentially positive and negative effects of using humor are presented here, with supporting examples. All of these effects are drawn from Buckman (1994); Dziegielewski, Jacinto, Laudandio, and Less-Rodriguez

(2003); Haig (1988); Kuhlman (1984); Lothane (2008a; 2008b); Lurie and Monahan (2015); Mosak (1987); Richman (2007; 1996); Scott, Hyer, and McKenzie (2015); Srivastava and Maurya (2014); and Strean (1994).

Benefits of Using Humor

Humor provides a playful context for discovery. This first point is illustrated by Laurie, a 30-year-old White Jewish social worker who made regular home visits to see her psychotic client.

Pride and Prejudice
"Sarah, a single 35-year-old White female, living alone in an apartment, had a 15-year history of schizophrenia characterized by frightening auditory hallucinations and delusions. The fact that she had few friends, was considered 'crazy' by her neighbors, and wanted desperately to have a boyfriend put her at high risk for sexual exploitation. Part of her intervention plan included learning appropriate social skills. Sarah was easily overwhelmed but was sociable by nature and wanted to be around people. We agreed that it would be helpful for her to learn social skills for these situations, so we organized a series of role plays for her to practice.

"Sarah was anxious around people and often 'giddy' in their presence. She had a limited attention span and was distractable, jumping from topic to topic. One of her strengths was that she had attended college for three years and majored in English literature. She was well read, and I tapped into this area as a means of helping Sarah stay focused during our role-play sessions.
'Who are the women in your favorite books who have the best manners?'
'Well, there's Elizabeth Bennet in* Pride and Prejudice.*'
'Yes, I saw the movie but didn't read the book. She was the "proper" sister, wasn't she? Maybe she could be a role model for how you talk to new people.'
'I don't know. She wasn't very pretty.'
'We're only talking about conversation here. She took care of her sisters, didn't she? And then she got this great guy in the end because of her personality. The little sister, Lydia, was a flirt, and she got into all kinds of trouble.'
'I don't know. I like Lydia, but I don't want to be like her.'
'But Elizabeth speaks well, right? She gets the message across but takes care of herself. Can she be your model?'
'We can see how it goes.'

"As we proceeded through our social skills exercises I would sometimes interject, 'Oh, that's wonderful; Elizabeth Bennet couldn't have done better' or 'Careful, Sarah, you're getting too personal there; you don't want to be like Lydia.' Sarah found the Jane Austen references fun. I was recognizing one of her interest areas and using those references to encourage her in a light manner, which she enjoyed."

The social worker's use of humor here was affiliative and playful and was effective in helping the disorganized client focus on their ongoing project of developing social skills.

Humor can be a sign of mastery (learning to laugh at a problem as one begins to surmount it). This benefit was illustrated earlier in the "Fingerprints" vignette.

Humor can reduce a client's tension, helping him or her to feel more able to proactively address a concern. This point is demonstrated in the next vignette, provided by 23-year-old Andrew, who, like his client, was an Asian American male.

Chewing Gum

"Tommy was an 11-year-old boy who lived with his mother, 4-year-old sister, and maternal grandparents. He was a sixth-grader who excelled academically but presented as very shy. During the initial assessment Tommy would nervously smile and avoid eye contact, often turning to his mother to answer my questions. One year earlier Tommy had been diagnosed with a brain tumor. He had two surgeries that removed the tumor but as a result he developed a strong fear of needles. This was unfortunate because he needed to complete a checkup every three months and get injections to monitor any further tumor growth. Tommy got so anxious that it took him two to three hours in the clinic to warm up to the idea of getting a shot. Tommy's primary care physician had referred him to my agency to work through his anxiety and fear of needles.

"I had worked with Tommy for a few months, seeing him weekly. While it was initially difficult to build rapport with him due to his shyness, he eventually became comfortable with me. His mother participated in our sessions. During one session, Tommy, his mom, and I engaged in a conversation about Tommy's habits when he got anxious about something. I had asked Tommy's mom how he responded at the hospital when he knew he was about to receive a shot. She said that his body tightened up and he shook his head in refusal to receive the shot. He would not say a word and sometimes cried uncontrollably.

"I asked about Tommy's responses to stressful situations in non-medical settings, and his mother shared an amusing story of a time when Tommy was nine years old and had been on vacation with his aunt and cousin. Tommy's aunt had been driving with him and his cousin when they got lost, which made Tommy nervous. He had been chewing gum at the time, and somehow he inadvertently took the gum out of his mouth and got it into his hair. Tommy only realized this had happened when his aunt later poked fun at him for the gum in his hair. They tried for an hour to get it out and eventually had to cut his hair. Both Tommy and his mom giggled over the funny memory.

"Toward the end of the session, we talked about the fact that the next session would be after Tommy's visit to the clinic, where he would need to have an IV line put into his arm. I asked him how nervous he was on a scale of 1 to 10, and he said "5." I joked that perhaps he could chew gum on his way to the clinic; that way, if I saw him with gum in his hair at our next session, I would know that he had been nervous about the IV line. Both Tommy and his mom thought this was hilarious, as they laughed over the visualization of him showing up for our session with a wad of gum in his hair.

"A practitioner's use of humor is tricky because it can be hard to predict how the client will perceive it. While I had built a strong relationship with Tommy and his mom, I did not want to give the impression that I was minimizing Tommy's anxiety but instead was attempting to be witty in a good-natured way to help him relax. I used to think that there was nothing professional about using humor. People come to social workers with serious issues. For some reason, I had thought it would be helpful to poke gentle fun at Tommy's anxiety.

"I deliberated after the fact about whether my joke had been appropriate. There were several factors I needed to consider: my alliances with Tommy and his mom, the joke itself, and their reaction to the joke. The fact that I had been working with Tommy for several months made it easier to justify my use of humor with him, as we had grown comfortable with each other and I was able to understand his sense of humor. I deliberated about the joke the most. I wanted to be sensitive to Tommy's anxiety around receiving the IV line and not allow my joke to minimize that anxiety. I think it was wise to ask him about his anxiety before I made the joke; if he had given me a number that was closer to 10, I do not think I would have made that joke. Furthermore, Tommy and his mom laughing at the story earlier in the session gave me a clue that it was safe territory. If Tommy or his mother had been upset with me, I would have tried to explain why I had made the comment. These reflections *helped me to understand the various factors related to humor and prepare me for future times when I think about using it. I feel better now about the idea of using humor as long as I try to anticipate what factors make it a positive or negative experience."*

An important point that Andrew made in this example is that he was prepared to apologize if his joke had come off badly. Apologizing for poorly received efforts at humor will usually prompt the client to forgive the "misfire," and then they can move on.

Humor demystifies the intervention process for clients who may feel intimidated and promotes the perception of the social worker as a "real" person. The following example of this point comes from an experienced male practitioner.

Color Blindness
"I am a color-blind social worker who has often used that fact to my advantage with clients as a means of helping them relax with me. I learned early in my career that many 'non–color-blind' clients found my condition amusing. If I ever had the opportunity to mention my color blindness in the context of some interaction and noticed that the client found it funny, I would occasionally refer back to it as a means of lightening the mood when an anxious or distressed client appeared to need relief during a painful exchange. I might ask: 'Now, that coat you're wearing today: Is that, uh, green, turquoise, or teal?' 'Do you see the painting on the wall here? I was just wondering: Is that sky violet?' The client would smile and correct me because I was usually wrong. The client was amused by the recurring theme and felt pleased that he or she possessed a quality that I lacked. I would often extend the moment by asking: 'Are you sure? I think I may be right on this one . . . Are you messing with me?' These kinds of exchanges worked especially well with clients who were artistically inclined, including one art school student who often laughed out loud in disbelief that I could be so 'impaired.' It also worked well with children, who were delighted to have a 'skill' that their social worker lacked. I think my joking about color blindness made me seem like a regular person to some clients, which is often helpful to the relationship."

This use of humor can be characterized as affiliative and relief-focused. It was intended not to allow the clients to defend against their negative feelings but rather to provide momentary relief.

Humor relaxes the adversarial position of a reluctant client. Some reluctant clients come to an initial session with a social worker prepared to be confronted harshly, in which case some lightness from the practitioner can help them relax their defenses. This is illustrated in the following brief vignette from Martha, an experienced 30-year-old Black substance use counselor.

The Sitter

"Sharon, a 22-year-old native of Ireland, was encouraged by her partner to seek help for reducing her substance use habits. Sharon did not agree that she had a problem and only came to the agency because of her partner's persistence. The client was polite in our first session but seemed uncomfortable because she anticipated that I would try to 'force' her to stop drinking. Sharon voiced this concern several times and resisted exploring her situation as a result. One day I said to her, 'Okay, Sharon, I'm going to tell you something about myself. Last year I agreed to watch my neighbor's 12-year-old son for a few evenings because she had to work late. She left me instructions about what her son was supposed to do, things like homework and cleaning the kitchen. Well, it was a disaster. I tried to be tough with him but couldn't, and he pretty much did what he wanted. He ate snacks, drank soda, played video games, and stayed up late. If I can't control a 12-year-old, do you really think I can coerce you into doing anything?' Sharon laughed and seemed to relax."

Martha told this story to convey to her client that she was not naturally authoritarian. It was a means of communicating that their relationship might not be as daunting as Sharon had anticipated. It was another use of the "relief" function.

Humor can introduce a different, less threatening perspective on a problem. A social worker showed a client with extreme social anxiety a cartoon drawing featuring 20 guests at a party, all sharing this same thought balloon: "I wish I had my act together like all the other people here." The purpose of the joke was to assure the client that all people deal with insecurity at times.

Humor can create a healthy distance between a client and his or her problem. Clients can often assume greater control of their challenges when they detach themselves from them emotionally to some degree. A humorous comment can sometimes move that process along, as in the following story related by Nate, a 32-year-old White male social worker.

An "A" for Effort

"Mike was a 30-year-old single White male who had been battling major depression for years. He had been making progress in his therapy and now wanted to take the major step of trying to reunite his family. His parents and two siblings had become strangers to each other over the years due to a long history of neglectful and abusive behaviors by the parents. Mike had felt responsible for this situation because his frequent outbursts of adolescent anger at all of his family members had contributed to their shared antagonism. I felt that the family problem was related to the behaviors of all the members and that any one of them who tried to bring the group together might fail. I wanted to offer Mike a certain perspective on the situation.

'Mike, do you know what the term "A for effort" means?'

'Yes, it means you tried hard and should get credit for that.'

'That's right. Did you ever have a grade school teacher who gave you an A for effort?'

'Sister Elizabeth Jane did that a lot in fifth grade. Once she gave me an A for effort when I wrote a terrible report about the big bang. She said the topic was "above my head" but was impressed that I took it on.'

'Okay. This could well be one of those projects. You think you are to blame for the family's disintegration, but I don't think so. I think everyone bears some responsibility. So I don't think that you can make this reunification happen by yourself.'

'But I want to try.'

'And that's great. But this may be one of the situations where the problem is really "above your head," and if your effort doesn't work out, you still deserve an A for effort. Do you get my point?'

'Yes, but I'm not sure I agree.'

'Go ahead and reach out to your parents, but if they refuse to see you, remember that you've tried. You took a big risk and it was well-meaning. However it turns out, remember that you've got another Sister Elizabeth Jane here giving you an A for effort.'"

Mike's effort to reunite his family did in fact fail, but Nate's use of humor in preparing him for that possibility helped Mike to see that he deserved credit for his effort, not the outcome.

Humor can provide immediate gratification for the client when addressing a challenge. To a *Star Wars* fan: "Excellent idea! I don't think Yoda could grasp this issue more clearly than you!"

Humor can help a client to relax when disclosing or discussing a difficult issue. The following example of this point illustrates the risk that a social worker can take when using humor with a client. Megan, a 25-year-old White social worker, upset her client with a spontaneous show of playfulness. She regretted her action but later realized that it was ultimately beneficial in leading to her client's self-disclosure about trauma in his past.

The Cockroach

"Carl was a nine-year-old White male who was placed into foster care one year ago due to his parents' physical abuse of him. His current home consisted of a foster mother, father, two sisters, and a brother. The foster mother ran a day-care service out of the house so Carl was able to interact with many other children. His foster parents had sought services from my agency due to his regular emotional outbursts, which consisted of defiant behavior and physical aggression. He occasionally threw objects and hit or kicked walls or furniture. Carl had been diagnosed with post-traumatic stress disorder.

"I had been working with Carl for six months as his intensive in-home counselor. We quickly built rapport through our shared sense of humor. We spent the first month of our work together joining through play. I taught him backgammon, which turned into his favorite game and a ritual in each of our sessions. After a few months I had more difficulty interacting with Carl, but for a good reason: His behavior at home had improved remarkably; he rarely had emotional outbursts anymore. Whenever he began to escalate, his foster mother was able to calm him with warm yet firm boundaries. My sessions with Carl had initially been focused on regulating his behaviors, so I began focusing more on his history of trauma. This was difficult for him.

"To help Carl process his history of trauma, I incorporated the use of a sand tray. As I said, Carl and I were often playful in our interactions but were now able to experience greater intensity when talking about his past. During one recent session, Carl and I were quietly exploring the miniatures within the sand tray, which included some realistic-looking bugs such as cockroaches, flies, and beetles. As we were sifting through the miniatures, I jokingly tossed the cockroach in the air, shouting and pretending to be scared. Carl screamed and ran across the room.

"Although this was intended as a joke, I had frightened Carl. When he realized the figurine was fake, however, he began to laugh. He came back and

tossed the other bugs at me, hoping he would startle me as well. We laughed together, but I also apologized. I worried that the cockroaches might have been a trigger for him. After we collected ourselves, I asked Carl if he had ever encountered real cockroaches. Although he could be quite hesitant to talk about personal experiences, he was open to talking about his experiences with bugs. He said that when he lived with his father, there were a lot of cockroaches in the apartment and he found them to be scary. I asked what he did when he encountered them, and he was happy to demonstrate. He took his shoe and began to smash the fake cockroach with it. I acknowledged his bravery for being able to take on the cockroaches. I explained again that I should have considered that he may have been afraid of them. Carl accepted my apology and began to playfully toss the bugs at me again.

"I brought up this encounter with my supervisor, who assured me that if we processed the incident it would probably do no harm to Carl or our relationship. She often encouraged my playfulness with my kids, saying it could help them relate to me more easily. In subsequent sessions with the sand tray, Carl would often find the cockroach, laugh at it, and smash it. In retrospect, I wish I had been more thoughtful in my use of humor in that earlier session. I still think about the triggering effects it had on him. Still, the encounter opened the door for Carl to talk about his experiences with his father. He became able to share his fears related to his upbringing. I was happy with the outcome of the encounter, but it did teach me to be more mindful of how I use humor. Because humor and playfulness are a major component of building and maintaining rapport with children, I will continue to use it in my work, although I will strive to be more mindful of when to use it by assessing its purpose, appropriateness, and timing."

Megan's story illustrates that well-meaning efforts at humor can backfire. It is always a risk, which is why an apology immediately following the comment is important.

Humor can take the "edge" off a painful interpretation. Ken used a joke to help his adult client work through painful reflections about her family.

Hair Color

"Kelly, my 40-year-old female client with longstanding family-of-origin conflicts, took great pride in her personal appearance and occasionally commented about how much fun it was to change her hairstyle. One week during a session she was struggling with the challenge of separating emotionally from

her father. At one point she began to cry, worrying that she would never be able to reconcile their differences. I said, 'Don't beat yourself up over this, Kelly. We're talking about changing family patterns that go back to your childhood. This would be hard for anyone. Let's face it, this will be much harder than working on your hair. The solution doesn't come in a bottle.' My comment broke the tension and Kelly chuckled. She backed off the issue at hand to give herself a break from the distress she had been feeling. I did make sure we got back to the topic in that same session."

It is evident again in this vignette that when using humor to provide temporary relief for a struggling client, it is important to quickly return to the issue at hand, so that humor is not modeled as an avoidance mechanism. Brief humorous interludes can constructively remind the client of the social worker's empathy and understanding of the difficulty of her emotional struggle.

Risks of Using Humor

Efforts at humor may be harmful to the worker/client relationship as well. Again, one can never be sure of how another person will react to a comment intended to be humorous (Gibson & Tantam, 2017). There are certain kinds of clients, or situations, where it should be assumed that the use of humor is clearly *not* appropriate. These include working with clients who are paranoid, who are actively suffering, who have a sense of superior moral standards, who are rigid and controlled (and perhaps afraid of feelings), or who see humor as frivolous. The potentially negative effects of using humor are as follows.

Humor can be a means of expressing veiled aggression (sarcasm). As discussed in Chapter 9, social workers can become angry with their clients at times, which is normal, and it is best for the intervention process if they understand the reasons for those feelings and deal with them directly. Suppressing those feelings may lead to their leaking out in damaging ways, such as sarcasm. For example, Miles was frustrated with the fact that his client Andrew, who experienced mild but persistent depression, had made little progress on his goals in the past six months. One day at the end of a session Miles went to the file and showed Andrew a session note that he had written three months earlier. He read it aloud and then said, "I think I'll just copy and paste this into today's note" and laughed. Miles was intending to make a serious point in a humorous way about his client being "stuck," but Andrew was offended and subsequently seemed to become more distrustful of the social worker. Miles later realized that his effort at humor had actually been a misguided expression of anger, using humor as a superiority function.

Humor can be resented by a client who feel that he or she is not being taken seriously. Chuck, a 26-year-old Black married male, felt that he had a good relationship with his client Fritz, a 35-year-old White male who was dealing with anxiety and depression related to a recent separation from his wife. He had become comfortable teasing his client now and then but learned too late that Fritz felt demeaned by his behaviors.

The Guitar Man

"Fritz was a musician who worked in lounges every night, playing his guitar and singing. His wife had learned that Fritz was having affairs with other women and she wanted a divorce. Fritz came to the agency on the advice of his attorney and said he wanted to stop drinking, decide on another occupation, and hopefully win back his wife's trust. We got along well. Fritz appreciated that he had someone to talk with who would not judge him.

"Fritz had learned to cope with his anxiety by becoming rigid in demeanor, interpersonally formal, and excessively polite. He rarely acknowledged any negative feelings and always said 'Thank you' when I (or anyone) responded to a comment or answered a question. I suggested to Fritz that he try to identify and express a broader range of feelings. As we worked on the issue I teased him by saying, 'At least if you're going to say "thank you" so much, how about doing it like Elvis; you know [mimicking the singer's delivery], "Thank you . . . thank you very much."' Fritz smiled but didn't respond verbally. One day after such an interchange I walked Fritz to the agency door and, as he left, said good-naturedly, 'Elvis has left the building!'

"Both of these efforts at humor were mistakes. The following week Fritz mentioned to his psychiatrist that he didn't think I took him seriously. He also felt that I was mocking him for 'claiming' to be a musician. After the psychiatrist shared this comment with me, I was devastated and apologized to Fritz the next time we met. We continued working together, but I don't think we ever regained our previous level of trust. I had made the mistake of not understanding the depth of my client's sensitivity and his fragile self-esteem. He perceived my comments as sarcastic; I should have kept quiet. Later it occurred to me that I had become frustrated with Fritz's slow progress and my comments, while good natured at first, had become a veiled expression of my feelings."

Humor may be perceived by the client as the practitioner's showing off or may be perceived by a client as seductive. The following vignette from Todd, a 25-year-old single Latino male, addresses both of these points. Todd's use of humor seemed appropriate to him but was perceived by his client as "showing off" his skills with quick banter. It also struck her as seductive, which frightened her and which she only expressed to him a few weeks later.

Points of Interest

"Beth was a 24-year-old single Black female with agoraphobia who had been unable to attend to her activities of daily living by herself for several years. During her intervention she stabilized and showed herself to have a good sense of humor as well. One day, to celebrate her new confidence, she talked to me about her desire to get out and drive around town, to enjoy the fall weather and her new confidence. Beth shared some 'points of interest' with me that she wanted to visit. I was pleased with her improvement and as a result was in a playful mood.

'I thought about going to the Historical Society museum.'
'Yeah, that's not bad, but this city has some of the region's best Starbucks, too. Shouldn't you start there?'
'Well, maybe. But the art museum is supposed to be pretty spectacular.'
'What's with you and museums? There's a new McDonald's much closer, just down the street. I think they carry gourmet coffees, too.'
'What's with me and museums? What's with you and coffee?'
'What's a point of interest without a good cup of coffee?'
'They probably don't allow coffee in the museums anyway.'
'That's another reason to avoid them.'

Beth laughed throughout the conversation but was concerned about Todd's tone, which she later admitted seemed more intrusive than usual, and rather seductive. Todd was shocked when she said this, as he felt that the exchange had been appropriate. At the time of the exchange he was sharing in his client's pleasure at having made progress, but he evidently became too casual, and his intentions were misunderstood. Further, because he had become fond of his client, Todd was using a tone that suggested that he was indeed flirting with her.

Humor can be used to avoid sensitive topics. In the following vignette Rhonda, a 24-year-old Latina woman, felt that her client was using humor as an avoidance mechanism. For that reason she struggled to avoid participating in his banter.

Laughing It Off

"Mr. Lucas was a patient in the spinal cord injury unit at the veterans' hospital. He was a retired army veteran and received his injury, incomplete paraplegia, three years ago following a motor vehicle accident. Mr. Lucas had the use of his arms and hands and used a wheelchair for mobility. He stated that his injury took time to adjust to and that it helped to use humor to deal with the reality of his situation. Mr. Lucas was in the hospital for a few days for his annual evaluation, which included a psychosocial assessment. This was our initial encounter.

"Whenever I met a patient for the first time I did my best to display professionalism. In most cases, the patient allowed me to lead the conversation and answered my questions, sometimes elaborating with stories. Mr. Lucas was unique in that he answered my questions in ways that were humorous. This started off harmlessly, such as making a joke about the size of his large family, but his self-deprecating jokes became difficult for me to abide, such as joking about his mental health and saying that he needed to get his mind right, 'but that'll never happen.' After making such a statement he would laugh heartily and wait for me to do the same. I tried to maintain a professional demeanor, but his responses were to either make more jokes or minimize what he had been joking about.

"Midway through the assessment, his spouse arrived. This compounded the situation as she also used jokes to talk about their problems. Mr. Lucas would then make statements such as 'this poor intern didn't know what she was getting into with us West Virginian folks.' I did not feel that this comment was meant to belittle me but was gentle self-deprecating talk. Mr. Lucas also made jokes about how he better not say certain things with his wife around, and she would give a faux-look of anger. He would then laugh and talk about their relationship being good. It was difficult to get clear answers from the pair due to their tendency to minimize or discuss serious matters in humorous ways.

"My concern was that the couple appeared to use humor to avoid talking about difficult subjects. I found this to be problematic because while I wanted them to be comfortable with me, I wanted to take what they had to say seriously. I did not want to laugh at potentially serious statements regarding their concerns. I had to quickly find a balance when working with Mr. Lucas and his spouse to show that I was a person with whom they could joke while also respecting the seriousness of their situation.

"Working with Mr. Lucas provided me with a difficult challenge of balancing my personal and professional selves. In terms of my personal self, I enjoy being light-hearted and engaging in humorous conversation. However, I realized that the self-deprecating talk in relation to the matters at hand was not appropriate. I found myself forcing myself to smile when comments were made that I did not think were amusing. I wanted to be accommodating to the couple since conversing in that manner was their preference. But since it was the first time meeting the patient, I did not want him to think I was laughing at what he was saying about himself, in case he was hoping that I would intervene and probe deeper. This experience gave me an opportunity to place what I would do in a social situation on the back burner and behave solely as a professional. I did not reinforce their self-deprecating talk. Whenever they said something that concerned me, I would emphasize that it seemed like something that should be explored further, and I would ask questions to explore their statements more deeply.

"The Lucas couple felt the need to frame things as funny before they could be talked about in depth. There were times where I felt that if I had joined them in laughing something off that we would not have had a productive conversation. For instance, the patient was having a hard time relationship-wise with his teenage son. He initially made a joking comment about how things were not great but that he assumed things would get better. Instead of agreeing and saying time would help, I asked how the son had been adjusting to the patient's injury. The son had not adjusted well to the changes around the injury, so we talked about that a bit further. This element of the family dynamic may not have arisen if I had not probed further. I felt as if the couple appreciated me asking probing questions. Through this experience I learned that humor can have positive impacts with patients but should be used on a case-by-case basis. I feel that indulging this patient's use of humor would not have been helpful."

Humor serves many purposes, and it is well known that people sometimes use humor to avoid facing their problems. This may be effective in part, but if taken too far it might become a denial mechanism. Rhonda was uncomfortable because she was trying to find a balance between supporting and limiting her client's therapeutic and possibly problematic uses of humor.

A Word About Gallows Humor

This chapter concludes with a brief consideration of *gallows humor*, which is not a form of humor that social workers and clients share with each other but rather one that human service professionals sometimes share with each other, usually after a stressful incident with a client. Gallows humor (so named because it is "dark") can be defined as any humor that makes fun of frightening client interactions that occur among professionals at an agency. It treats those situations in a sarcastic way as a means of managing the high levels of stress they provoke (Craun & Bourke, 2014). The humor may seem inappropriate and demeaning to clients and some (uninvolved) staff, but the participants laugh anyway. While sarcasm is always involved, gallows humor can in fact be helpful to social workers' professional functioning when it helps to relieve tensions that might inhibit the quality of their work, distances them from traumatic aspects of their work, and helps them to foster cohesion as a team (Sullivan, 2013). For example, a small group of social workers may share the experience of having to physically restrain an out-of-control psychotic client who is threatening others in the waiting room of an agency. They complete the task as competently and respectfully as they can, but afterwards in the break room they work off their tension by laughing about certain elements of the episode, likening the client to an animal and themselves as big-game hunters.

While some social workers will disagree with this statement, gallows humor is not synonymous with cruel humor (Watson, 2011). Its constructiveness is most apparent when it is specific to a situation and a participant. In the example just given, the social workers would be using the humor appropriately if they did not make fun of the client after the event. If the humor is generalized to other clients, other staff, or the agency in general, however, it might become destructive. Gallows humor can have a negative effect to the extent that it runs the risk of bolstering one's coping and self-esteem by negatively valuing other staff or clients. It may also be discriminatory when used only within certain staff groups, in which case the cohesion of a few people may derive from separating themselves from those who are outside that group. For example, the social workers in the above example may come to separate themselves from the psychology staff, whom they perceive (rightly or wrongly) as tending to avoid difficult confrontations. Long after the incident is over, the social workers may share their negative attitude toward the psychology staff based on one or several incidents, which is clearly not helpful for promoting agency teamwork. Another concern found in one literature review is that the frequent use of gallows humor is an indicator of psychological distress among staff (Craun & Bourke, 2014).

Presented here are guidelines for distinguishing the appropriate and inappropriate use of gallows humor:

Who or what is the true target? If the target of the humor is the anxiety-provoking situation itself, and not the clients or other staff who are "outside" the situation, it is probably being used appropriately.

Who is listening? No one outside the small number of involved staff should hear what is being said. Otherwise, feelings could be hurt and relationships damaged.

Who is harmed? If the participants can go back to their clients and coworkers after having worked off their stress, and their attitudes continue to be positive about those persons, it is likely that no harm has been done.

What is the underlying intention? The humor should be used as a helpful defense mechanism, not an intention to denigrate anyone.

What impact might the humor have on the practitioner? Social workers need to be sure through reflection or sharing with trusted peers that their occasional use of gallows humor does not have a cumulative effect of feeling cut off emotionally from their clients.

Could the humor harm the way future care is delivered? This could occur if the humor biases listeners against working with certain types of clients or makes the provider callous.

Can it harm the profession? The advancement of the department or the profession could be harmed, or held back, if using gallows humor diverts energy from addressing structural agency problems that contribute to the possibility of dangerous situations. Perhaps, for example, a rising frequency of staff/client altercations should be dealt with through in-service self-defense and restraint trainings.

How often does the provider joke like this? As noted earlier, the frequent use of this coping technique may indicate that the social worker needs help in expanding his or her range of coping mechanisms.

Most importantly, social workers should be aware, if they are not already, that gallows humor is common in the human services, and its use is not necessarily problematic, so long as the practitioner considers its nature and consequences. It is not necessarily a reflection of one's attitudes about the other persons, and the practitioner need not feel guilty about occasionally indulging in it.

Summary

Humor can be a powerful tool for interpersonal communication, but its use is suspect in the social work profession, where practitioners and clients meet about serious issues and the injection of humor can seem insensitive. Still, many people are skilled at using humor in ways that are constructive for building relationships and can help clients bear their pain more effectively. The purpose of this chapter has been to show how a social worker's use of humor can have certain benefits for the professional relationship, although it carries risks as well. Various principles that can guide social workers toward the appropriate uses of humor while understanding its risks were presented.

13
The Worker/Client Relationship in Technology-Assisted Interventions

Almost all of the material in this book thus far has focused on in-person interactions between social workers and their clients. Communications modalities are changing, however, and there has been a steady increase in the range and nature of distance interactions among people. Such practices as texting, emailing, social networking, and blogging have not only eased the process of keeping in touch with others but may also be fundamentally changing the nature of relationships. Likewise, technological interactions have become more common in human services practice. Terms such as "e-professionalism," "digital literacy," and the "digital professional" have come into use to characterize the online practitioner (Beaumont, Chester, & Rideout, 2017).

Not surprisingly, there has been some resistance to technology-assisted intervention among both social workers and clients. Some of this is generationally based (Simpson, 2013). Many people over 40 years of age or so are uncomfortable with new electronic practices, as they grew up in a different and simpler communications era. Younger persons, however, perceive these practices as natural. Additionally, many social workers are skeptical about the ways in which communication technology affects the quality of service provision. Clients, too, often express ambivalence about using new technologies, although they seem to adapt to them quickly (Schulze et al., 2019).

The worldwide COVID-19 crisis may become known as the tipping point toward the widespread use of online interventions because, with the need for social distancing, health professionals from all disciplines have been forced to use them (Bashshur, Doarn, Frenk, Kvedar, & Woolliscroft, 2020; Perrin et al., 2020). Given the inevitability of ongoing developments in this area, social workers should embrace the opportunities afforded by online therapies rather than resist them. Discounting their relevance only prohibits a full understanding of their positive therapeutic potential, not the least of which is their facilitation of contact with hard-to-reach clients. Still, online interventions have not yet been subject to extensive evaluation. The purposes of this chapter are to review various types of distance interventions and examine their effects on the quality of worker/client relationships.

Types of Communication Technology

Many types of information and communication technology have been incorporated into social work interventions (Irvine et al., 2020; LaMendola, 2010; Stromm-Gottfried, Thomas, & Anderson, 2014; Turner, 2016a; 2016b). They include:

- Telephone contact
- Email
- Blogs (journals or op-ed writings)
- Twitter (micro-blogs)
- Chatrooms (internet "locations" where people with a common interest can log on, simultaneously or at their convenience, to communicate about a designated topic)
- Webcams
- Smartphone apps to track symptoms or generate interactive programs
- Recording devices on smartphones for client use in practicing intervention-related skills
- Text messaging
- Electronic communities as sites for support groups
- Resource information sites
- Geographic information systems where social workers can locate services and make referrals
- Podcasts and videocasts (subscription-based downloads of audio files).

Several of these interventions will be discussed in this chapter. This first vignette provides an example of the value of one type of online technology (email) for intervention but also its limitations when not used in a carefully planned manner. It is provided by Harriet, a 27-year-old Black female who typically worked with clients in person but made an exception with one client to minimize her barriers to treatment participation.

Email

"Patty was a 55-year-old White married female with two children. She was referred to the behavioral health unit of my agency by her medical provider due to his concerns about spousal abuse. According to her provider, Patty had presented numerous times with her husband James, who was said to be verbally aggressive toward Patty during those appointments. At their last appointment Patty had come with her mother, and the medical provider noticed a large bruise on Patty's arm. He questioned Patty and her mother about this. Her mother confirmed that Patty's husband had been abusing her, but Patty said, 'It's nothing.' She said that James had been drinking and became angry when Patty hid his keys, as he was attempting to drive away. James grabbed Patty's arms and began shaking her, demanding that she return his keys. Patty said that he 'only does this when he is drinking,' and thus she did not perceive his actions as abusive. Patty's medical provider felt that she might benefit from speaking with a behavioral health clinician, and I was asked to meet with the client.

"Patty and I had met face to face three times. During our first encounter, I met with both Patty and her mother. We discussed Patty's background of domestic abuse and how to address it. Though Patty still struggled with the idea that she was experiencing domestic violence, she agreed to meet with me again. At our next visit, however, Patty arrived with James, who despite my encouragement refused to allow Patty to see me alone. To gain their trust, and with Patty's agreement, I allowed James to stay and told him that Patty and I were meeting because she had disclosed an emerging depression to her medical provider. This was not entirely true, but because of James's presence that was the issue we focused on. At the end of the session, James said that Patty would not be returning to my office, as he did not think she was depressed. While I was disappointed, I was aware that Patty was scheduled for a medical appointment the following week and, hoping that her mother would accompany her, made plans to see her then.

"Patty attended her medical appointment and I was able to spend time with her. I attempted to provide her with written material that included local resources for domestic violence victims, but she declined, saying that her husband would find them. Patty also declined to allow me to call her cellphone, saying that James reviewed her incoming and outgoing calls. I suggested that, although not ideal, we could communicate via email while she was at work if her employer would allow this. Patty agreed, noting that her employer was aware of her domestic situation. I had little experience working with clients via email, but since Patty's well-being was my major concern, I decided to try it.

"I gave my email address to Patty. We also developed a plan for me to classify Patty's meeting with me as medical appointments, as it was common for James to call the agency to inquire about her meetings. Patty agreed to this plan. James, however, questioned Patty a few nights later after receiving a routine agency phone call reminding Patty of her appointment. Patty attempted to make an excuse for needing to see her medical provider, but James did not believe her.

"The next day, I received a message from Patty stating that James had become intoxicated the previous night and began yelling at her, later forcing her to engage in sex with him. Patty did not feel as though this was domestic violence as the couple was married. I felt that it was important to tell her that this was in fact abuse, and that it was unacceptable. We had a brief interchange discussing ways to maintain her safety, including an exit plan. We decided that we would continue to communicate via instant messenger and email for the time being.

"Following this encounter, I had many email exchanges with Patty but found it difficult to work with her in this way. I could not assess her moods or reactions to my comments. I never felt sure what she was truly thinking or failing to disclose to me. My inability to see her was negatively affecting our bond. I was also concerned that as a student, I could not reach out to Patty as quickly as I would have liked. I found myself wanting to contact Patty on days that I was not at the agency, but such behavior from students was not permitted. Though it would have been easy for me to check my email from home to ensure that Patty was safe, this would have violated my professional and ethical duty within the agency, as I was not providing this service to other clients. Further, I feared that if I did not communicate with Patty more often, her motivation to change might wane.

"To ease my concerns, I continually updated Patty on my schedule and encouraged her to contact me at the agency if a crisis arose. I would not normally allow clients to have my schedule, but given my sense that Patty understood the boundaries of contact I made an exception. It did seem that this was helpful to her in some ways. I believed that her ability to engage with me via email may have alleviated some of her fears that her spouse would discover our encounters. Patty and I were also able to develop a clear safety plan, and she was able to keep me updated on relevant events that occurred in her life.

The limitations of our communication were that it allowed my client little time for self-reflection in my presence and narrowed the focus of my intervention. Ultimately, Patty stopped communicating with me after a few weeks and I never heard from her again. I felt that I had failed her, and I still wonder how a more therapeutic relationship might develop via email."

Harriet, who had wanted to work with Patty from a person-centered perspective along with an initial focus on safety planning, had not planned on using the email format as her major intervention modality. Without having had prior experience with it, and without any existing agency protocols about the practice, she was never comfortable with it. She was particularly concerned that the absence of verbal interaction and her inability to assess Patty's nonverbal expressions hindered their ability to build a strong relationship. Still, Harriet recognized that email provided the best possible means at the time for her to help Patty through her critical problem situation. Another issue evident in this story is that the agency had not taken any measures to develop formal policies around some types of distance interventions. Had the agency done so, Harriet may have had better guidelines available to her.

There are clearly benefits and limitations to all technological interventions. One emerging theoretical perspective, social presence theory, articulates their positive potential as resources for social work practice from a relationship perspective.

Social Presence Theory

A theory of human behavior known as social presence helps to account for how significant relationships can be developed and maintained through technology-mediated communication (Cui, Lockee, & Meng, 2013; LaMendola, 2010). This theory asserts that people develop systems of association and attachment through various types of contact. New communication technologies do not necessarily alter the nature of traditional face-to-face social bonds and in fact facilitate new opportunities for their expression. Regarding social work practice, social presence theory suggests four ways that technology can positively affect the worker/client relationship:

> *Increased opportunities for bonding* (through multiple methods of social presence)

An enhanced sense of partnership (clients experience a greater sense of participation in the intervention process)

Enhanced client confidence in the practitioner (who is perceived as being more available)

A client's greater sense of openness (clients feel more free to share sensitive information without being judged when not in the social worker's physical presence).

For social workers concerned about the additional workload required by these practices (more contact means more charting, for example), it is said that the intensity of online interactions can be controlled by establishing structured protocols appropriate to each circumstance.

The concept of social presence was examined in a qualitative study in England where eight adolescent clients (aged 16 to 19 years) and five caregivers (aged 35 to 39 years) were interviewed in focus groups about the kinds of relationships they sought with each other (Simpson, 2017). All of the clients had worked with primary-care social workers and adjunctive case managers. The social workers were required by their employers to utilize face-to-face interventions, while the case managers supported the work of the primary providers through occasional texting and phone calls to clients. The results of the focus groups indicated that all respondents sought a positive working relationship with their providers, and those relationships were considered optimal when they included regular phone and texting contact. Perhaps because of this, the clients unanimously felt more positively about their relationships with the case managers. In fact, they registered some complaints about their social workers' limited availability, which they interpreted as evidence of less caring. The case managers made use of a range of communication methods and by doing so conveyed a stronger sense of their presence, engagement, and involvement with the clients. The authors of the study concluded that, with adolescent clients, the best way to promote a positive working relationship is by establishing a broad sense of social presence. Of course, a client's desire for more time with a practitioner does not mean that doing so is professionally indicated.

Examples of Technology-Assisted Interventions

Before considering their effects on the quality of the worker/client relationship, we will present some examples of technology-assisted interventions to give an idea of their range. Several systematic reviews and meta-analyses indicate that these interventions may at times be as effective as face-to-face interventions, especially when utilizing cognitive-behavioral and educational approaches, which are relatively task-focused (Chan, 2016; Gros et al., 2013; Irvine et al., 2020; Osenbach, O'Brien, Mishkind, & Smolenski, 2013; Ramsey & Montgomery, 2014; Ross, 2020). Some are rather simple in nature while others are more complex.

A group of researchers in the Netherlands interviewed therapists and clients at three agencies for their opinions about the suitability of a hybrid (combining face-to-face and online components) intervention for persons with depression (Van der Vaart et al., 2014). According to these researchers, systematic reviews and meta-analyses indicate that online treatments for depression are often as effective as face-to-face interventions, but some level of in-person support increases their effectiveness. The authors interviewed 12 practitioners and six clients and found that both groups supported the desirability of such a program. Respondents felt that face-to-face sessions were important but denied that additional online components such as phone calls, text messages, online learning resources, and assignments might be too impersonal to be helpful. Clients stated that these features could help them better follow the structure of the intervention, give them more responsibility for their progress, and help them to better prepare for in-person sessions. Practitioners agreed that they would be able to provide clients with useful supplemental intervention materials online. All respondents agreed that face-to-face sessions were necessary for allowing clients to process their thoughts and feelings in detail, and that these sessions were most important at the beginning of treatment. Regarding the desired ratio of online and face-to-face sessions, practitioners wanted to see their clients in person for most contacts (75%) while clients would be content with half or slightly more of their contacts occurring online, partly due to its convenience. All respondents agreed that online therapy would not be suitable for clients with severe depression.

In another qualitative study, 20 adolescents aged 14 to 16 years who had been clients at a mental health agency in the eastern United States were interviewed for their opinions about their practitioners using social media sites, including Facebook, for maintaining therapeutic contact with them (Van Rensburg, Klingensmith, McClaughline, Qayyum, & van Schalkwyk, 2015). The respondents, who routinely used social media in their personal lives, all favored the idea, with three themes emerging in their comments.

First, clients emphasized the perceived benefit of increased access to their provider because of increased feedback, contact outside of scheduled appointments, and a positive sense of social presence. The adolescents admitted that they might experience anxiety if the provider's response time was perceived to be slow. A second theme was the clients' greater perceived ease in opening up to the practitioner online, as this would resemble their natural style of communication with friends and family. Respondents all acknowledged, however, that the loss of nonverbal communication could be problematic. The third theme involved the capacity for better mental status monitoring, as the provider could get a better longitudinal sense of a client's functioning and be made quickly aware if personal concerns emerged. The researchers concluded that social media contact should be considered as a viable part of intervention, although there are ethical risks to the process, including preserving the confidentiality of online communications and making sure that clients are competent to use the requisite technology.

An experimental study of clients with bulimia suggested that the use of printable online materials may support recovery over the long term. Noting that mental health services using online technologies have demonstrated promise in treating bulimia, a group of researchers recruited 179 adults and randomly assigned them to either online chatroom or comparable face-to-face interventions of three to five clients each (Zerwas et al., 2017). Clients in both types of therapist-led groups participated in 16 cognitive-behavioral sessions of 90 minutes delivered over 20 weeks that included modules on psychoeducation, self-monitoring, normalization of meals, cue identification, challenging automatic thoughts, thought restructuring, chaining, and relapse prevention. At the end of treatment, outcomes in the face-to-face group format were superior to those for the online group, but at one-year follow-up those differences disappeared. The authors speculated that the online clients were able to catch up to their peers by continuing to utilize the online manuals and worksheets during the follow-up period. The authors added that in absolute terms either program led to abstinence for only a minority (14% to 30%) of participants, although these rates align with norms found in the literature.

Another type of internet cognitive-behavioral therapy (ICBT) for persons with depression and anxiety was based on a research-based assumption that they are effective, with therapist-assisted programs being more so (Pugh, 2012). The author developed a therapist-assisted ICBT program for Saskatchewan residents in which participants, screened for admission, can access program materials over 12 modules through texts, graphics, animation, audio, video, and online activities. Clients complete check-in questions and mood ratings at the beginning of each module, which are then submitted and reviewed by their practitioners on a weekly basis to track their progress. Following each module, clients complete offline activities that are also reviewed. Practitioners can determine which modules the clients have completed and how often each of the module pages was visited. More than 45 practitioners provided the service to over 300 regional residents, with results indicating that the program is beneficial, based on participants' statistically significant reductions in anxiety, depression, panic, work, and social adjustment issues. The author states that these outcomes compare favorably with those reported for face-to-face therapy and remain significant when considering both partial and full treatment completion. Ratings of treatment satisfaction and therapeutic alliance were also high.

The FearLess program, developed in Australia, represents an attempt to provide a self-help intervention for persons experiencing anxiety (Kelson, Lam, Keep, & Campbell, 2017). The program provides anxiety-related information and acceptance and commitment therapy–based exercises in nine modules, each of which has a completion time of 5 to 30 minutes. The entire program requires a maximum of 4.5 hours to complete over a two-week period. Educational content is delivered with graphics and text written for a broad adult audience. Modules address the completion of anxiety inventories, exercises including breathing, cognitive diffusion, anxiety body scans, values prioritization, goals creation, and online resources that can be used for further work. With 40 participants aged 18 to 25 years in the pilot program, the intervention received moderately positive ratings regarding participant acceptability, treatment satisfaction, and perceived value. Small to moderate improvements were found for target measures of anxiety, depression, and psychological flexibility but not stress. Modules were rated moderately to extremely helpful by over 50% of the sample, and the 25% dropout rate was said to be comparable to rates found in other online programs.

Finally, TalkSpace is one of several online mobile therapy companies that provide psychotherapy services with licensed professionals through a website or app for adults (Canady, 2015). It is a monthly subscription service with several options for intervention, all of which are less expensive than equivalent in-person therapy. Based on assessment information clients are paired with a therapist (whom they never meet or speak with in advance) by an intake specialist, or they can select a therapist through a process based on a matching algorithm. (All therapists who participate in TalkSpace are screened.) Intervention approaches reflect various theoretical orientations. The platform works through unlimited texting where therapists respond to their clients once or twice per day, depending on the plan. Like traditional therapy, clients work with their therapists in a structured environment to set goals and work through their challenges. Clients are encouraged to provide ongoing feedback to their therapists. TalkSpace can provide access to intervention to those with mobility issues as well as those who are nonverbal, reside in rural areas, or are traveling.

These program examples are not intended to be exhaustive but provide a general sense of how technology-assisted interventions can be implemented.

Summary of the Benefits and Limitations of Technology-Assisted Intervention

The relative benefits and limitations of online intervention are often noted in the literature (Chan, 2016; Irvine et al., 2020; Loue, 2016; Mattison, 2012; Swart, 2015). Benefits include client convenience and increased service access, which is especially important for persons who are homebound or live at a distance from service providers. The opportunity for various types of contact with the social worker helps many clients to feel more supported. It has also been consistently demonstrated that when clients communicate with providers at a physical distance, they engage in more honest self-disclosure, being less likely to feel intimidated or judged. Further, because of the delay in the timing of reciprocal communications, clients have more time to reflect on their thoughts and feelings before responding to a practitioner, which may lead to more substantive communications, especially from those who communicate better in writing. Practitioner prompts utilized with some online interventions make clients more likely to complete any homework tasks that may be prescribed. Finally, some clients experience technology-assisted intervention as a status equalizer with their providers and experience a greater sense of ownership and control of the process, which can be empowering.

Regarding limitations, there is an obvious absence of verbal and visual cues in online interaction that can adversely affect the clarity of communication, with the possibility of misinterpreting written messages. Time delays in communication may be problematic for some clients who desire quick feedback, and poor computer and phone skills may make it difficult for others to participate effectively. Increased availability demands on the social worker, when they occur, may create workload stress. Beyond problems associated with the intervention process are issues related to third-party reimbursement, and legal issues may emerge when, for example, a client lives in a state where the provider is not licensed to practice. Finally, some types of clients may not be appropriate for online interventions, including those who are psychotic or suicidal, those who are active substance users, those who experience frequent crises, and others who require immediate attention.

There is also some literature that specifically focuses on the effects of technology on the quality of the worker/client relationship.

The Worker/Client Relationship

The research is limited, but there have been some studies done on the topic of how the practitioner/client relationship can be developed with online interventions. In one small empirical study in the Netherlands researchers evaluated the capacity of five social workers to develop positive working relationships through an online chat application with adolescent clients seeking help with a variety of psychosocial problems (Van der Luitgaarden & van der Tier, 2018). The purpose of the program was for the social workers, in one session lasting 20 to 60 minutes, to engage in assessments and treatment planning with their clients, followed by either a single chatroom intervention or a referral to other services. The researchers assessed five elements of relationship development through 10 session transcript reviews and interviews with all participating social workers: engagement in the relationship; engagement in change work; clarity of communication; mutual agreement on problems, tasks, and goals; and collaboration.

The researchers concluded that some aspects of the service facilitated a working alliance while others did not. Worker and client engagement in the process was successful, probably because the beginning protocols were straightforward, but client engagement in change work was not evident. Further, while the text communications seemed clear, providers tended to focus on specific problems and solutions (sometimes called "channel reduction") at the expense of allowing clients the opportunity to reflect and elaborate on more general concerns. There was often mutual agreement on problems, tasks, and goals, but again the workers tended to take a dominant role in defining them. The social workers also tended to be dominant in promoting collaboration, and they admitted that their inability to assess the client's nonverbal behaviors accounted for this. The social workers perceived themselves as having limited online intervention skills and commented on the slowness of typing on both sides. The authors concluded that the program was minimally successful in developing good working relationships. They recommended that the social workers should ask fewer questions and allow clients more time to formulate and share responses.

Two systematic literature reviews have concluded that it is possible to develop a positive therapeutic alliance with client over the telephone and that the process is enhanced when the practitioner is careful to sustain a tone of voice that communicates empathy and provides much validation of the client's situation (Brenes, Ingram, & Danhauer, 2011; Irvine et al., 2020). For example, a mixed-methods study with 49 adolescent clients in the United Kingdom focused on the working alliance in telephone intervention, which the author believed had more existing empirical support than other types of online intervention (Hanley, 2009). The author investigated whether young people accessing online counseling would report evidence of a working alliance, what features of such an alliance might emerge, and if there would be a correlation between a positive alliance and positive intervention outcomes. Participating clients competed a working alliance questionnaire, pre- and post-intervention problem assessments, and an online interview. Results indicated that clients reported a high (17.4%) or medium (58.7%) working alliance and that the adolescents liked the nature of the service. They felt more free to talk about their issues with a greater sense of anonymity and appreciated both the flexibility of times offered for the service and the reduced perceived power differential with the practitioner. Providers, on the other hand, were concerned that the grammar used by the adolescents was poor and they tended to misinterpret messages as a result.

Another mixed-methods study of 15 clients and five providers of online therapy examined whether the working alliance might be comparable to clients who receive face-to-face intervention for problems focused on relationship concerns and depression (Cook & Doyle, 2002). The convenience sample of online clients, who received various types of online therapy (chatroom, text, or email), was compared to a convenience sample of 25 clients receiving face-to-face interventions. In addition to completing working alliance questionnaires, all clients were interviewed after the intervention about the quality of their experience. Results indicated that the working alliance was rated more highly by the online clients, although not significantly so. There was a significant difference, however, on the task agreement subscale, which was higher for the online group. The researchers speculated that written communications about tasks leave less room for misinterpretation. They admitted that their study had many limitations, but they believe it supports the possibility of developing effective worker/client relationships online.

Two related studies did not focus on the overall quality of the relationship per se but considered the importance of practitioners' attending to expectation management with clients at the beginning of online therapy as a means of securing their engagement in the process (Ekberg, Barnes, Kessler, Malpass, & Shaw, 2014; Ekberg et al., 2015). The clients were accessing a program that provided up to 10 hour-long sessions of cognitive-behavioral therapy for depression from 1 of 15 therapists. In the study three types of first-session online orientation were monitored for 176 client/therapist dyads: (1) giving comprehensive projections of the activities involved in therapy for the first and subsequent sessions ($n = 36$); (2) outlining what would happen only in the first session ($n = 108$); and (3) making no effort to manage clients' expectations ($n = 32$). Through a study of transcripts, it was found that the clients who experienced comprehensive expectation management demonstrated a higher level of engagement and fewer points of confusion about intervention processes, and they stayed in therapy more than a session longer (1.2) than the average of seven sessions attended by those clients who did not have their expectations managed at the outset. These findings are consistent with literature reviews by Gros et al. (2013) and Simpson and Reid (2014), who found that clients are more likely to connect with their providers when both parties have a positive attitude about the modality, a state of affairs that is more likely to occur when the practitioner takes time to orient the client to its nature.

To summarize, positive relationships with clients during technology-assisted interventions are facilitated when the social worker does the following:

- Becomes comfortable with using the technology
- Understands the benefits and limitations of the modality being used
- Thoroughly orients the client to the modality
- Conveys a positive attitude to the client about the usefulness of the modality
- Prepares for sessions with a level of structure that is appropriate to the modality

- Is patient with client interactions, especially if technical problems occur during the interaction
- Encourages client interaction if its level appears to diminish because of the physical distancing
- Clarifies the substance and meaning of client communications in the absence of nonverbal cues
- Is more careful to communicate empathy in the absence of nonverbal cues
- Provides feedback, and solicits client feedback, at the end of each session about its quality, especially during the early interactions
- Slows down his or her pace of talking and provides much validation during telephone interactions
- Is attentive to self-care so that any intervention-related stresses do not negatively interfere with the quality of the relationship.

Of course, it is difficult to make a standard list of recommendations because each technology-assisted intervention is unique. Practitioners will develop their own styles based on what seems to work in their circumstances.

What follows are practice vignettes that demonstrate how two social workers had some success in developing positive relationships with their clients during telephone and computer-assisted interventions. The first of these is provided by Destiny, a 24-year-old Black female placed in the mental health unit of a Veterans Affairs (VA) hospital. She describes a standard hospital telephone intervention that was made available to some veterans.

The Telephone Assessment

"Althea was a 31-year-old married Black combat veteran with two children. Her spouse had a full-time job outside the military and Althea was a stay-at-home parent. Althea had been referred to the VA behavioral health clinic because of reports from her physician that she was depressed, with regular thoughts of suicide. He added that chronic pain resulting from injuries received during her military service was a trigger for the client's low moods. The referral indicated that Althea denied any previous history of mental health problems and adamantly stated that she would not come to our agency for any appointments unless she deemed it 'vital.' She did not want to believe that she had an emotional problem.

"Althea had been placed on our behavioral health list of veterans who needed to be contacted via phone for an initial assessment due to their reported transportation limitations. There were dozens of such persons on this list, and they unfortunately tended to be given less priority from staff because our in-person demands for service were high and the motivation of the 'list' clients to receive help was considered questionable. I repeatedly tried to contact Althea by phone, but she proved difficult to reach. After three such failed attempts staff are permitted to close out the case, but I did not want to let Althea go because of the report that emphasized the severity of her low mood. I finally reached her on my fifth attempt and she agreed to talk with me to discuss her situation.

"I felt that this initial phone contact would be critical regarding her decision to accept help, given that she had thus far been resistant. During our conversation I worked hard to create an immediate and trusting rapport with Althea. I was conscious of my need to communicate empathy in my inflections, show patience, and be nonjudgmental in my responses. Even before reaching Althea I had been careful to avoid 'bombarding' her with daily calls. I only called her and left messages every three days in case my outreach efforts annoyed her. I also decided that it would be clinically appropriate to spend extra time with Althea (more than an hour) given her recent suicidal ideation. I think we spent an hour and a half on the phone that day. I learned that Althea's symptoms were still severe, and I candidly shared my concerns about her welfare. Eventually she agreed to accept the VA's mental health services if they could be provided via telehealth, because of her difficulty getting to the agency in person. The hospital permitted the use of this online intervention (where the involved parties could see each other) if it could be justified by the clinician involved. This modality was perceived as being less than ideal at the agency due to the possibility of the practitioner's being less emotionally attuned to the other person and the risk of each participant being distracted by other stimuli during the interaction. The issues of travel and child care did, however, make this seem appropriate in Althea's case.

"I did not work with Althea after that phone call. My job was to complete the assessment and then refer her to another professional at the agency. I later learned that she was consistent in keeping her telehealth appointments. This intervention was a learning experience for me because it reminded me that all persons deserve access to professional services in any way possible, and that just because I haven't seen someone's face, it doesn't mean they should be less of a service priority. I also learned that when on the phone a social worker *needs to concentrate especially hard on the full meaning of a client's statements because the inability to observe nonverbal cues is a problem."*

It is interesting that Destiny's department viewed the telehealth intervention as suboptimal, which appears to be a prevailing belief in the absence of comparative research evidence. Whether such an assumption is true, the service certainly does bring help to people who otherwise could not receive it. Destiny is to be credited with recognizing her need to create a constructive relationship with Althea on the phone and being aware of some of the challenges to doing so. Knowing that the outcome of this conversation would determine whether her client decided to participate in ongoing therapy, Destiny took more time than would have been allotted for an in-person session so that she could effectively convey the empathy that would be a key to engaging Althea in the service system.

The next vignette comes from George, a 45-year-old Black social worker employed at a private-practice agency. He describes some of the challenges of maintaining good working relationships with clients when meeting with them through a telehealth intervention. George worked individually with adult clients who experienced a variety of problems, including mood, personality, and psychotic disorders. He was new to the online modality but was forced to learn it due to social distancing mandates resulting from the coronavirus pandemic.

Accommodating the Pandemic

"During the spring of 2020, the 30 or so practitioners at my agency had to start meeting with their clients online due to the spread of the coronavirus pandemic. The agency was closed to in-person meetings for six months and all of us had to learn to use Zoom to keep working. Learning the Zoom basics was not difficult, but for myself and most of the other staff it felt like the relationships with our clients changed adversely, at least for a while. Among the concerns I had was that my clients seemed so far away, emotionally as well as physically, which lessened the intensity of our interaction. I made a point to talk with my clients during our first sessions about how the modality worked, and then at the end of each session I asked them to share their reactions to it. My clients, as well as myself, all admitted that the setting felt awkward,

although I must admit that they seemed to adapt to the new format more quickly than I did.

"At first, as I said, I felt like there was an emotional distance between us that got in the way of the depth of our communications. Our interactions felt more formal. Our ranges of physical motion were restricted, as we needed to stay centered on the screen. This made it harder for me to assess their mental status, and they seemed to talk less. For my part, I became more verbally active, feeling that I needed to take more responsibility for focusing our conversations on relevant content. This sense of additional responsibility was draining for me. Once we all got used to the online modality, the substance of our interactions improved, however, and I can't say that the quality of the work being done suffered. Still, I worried that the strength of our alliance had diminished in the less personal atmosphere created by the setting.

"What did not change over time, however, was the added stress I accumulated over the course of a working day. I noticed that sitting in front of a computer screen for so many hours had adverse effects on me, a situation that was compounded after my sessions in that I had to continue working on the computer to get my notes written. Further, my work became a lonely experience, given that I did not have the pleasure and support of interacting with my colleagues around the office. In fact, during the pandemic I almost never encountered other colleagues, as almost everyone worked from home, and in addition to feeling isolated I missed my usual opportunities to ask for their input about my cases.

"Fortunately, I did not work with children, as so many of my colleagues did. I learned that they were having particular difficulty with the online format because they were accustomed to providing play therapy, which was quite difficult to organize online. Their agency offices were filled with toys and games, and they were accustomed to spending their client hours engaged with kids in that way. They felt that there was less that they could provide to their clients online. Children also have a difficult time sitting still in one place for very long, of course, and they became easily distracted in front of their computers at home. Those sessions were often less substantive and shorter as a result.

"My takeaway from the online therapy experience is that it was difficult in part because it was new. I had never worked this way before, so it felt uncomfortable, but as time went by I adjusted to the format and became more comfortable with it. I do feel that there was always something missing from my sessions with regard to the intensity of the work, but I tried to adjust my *behavior to account for it, again becoming more verbal and probably more confrontational so that I was able to work productively on my clients' issues."*

George had been forced to learn this form of online intervention because of agency mandates related to the COVID-19 pandemic. Being new to the modality, he noticed that it felt awkward and the bond between him and his clients seemed weaker due to their physical distance. With experience his attitudes improved, although he recognized that he had to adjust his behaviors to ensure that his sessions were productive (talking more and continually asking clients for feedback about the process). George never came to feel that his relationships with his clients were as positive as before. He observed, too, that coworkers who provided play therapy were seriously disadvantaged by distance interventions. Interestingly, George became aware of stresses inherent in the modality related to continuous online work and the absence of other staff as support resources. These adverse effects of online intervention and the increased need for self-care have begun to receive attention in the literature (Brown, 2020). Social workers must agency supports to maintain their usual level of energy for intervening with clients, such as taking more breaks, arranging to be in contact with coworkers, perhaps conducting online mutual support meetings with coworkers, and receiving ongoing staff development around the effective use of technology.

Ethical Issues

The use of technology-assisted interventions has also given rise to ethical concerns in social work and other helping professions (Broddy & Dominelli, 2017; Reamer, 2018; Stromm-Gottfried, Thomas, & Anderson, 2014; Swart, 2015). These include challenges in receiving informed client consent, establishing competence in practice, managing abrupt service interruptions due to technology failure, managing records, and engaging in supervision and consultation online. It may also be easier to for social workers to cross boundaries and develop dual relationships with clients in online practice. For example, in one study 83% of social work students said they would accept a Facebook friend request from a client and two-thirds admitted to venting to their online friends about their field placement experiences (Voshel & Wesala, 2015).

There are also ethical concerns related to privacy (including the permanence of online communication), confidentiality, security, and controlling the amount of information clients and practitioners may find about each other online. In response to these concerns, the National Association of Social Workers (NASW) revised its code of ethics in 2017 to include 19 new or revised standards about technological practice (NASW, 2017a). That same year a taskforce including members of NASW, the Association of Social Work Boards, the Council on Social Work Education, and Clinical Social Work Associations published a manual entitled *Standards for Technology in Social Work Practice* (NASW, 2017b). At a minimum, social workers should be aware of the complexities of online interaction and help their clients to become digitally and ethically literate (Karpman & Drisko, 2016). Agencies must also assume responsibility for developing policies about online interventions for their staff.

The following is an example of an ethical violation committed by an experienced social worker related to online intervention. It seems that the social worker had no awareness of the boundary issue involved, which points to the need for professional development in online relationship management. The story is relayed by the person's supervisee, a 25-year-old White social worker named Taylor.

The Facebook Friend

"I recently worked with William, a 50-year-old Black male who was admitted to our hospital's hospice unit. William was in his second marriage, to Ahjanae, a 35-year-old stay-at-home parent. They had an 11-month-old daughter together and several stepchildren whom William had adopted. William had recently broken several bones in his arms and ribs in a fall from a ladder. During the resulting examination the physician was surprised to discover that William had bone cancer, a condition that had made his bones frail. Sadly, his condition progressed rapidly. William was admitted to our hospital and soon moved to the hospice unit. He passed away after only three weeks. My role in the intervention was to meet with Ahjanae, along with my supervisor, to provide her with support resources and help her plan for her life after William passed. We also had two more meetings with her after William died. Ahjanae was distraught about her loss, and she had little evident support to help her grieve or attend to her young daughter.

"This is where my supervisor's [a 45-year-old single White female] behavior began to concern me. Just after we closed William's file she looked up Ahjanae on Facebook and sent her a friend request, which was accepted. I wondered about the ethics of this action, because it appeared to me to create an inappropriate dual relationship. Sure enough, my supervisor began sending regular messages to Ahjanae, communicating her ongoing concern about her emotional well-being. Ahjanae always responded in detail, and they gradually began sharing more personal information, including family photographs. When I asked my supervisor about the ethics of this activity she showed no qualms about it, stating that the wife had little support and was in need of reassurance from a friend. I wondered if my supervisor was doing this to get her own social support needs met. She often talked with me and other staff about how Ahjanae was doing and made complimentary remarks about the posted photographs of the client's family. I didn't do anything about the situation because of my status as a student, although it bothered me. Their friendship continued even after I left the agency.

"Nowadays social workers and their clients can find information about each other rather easily. I have been taught that, as tempting as it might be, social workers should not search their clients on the internet. This case also sensitized me to the fact that clients might find their social workers online and make friend requests of their own, perhaps after the intervention ends. Nevertheless, the relationship is supposed to end with the service termination and the client should be referred for support elsewhere. My supervisor, though, once said that we should never dismiss a friend request out of hand, but consider how it might be therapeutic. That was her point of view, but it didn't make sense to me, and I have not followed that advice."

It appears that Taylor's supervisor was giving in to a personal inclination that was at odds with the profession's values, although she rationalized her actions as being professional. The NASW Code of Ethics (2017a) states that social workers should not communicate with clients using technology for personal or non-work-related purposes in order to maintain appropriate boundaries. The availability of personal information on professional websites or other media can cause boundary confusion, inappropriate dual relationships, or harm to clients when they perceive that they can have personal relationships with their providers. This demonstrates the ambiguity about the nature of modern-day worker/client relationships. It would have been appropriate for Taylor's supervisor to arrange to help the client secure her own social support resources, perhaps by referral to another practitioner after she was no longer involved in the hospice program.

Summary

While the safe and effective delivery of technology-assisted interventions remains a challenge, they can be quite helpful for clients, and it is evident that positive worker/client relationships are possible through these media. With the worldwide onset of the COVID-19 pandemic it has become almost mandatory that human service practitioners become competent in these forms of service delivery. The demand for technological services will continue to increase, largely due to the fact that they allow for expanded service delivery access for clients and will possibly revise how professionals conceptualize the scope of practice. This chapter has described the various ways in which social workers will need to make some adjustments in how they develop relationships with their clients, including 12 recommendations for doing so. The manner in which these relationships can be sustained will become more evident with further research.

References

Abbot, A. A. (2003). Understanding transference and countertransference: Risk management strategies for preventing sexual misconduct and other boundary violations in social work practice. *Psychoanalytic Social Work, 10*(2), 21–41.

Accurso, E. C., & Garland, A. F. (2015). Child, caregiver, and therapist perspectives on therapeutic alliance in usual care child psychotherapy. *Psychological Assessment, 27*(1), 347–352.

Adamowich, T., Kumsa, M. K., Rego, C., Stoddart, J., & Vito, R. (2014). Playing hide-and-seek: Searching for the use of self in reflective social work practice. *Reflective Practice, 15*(2), 131–143.

Ainsworth, M. S., Blehar, M. C., & Waters, E. (1978). *Patterns of attachment: A psychological study of the strange situation.* Oxford: Lawrence Erlbaum.

Alyn, J. H. (1988). The politics of touch in therapy: A response to Willison and Masson. *Journal of Counseling and Development, 66,* 432–433.

American Psychiatric Association. (2012). *Diagnostic and statistical manual of mental disorders (5th ed.).* Arlington, VA: Author.

Andrews, F., Griffiths, N., Harrison, L., & Stagnatti, A. (2013). Expectations of parents on low incomes and therapists who work with parents on low incomes of the first therapy session. *Australian Occupational Therapy Journal, 60*(6), 436–444.

Association of Social Work Boards. (2018). *Model social work practice act.* Culpepper, VA: Author.

Ayotte, M., Lanctot, N., & Tourigny, M. (2017). The association between the working alliance with adolescent girls in residential care and their trauma-related symptoms in emerging adulthood. *Child and Youth Care Forum, 46,* 601–620.

Ayotte, M., Lanctot, N., & Tourigny, M. (2015). Pre-treatment profiles of adolescent girls as predictors of the strength of their working alliances with practitioners in residential care settings. *Child and Youth Services Review, 53,* 61–69.

Bachelor, A. (2013). Clients' and therapists' views of the therapeutic alliance: Similarities, differences, and relationship to therapy outcome. *Clinical Psychology and Psychotherapy, 20,* 118–135.

Baldwin, E. N. (2014). Recognizing guilt and shame: Therapeutic ruptures with parents of children in psychotherapy. *Psychoanalytic Social Work, 21,* 2–18.

Balkin, R. S., & Schmit, E. L. (2018). A humanistic framework using nonlinear analysis to evaluate the working alliance and coping for adolescents in crisis. *Journal of Humanistic Counseling, 57,* 2–13.

Barnard, C. P., & Kuehl, B. P. (1995). Ongoing evaluation: In-session procedures for enhancing the working alliance and therapeutic effectiveness. *American Journal of Family Therapy, 23*(2), 161–172.

Bartholomew, T. T., Gundel, B. E., & Scheel, M. J. (2017). The relationship between alliance ruptures and hope for change through counseling: A mixed methods study. *Counseling Psychology Quarterly, 30*(1), 1–19.

Bashshur, R., Doarn, C. R., Frenk, J. M., Kvedar, J. C., & Woolliscroft, J. O. (2020). Telemedicine and the COVID-19 pandemic: Lessons for the future. *Telemedicine & e-Health, 26*(5), 571–573.

Baum, N. (2007). Therapists' responses to treatment termination: An inquiry into the variables that contribute to therapists' experiences. *Clinical Social Work Journal, 35*, 97–106.

Baum, N. (2005). Correlates of clients' emotional and behavioral responses to treatment termination. *Clinical Social Work Journal, 33*(3), 309–326.

Beaumont, E., Chester, P., & Rideout, H. (2017). Navigating ethical challenges in social media: Social work student and practitioner perspectives. *Australian Social Work, 70*(2), 221–228.

Beck, J. (2011). *Cognitive theory: Basics and beyond (2nd ed.)*. New York: Guilford.

Bernhard, G., Knibbe, R. A., van Wolff, A., Dingoyan, D., Schulz, H., & Mosko, M. (2015). Development and psychometric evaluation of an instrument to assess cross-cultural competence of healthcare professionals. (CCCHP). *PLoS One, 10*(12): e0144049. doi:10.1371/journal.pone.0144049.

Bernsen, A., Tabachnick, B. G., & Pope, K. P. (1994). National survey of social workers' sexual attraction to their clients: Results, implications, and comparison to psychologists. *Ethics & Behavior, 4*(4), 369–388.

Berzoff, J. (2016). Relational and intersubjective theories. In J. Berzoff, L. M. Flanagan, & P. Hertz (Eds.), *Inside out and outside in: Psychodynamic clinical theory and psychopathology in contemporary multicultural contexts* (pp. 249–268). Lanham, MD: Rowman & Littlefield.

Borden, W. (2000). The relational paradigm in contemporary psychoanalysis: Toward a psychodynamically informed social work perspective. *Social Service Review, 74*(3), 352–379.

Bowen, M. (1978). *Family therapy in clinical practice*. Northvale, NJ: Jason Aronson.

Brenes, G., Ingram, C. W., & Danhauer, S. C. (2011). Benefits and challenges of conducting psychotherapy by telephone. *Professional Psychology: Research and Practice, 42*(6), 543–549.

Broddy, J., & Dominelli, L. (2017). Social media and social work: The challenges of a new ethical space. *Australian Social Work, 70*(2), 172–184.

Broderick, P. C., & Blewitt, P. (2020). *The life span: Human development for helping professionals (5th ed.)*. Hoboken, NJ: Pearson.

Brown, J. (2015). Specific techniques vs. common factors: Psychotherapy integration and its role in ethical practice. *American Journal of Psychotherapy, 69*(3), 301–316.

Brown, M. (2019). Constructing accountability: The development and delegation of outcome evaluation in American social work. *Social Service Review, 93*(4), 712–763.

Brown, S. (2020). Working remotely. *Therapy Today, 31*(4), 21–24.

Bruhn, J. G., Levine, H. G., & Levine, P. L. (2002). *Managing boundaries in the health professions*. Clinton Corners, NY: Elliot Werner Publications.

Buckman, E. S. (Ed.) (1994). *The handbook of humor: Clinical applications in psychotherapy*. Malabar, FL: Krieger Press.

Burdick, K. E., Braga, R. J., Goldberg, J. F., & Malhotra, A. K. (2007). Cognitive dysfunction in bipolar disorder: Future place of pharmacotherapy. *CNS Drugs, 21*(12), 971–981.

Burston, D., & Frie, R. (2006). *Psychotherapy as a human science*. Pittsburgh: Duquesne University Press.

Calmes, S. A., Piazza, N. J., & Laux, J. M. (2013). The use of touch in counseling: An ethical decision-making model. *Counseling and Values, 58*, 59–68.

Cameron, M. (2014). This is common factors. *Clinical Social Work Journal, 42*, 151–160.

Cameron, M., & Keenan, E. K. (2010). The common factors model: Implications for transtheoretical clinical social work. *Social Work, 55*(1), 63–73.

Campbell, R. J. (2009). *Campbell's psychiatric dictionary (9th ed.)*. New York: Oxford University Press.

Canady, V. A. (2015). Study finds text-based therapy delivery convenient, accessible. *Mental Health Weekly, 25*(28), 3–5.

Capaldi, S., Asnaani, A., Zandberg, L. J., Carpenter, J. K., & Fioa, E. B. (2016). Therapeutic alliance during prolonged exposure versus client-centered therapy for adolescent posttraumatic stress disorder. *Journal of Clinical Psychology, 72*(10), 1026–1036.

Carlson, E. A. (1998). A prospective longitudinal study of attachment disorganization/disorientation. *Child Development, 69*(4), 1107–1128.

Cartwright, C., Rhodes, P., King, R., & Shires, A. (2014). Experiences of countertransference: Reports of clinical psychology students. *Australian Psychologist, 49*, 232–240.

Cash, S. K., Hardy, G. E., Kellett, S., & Parry, G. (2014). Ruptures and resolution during cognitive-behaviour therapy with patients with borderline personality disorder. *Psychotherapy Research, 24*(2), 132–145.

Celenza, A. (2010). The guilty pleasure of erotic countertransference: Searching for radial true. *Studies in Gender and Sexuality, 11*, 175–183.

Chan, C. (2016). A scoping review of social media use in social work practice. *Journal of Evidence-Informed Social Work, 13*, 263–276.

Charlesworth, L. W. (2019). Middle childhood. In E. D. Hutchison (Ed.), *Dimensions of human behavior: The changing life course (6th ed.)* (pp. 153–188). Thousand Oaks, CA: Sage.

Cheng, T. C., & Lo, C. C. (2016). Linking worker–parent working alliance to parent progress in child welfare: A longitudinal analysis. *Child and Youth Services Review, 71*, 10–16.

Clapton, K. (2013). Developing professional boundaries guidance for social workers. *Journal of Adult Protection, 15*(1), 37–44.

Clark, P., Cole, C., & Robertson, J. M. (2014). Creating a safety net: Transferring to a new therapist in a training setting. *Contemporary Family Therapy, 36*, 172–189.

Clark, P., Robertson, J. M., Keen, R., & Cole, C. (2011). Outcomes of transfers in a training setting. *American Journal of Family Therapy, 39*, 214–225.

Cook, J. E., & Doyle, C. (2002). Working alliance in online therapy as compared to face-to-face therapy: Preliminary results. *CyberPsychology & Behavior, 5*(2), 95–105.

Cooper, F. (2012). *Professional boundaries in social work and social care: A practical guide to understanding, maintaining, and managing your professional boundaries*. Philadelphia: Jessica Kingsley Publishers.

Corcoran, J. (2014). *Collaborative cognitive-behavioral intervention in social work practice: A workbook*. New York: Oxford University Press.

Council on Social Work Education. (2015). *2015 Educational and policy accreditation standards for baccalaureate and master's social work programs*. Washington, DC: National Association of Social Workers.

Couthino, J., Ribeiro, E., Hill, C., & Safran, J. (2011). Therapists' and clients' experiences of alliance ruptures: A qualitative study. *Psychotherapy Research, 21*(5), 525–540.

Cox, K., Sullivan, N., Reiman, J., & Vang, C. (2009). Highlighting the role of cross-cultural competence in ethically sound practice. *Journal of Social Work and Values, 6*(1). https://www.nlasw.ca/sites/default/files/inline-files/cultural_competency_standards.pdf.

Craun, S. W., & Bourke, M. L. (2014). The use of humor to cope with secondary traumatic stress. *Journal of Child Sexual Abuse, 23,* 840–852.

Crawford, E. A., Frank, H. E., Palitz, S. A., Davis, J. P., & Kendall, P. C. (2017). Process factors associated with improved outcomes in CBT for anxious youth: Therapeutic content, alliance, and therapist actions. *Cognitive Therapy Research, 42,* 172–183.

Creed, T. A., & Kendall, P. C. (2005). Therapist alliance-building behavior with a cognitive-behavioral treatment for anxiety in youth. *Journal of Consulting & Clinical Psychology, 73*(3), 498–505.

Cui, G., Lockee, B., & Meng, C. (2013). Building modern online social presence: A review of social presence theory and its instructional design implications for future trends. *Education and Information Technologies, 18,* 661–685.

Cuijpers, P., Driessen, E., Hollon, S. D., van Oppen, P., Barth, J., & Andersson, G. (2012). The efficacy of non-directive supportive therapy for adult depression: A meta-analysis. *Clinical Psychology Review, 32,* 280–291.

Dahl, H. J., Høglend, P., Ulberg, R., Amlo, S., Gabbard, G. O., Perry, J. C., & Crits Christoph, P. (2017). Does therapists' disengaged feelings influence the effect of countertransference work? A study on countertransference. *Clinical Psychology and Psychotherapy, 24,* 462–474.

Dalenberg, C. J. (2014). On building a science of common factors in trauma therapy. *Journal of Trauma and Dissociation, 15*(4), 373–383.

Dalenberg, C. J. (2004). Maintaining the safe and effective therapeutic environment in the context of distrust and anger: Countertransference and complex trauma. *Psychotherapy: Research, Practice, Training, 71,* 438–447.

Daniels, R. A., Holdsworth, E., & Tramontano, C. (2017). Relating therapist characteristics to client engagement and the therapeutic alliance in an adolescent custodial group substance misuse treatment program. *Substance Use and Misuse, 52*(9), 1139–1150.

Davidson, J. C. (2005). Professional relationship boundaries: A social work teaching module. *Social Work Education, 24*(5), 511–533.

Decety, J., Meidenbauer, K. L., & Cowell, J. M. (2018). The development of cognitive empathy and concern in preschool children: A behavioral neuroscience perspective. *Developmental Science, 21,* 1–12.

Denzin, N. K. (2001). *Interpretive interactionism.* Thousand Oaks, CA: Sage.

Dewane, C. J. (2006). Use of self: A primer revisited. *Clinical Social Work Journal, 34*(4), 543–558.

Diamond, G. M., Diamond, G. S., & Liddle, H. A. (2000). The therapist–parent alliance in family-based therapy for adolescents. *Psychotherapy in Practice, 56*(8), 1037–1050.

Diamond, G. M., Liddle, H. A., Hogue, A., & Dakof, G. A. (1999). Alliance-building interventions with adolescents in family therapy: A process study. *Psychotherapy, 36*(4), 355–368.

Diamond, L. M., & Fagundes, C. P. (2010). Psychobiological research on attachment. *Journal of Social and Personal Relationships, 27*(2), 218–225.

Dietz, C., & Thompson, J. (2004). Rethinking boundaries: Ethical dilemmas in the social worker–client relationship. *Journal of Progressive Human Services, 15*(2), 1–24.

Dilks, S., Tasker, F., & Wren, B. (2008). Building bridges to observational perspectives: A grounded theory of therapy processes in psychosis. *Psychology and Psychotherapy: Theory, Research and Practice, 81,* 209–229.

Doran, J. M. (2016). The working alliance: Where have we been, where are we going? *Psychotherapy Research, 26*(2), 146–163.

Dorros, S., Hanzal, A., & Segrin, C. (2008). The Big Five personality traits and perceptions of touch to intimate and nonintimate body regions. *Journal of Research in Personality, 42,* 1067–1073.

Drisko, J. M., & Grady, M. D. (2012). *Evidence-based practice in clinical social work.* Boston: Springer.

Dziegielewski, S. A., Jacinto, G. A., Laudandio, A., & Less-Rodriguez, L. (2003). Humor: An essential communication tool in therapy. *International Journal of Mental Health, 32*(3), 74–90.

Early, B., & Grady, M. (2017). Embracing the contribution of both behavior and cognitive theories to cognitive-behavioral therapy: Maximizing the richness. *Clinical Social Work Journal, 45*(1), 39–48.

Edwards, J. K., & Bess, J. M. (1998). Developing effectiveness in the therapeutic use of self. *Clinical Social Work Journal, 26*(1), 89–105.

Ekberg, S., Barnes, R. K., Kessler, D. S., Malpass, A., & Shaw, A. R. G. (2014). Managing clients' expectations at the outset of online cognitive-behavioural therapy (CBT) for depression. *Health Expectations, 19,* 557–569.

Ekberg, S., Barnes, R. K., Kessler, D. S., Mirza, S., Montgomery, A. A., Malpass, A., & Shaw, A. R. G. (2015). Relationship between expectation management and client retention in online cognitive behavioural therapy. *Behavioural and Cognitive Psychotherapy, 43,* 732–743.

Ekman, E., & Krasner, M. (2017). Empathy in medicine: Neuroscience, education and challenges. *Medical Teacher, 39*(2), 164–173.

Eubanks, C. F., Lubitz, J., Muran, J. C., & Safran, J. D. (2019). Rupture Resolution Rating System (3RS): Development and validation. *Psychotherapy Research, 29*(3), 306–319.

Eyckmans, S. (2009). Handle with care: Touch as a therapeutic tool. *Gestalt Journal of Australia and New Zealand, 6*(1), 40–53.

Farlex, Inc. (2019). *The free dictionary.* www.thefreedictionary.com.

Farmer, R. F., & Chapman, A. L. (2016). *Behavioral intervention in cognitive behavioral therapy: Practical guidance for putting theory into action.* Washington, DC: American Psychological Association.

Fava, G. A., Ruini, C., & Rafanelli, C., (2005). Sequential treatment of mood and anxiety disorders. *Journal of Clinical Psychiatry, 66*(11), 1392–1400.

Fjermestad, K. W., McLeod, B. D., Heiervang, E. R., Havik, O. E., Ost, L.-G., & Haugland, B. S. M. (2012). Factor structure and validity of the therapy process observational coding system for Child Psychotherapy-Alliance Scale. *Journal of Clinical Child & Adolescent Psychiatry, 41*(2), 246–254.

Flanagan, L. M. (2016). Object relations theory. In J. Berzoff, L. M. Flanagan, & P. Hertz (Eds.), *Inside out and outside in: Psychodynamic clinical theory and psychopathology in contemporary multicultural contexts* (pp. 123–165). Lanham, MD: Rowman and Littlefield.

Forte, J. A. (2014). *An introduction to using theory in social work practice.* New York: Routledge.

Frank, J. D. (1961). *Persuasion and healing: A comparative study of psychotherapy.* Baltimore: Johns Hopkins University Press.

Frank, J. D., & Frank, J. B. (1993). *Persuasion and healing: A comparative study of psychotherapy (3rd ed.).* Baltimore: Johns Hopkins University Press.

Franzini, L. R. (2001). Humor in therapy: The case for training therapists in its uses and risks. *Journal of General Psychology, 128*(2), 170–193.

Freedberg, S. (2009). *Relational theory for social work practice: A feminist perspective.* New York: Routledge.

Freeman, E. (2011). *Narrative approaches in social work practice: A life span, culturally centered, strengths perspective.* Springfield, IL: Charles C. Thomas.

Frey, L. L. (2013). Relational-cultural therapy: Theory, research, and application to counseling competencies. *Professional Psychology: Research and Practice, 44*(3), 177–185.

Friedrich, M., & Leiper, R. (2006). Countertransference reactions in therapeutic work with incestuous sexual abusers. *Journal of Child Sexual Abuse, 15*(1), 51–68.

Fromm-Reichmann, F. (1952). Some aspects of psychoanalytic psychotherapy with schizophrenics. In E. B. Brody & F. C. Redlich (Eds.), *Psychotherapy with schizophrenics* (pp. 89–111). Madison, CT: International Universities Press, Inc.

Fuertes, J. W., Toprovsky, A., Reyes, M., & Osbourne, J. B. (2017). The physician–patient working alliance: Theory, research, and future possibilities. *Patient Education and Counseling, 100*(4), 610–615.

Gelso, C. J., Rojas, A. E., & Marmarosh, C. (2013). Love and sexuality in the therapeutic relationship. *Journal of Clinical Psychology: In Session, 70*(2), 123–134.

Gibson, N., & Tantam, D. (2017). The best medicine? The nature of humour and its significance for the process of psychotherapy. *Existential Analysis, 28*(2), 272–286.

Giovazolias, T., & Davis, P. (2001). How common is sexual attraction toward clients? The experiences of sexual attraction of counseling psychologists toward their clients and its impact on the therapeutic process. *Counselling Psychology Quarterly, 14*(4), 281–286.

Goldstein, E. G. (1995). *Ego psychology and social work practice (2nd ed.).* New York: Free Press.

Goldstein, E. G., Miehls, D., & Ringel, S. (2009). *Advanced clinical social work practice: Relational principles and techniques.* New York: Columbia University Press.

Goodman, G. (2005). "I feel stupid and contagious:" Countertransference reactions of fledgling clinicians to patients who have negative therapeutic reactions. *American Journal of Psychotherapy, 59*(2), 149–168.

Gordon, J., & Dunworth, M. (2017). The fall and rise of "use of self"? An exploration of the positioning of use of self in social work education. *Social Work Education, 36*(5), 591–603.

Gordon, R. M., Gazzillo, F., Blake, A., Bornstein, R. F., Etzi, J., Lingiardi, V., McWilliams, N., Rothery, C., & Tasso, A. F. (2016). The relationship between theoretical orientation and countertransference expectations: Implications for ethical dilemmas and risk management. *Clinical Psychology and Psychotherapy, 23*, 236–245.

Grant, J. G., & Mandell, D. (2016). Boundaries and relationships between service users and service providers in community mental health services. *Social Work in Mental Health, 14*(6), 696–713.

Gray, A. J. (2010). Whatever happened to the soul? Some theological implications of neuroscience. *Mental Health, Religion, and Culture, 13*(6), 637–648.

Green, L. B. (2006). The value of hate in the countertransference. *Clinical Social Work Journal, 34*(2), 187–199.

Gros, D. F., Morland, L. A., Greene, C. J., Aciernao, R., Strachan, M., Egede, L. E., Tuerk, P. W., Myrick, H., & Frueh, B. C. (2013). Delivery of evidence-based psychotherapy via video telehealth. *Journal of Psychopathological Behavior Assessment, 35*, 506–521.

Haig, R. A. (1988). *The anatomy of humor: Bio-psycho-social and therapeutic perspectives.* Springfield, IL: Charles C. Thomas.

Hall, C., Slembrouck, S., Haigh, E., & Lee, A. (2010). The management of professional roles during boundary work in child welfare. *International Journal of Social Welfare, 19*, 348–357.

Hanley, T. (2009). The working alliance in online therapy with young people: Preliminary results. *British Journal of Guidance and Counselling, 37*(3), 257–269.

Harris, S. M., & Harringer, D. J. (2009). Sexual attraction in conjoint therapy. *American Journal of Family Therapy, 37*, 209–216.

Harrison, C., Jones, R. S. P., & Huws, J. C. (2012). "We're people who don't touch": Exploring clinical psychologists' perspectives on their use of touch in therapy. *Counseling Psychology Quarterly, 25*(3), 277–287.

Havens, L. L. (1996). *A safe place: Laying the groundwork of psychotherapy.* Cambridge, MA: Harvard University Press, 1989.

Hawley, K. M., & Garland, A. F. (2008). Working alliance in adolescent outpatient therapy: Youth, parent and therapist reports and associations with therapy outcomes. *Child and Youth Care Forum, 37*, 59–74.

Hayes, J. A. (2014). "Well I got a few of my own": Therapists' reactions to attraction, sex, and love in psychotherapy. *Journal of Clinical Psychology: In Session, 70*(2), 119–122.

Heinonen, E., Lindfors, O., Härkänen, T., Virtala, E., Jääskeläinen, T., & Knekt, P. (2014). Therapists' professional and personal characteristics as predictors of working alliance in short-term and long-term psychotherapies. *Clinical Psychology and Psychotherapy, 21*, 475–494.

Henriksen, M. G., Raballo, A., & Parnas, J. (2015). The pathogenesis of auditory verbal hallucinations in schizophrenia: A clinical-phenomenological account. *Philosophy, Psychiatry, & Psychology, 22*(3), 165–181.

Hepworth, D. H., Rooney, R. H., Rooney, G. D., & Strom-Gottfried, K. (2017). *Direct social work practice: Theories and skills (10th ed.).* Boston: Cengage.

Herlihy, B., & Corey, G. (2015). *Boundary issues in counseling: Multiple roles and responsibilities (3rd ed.).* Alexandria, VA: American Counseling Association.

Hewitt, J., & Coffey, M. (2005). Therapeutic working relationships with people with schizophrenia: Literature review. *Journal of Advanced Nursing, 52*(5), 561–570.

Hill, C. E., & Knox, S. (2009). Processing the therapeutic relationship. *Psychotherapy Research, 19*(1), 13–29.

Hingley-Jones, H., & Ruch, G. (2016). "Stumbling through"? Relationship-based social work practice in austere times. *Journal of Social Work Practice, 30*(3), 235–248.

Høglend, P., Hersoug, A. G., Bøgwald, K., Amlo, S., Marble, A., Sørbye, Ø., Røssberg, J. I., Ulberg, R., Gabbard, G. O., & Crits-Christoph, P. (2011). Effects of transference work in the context of therapeutic alliance and quality of object relations. *Journal of Consulting and Clinical Psychology, 79*(5), 697–706.

Horvath, A., & Greenberg, L. (Eds.) (1994). *The working alliance: Theory, research, and practice.* New York: Wiley.

Hunter, M., & Struve, J. (1998). Challenging the taboo: Support for the ethical use of touch in psychotherapy with sexually compulsive/addicted clients. *Sexual Addiction & Compulsivity, 5*, 141–148.

Hutchison, S. L., Karpov, I., Crisan, A. B., Hulsey, E., & Dan, D. (2018). Association of therapeutic alliance with outcomes over two years in youth and family service. *Community Mental Health Journal, 54*, 935–943.

Irvine, A., Drew, P., Bower, P., Brooks, H., Gellatly, J., Armitage, C. J., Barkham, M., McMillan, D., & Bee, P. (2020). Are there interactional differences between telephone and face-to-face psychological therapy? A systematic review of comparative studies. *Journal of Affective Disorders, 265*, 120–131.

James, R. K., & Gilliland, B. E. (2017). *Crisis intervention strategies (8th ed.)*. Pacific Grove, CA: Cengage.

Jordan, S. (2017). Relationship-based social work practice: The case for considering the centrality of humour in creating and maintaining relationships. *Journal of Social Work Practice, 31*(1), 95–110.

Kachele, H., Erhardt, I., Seybert, C., & Buchholz, M. B. (2015). Countertransference as object of empirical research? *International Forum of Psychoanalysis, 24*(2), 96–108.

Karpman, H. E., & Drisko, J. (2016). Social media policy in social work education: A review and recommendations. *Journal of Social Work Education, 52*(4), 398–408.

Katz, J. S. (2010). Reconsidering therapeutic neutrality. *Clinical Social Work Journal, 38*, 306–315.

Kaushik, A. (2017). Use of self in social work: Rhetoric or reality. *Journal of Social Work Values and Ethics, 14*(1), 21–29.

Kazdin, A. E., & McWhinney, E. (2018). Therapeutic alliance, perceived treatment barriers, and therapeutic change in the treatment of children with conduct problems. *Journal of Child and Family Studies, 27*, 240–252.

Keefe, R. S., & Kraus, M. S. (2012). Clues to the cognitive and perceptual origins of social isolation in psychosis and schizophrenia. *American Journal of Psychiatry, 169*(4), 354–357.

Keenan, E. K., Tsang, A. K. T., Bogo, M., & George, U. (2005). Micro-ruptures and repairs in the beginning phase of cross-cultural psychotherapy. *Clinical Social Work Journal, 33*(3), 271–289.

Kelson, J. N., Lam, M. K., Keep, M., & Campbell, A. J. (2017). Development and evaluation of an online acceptance and commitment therapy program for anxiety: Phase I iterative design. *Journal of Technology in Human Services, 35*(2), 135–151.

Kemp, N. (2011). Provocative Change Works™: Improvisation and humor in therapy and coaching. In L. M. Hall & S. R. Charvet (Eds.), *Innovations in NLP for challenging times* (pp. 155–167). Norwalk, CT: Crown House Publishing Limited.

Kerns, C. M., Collier, A., Lewin, A. B., & Storch, E. A. (2018). Therapeutic alliance in youth with autism spectrum disorder receiving cognitive-behavioral treatment for anxiety. *Autism, 22*(5), 636–640.

Kirby, V. (2019). Seduction in the counselling room. *Therapy Today, 30*(5), 30–32.

Kirsch, V., Keller, F., Tutus, D., & Goldbeck, L. (2018). Treatment expectancy, working alliance, and outcome of trauma-focused cognitive behavioral therapy with children and adolescents. *Child and Adolescent Psychiatry and Mental Health, 12*, 1–16.

Knox, S., Adrians, N., Everson, E., Hess, S., Hill, C., & Crook-Lynn, R. (2011). Clients' perspectives on therapy termination. *Psychotherapy Research, 21*(2), 154–167.

Kuhlman, T. L. (1984). *Humor and psychotherapy*. Homewood, IL: Dow Jones-Irwin.

Labouliere, C. D., Reyes, J. P., Shirk, S., & Karver, M. (2017). Therapeutic alliance with depressed adolescents: Predictor or outcome? Disentangling temporal confounds to understand early improvement. *Journal of Clinical Child & Adolescent Psychology, 46*(4), 600–610.

LaMendola, W. (2010). Social work and social presence in an online world. *Journal of Technology in Human Services, 28*, 108–119.

Lamers, A., & Vermeiren, R. (2015). Assessment of the therapeutic alliance of youth and parents with team members in youth residential psychiatry. *Clinical Child Psychology and Psychiatry, 20*(4), 640–656.

Lavarenne, A., Segal, E., & Sigman, M. (2013). Containing psychotic patients with fragile boundaries: A single-session group case study. *American Journal of Psychotherapy, 67*(3), 293–302.

Lawson, M. A. (2015). Gender implications of the touch taboo in psychotherapy: A feminist rhetorical analysis. *Women & Language, 38*(2), 55–59.

Lee, E. (2011). Cultural significance of cross-cultural competencies (CCC) in social work practice. *Journal of Social Work Practice, 25*(2), 185–203.

Levy, K., & Scala, J. W. (2012). Transference, transference interpretations, and transference-focused psychotherapies. *Psychotherapy, 49*(3), 391–403.

Liebman, R. E., & Burnette, M. (2013). It's not you, it's me: An examination of clinician and client-level influences on countertransference toward borderline personality disorder. *American Journal of Orthopsychiatry, 83*(1), 115–125.

Liechty, J. (2018). Exploring use of self: Moving beyond definitional challenges. *Journal of Social Work Education, 54*(1), 148–182.

Lincoln, T. N., Hartmann, M., Kother, U., & Moritz, S. (2015). Do people with psychosis have specific difficulties regulating emotions? *Clinical Psychology and Psychotherapy, 22*(6), 637–646.

Linn-Walton, R., & Pardasani, M. (2014). Dislikable clients or countertransference? A clinician's perspective. *Clinical Supervisor, 33*, 100–121.

Littell, J. H., Corcoran, J., & Pillai, V. (2008). *Systematic reviews and meta-analysis.* New York: Oxford University Press.

Locati, F., Rossi, G., & Parolin, L. (2019). Interactive dynamics among therapist interventions, therapeutic alliance and metacognition in the early stages of the psychotherapeutic process. *Psychotherapy Research, 29*(1), 112–122.

Lothane, Z. (2008a). The uses of humor in life, neurosis and in psychotherapy: Part 1. *International Forum of Psychoanalysis, 17*, 180–188.

Lothane, Z. (2008b). The uses of humor in life, neurosis and in psychotherapy: Part 2. *International Forum of Psychoanalysis, 17*, 232–239.

Loue, S. (2016). Ethical use of electronic media in social work practice. *Revista Romaneasca pentru Educatie Multidimensionala, 8*(2), 21–30.

Lubove, R. (1965). *The professional altruist: The emergence of social work as a career, 1890–1930.* Cambridge, MA: Harvard University Press.

Lurie, A., & Monahan, K. (2015). Humor, aging, and life review: Survival through the use of humor. *Social Work in Mental Health, 13*, 82–91.

Lynch, R., & Garrett, P. M. (2010). "More than words": Touch practices in child and family social work. *Child and Family Social Work Journal, 15*, 389–398.

Madigan, S. (2019). *Narrative therapy (2nd ed.).* Washington, DC: American Psychological Association.

Magid, B., & Shane, E. (2017). Relational self psychology. *Psychoanalysis: Self and Context, 12*(1), 3–19.

Manso, A., Rauktis, M. E., & Boyd, A. S. (2008). Youth expectations about therapeutic alliance in a residential setting. *Residential Treatment for Children and Youth, 25*(1), 55–72.

Markin, R. D., McCarthy, K. S., & Barber, J. P. (2013). Transference, countertransference, emotional expression, and session quality over the course of supportive expressive therapy: The raters' perspective. *Psychotherapy Research, 23*(2), 152–168.

Marrone, M. (2014). *Attachment and interaction: From Bowlby to current clinical theory and practice.* London: Jessica Kingsley Publishers.

Martin, C., Godfrey, M., Meekums, B., & Madill, A. (2011). Managing boundaries under pressure: A qualitative study of therapists' experiences of sexual attraction in therapy. *Counselling and Psychotherapy Research, 11*(4), 248–256.

Martin, R., & Kuiper, N. A. (2016). Three decades investigating humor and laughter: An interview with Professor Rod Martin. *Europe's Journal of Psychology, 12*(3), 498–512.

Mattison, M. (2012). Social work practice in the digital age: Therapeutic e-mail as a direct practice methodology. *Social Work, 57*(3), 249–258.

McCarter, S. A. (2019). Adolescence. In E. D. Hutchison (Ed.), *Dimensions of human behavior: The changing life course (6th ed.)* (pp. 189–230). Thousand Oaks, CA: Sage.

McDaniel, E., & Andersen, P. A. (1998). International patterns of interpersonal tactile communication: A field study. *Journal of Nonverbal Behavior, 22*(1), 59–75.

McNeil-Haber, F. M. (2004). Ethical considerations in the use of nonerotic touch in psychotherapy with children. *Ethics & Behavior, 14*(2), 123–140.

Mechanic, D. (2008). *Mental health and social policy: Beyond managed care (5th ed.).* Boston: Pearson.

Miller, S. D., Duncan, B. L., & Hubble, M. A. (2005). Outcome-informed clinical work. In J. C. Norcross & M. R. Goldfried (Eds.), *Handbook of psychotherapy integration (2nd ed.)* (pp. 84–102). New York: Oxford University Press.

Minuchin, S., Lee, W., & Simon, G. M. (2006). *Mastering family therapy: Journeys of growth and transformation (2nd ed.).* Hoboken, NJ: Wiley.

Moesender, L., Ribeiro, E., Muran, J. C., & Caspar, F. (2019). The impact of confrontations by therapists on impairment and utilization of the therapeutic alliance. *Psychotherapy Research, 29*(3), 293–305.

Moggi, F., Brodbeck, J., & Hirsbrunner, H. (2000). Therapist–patient sexual involvement: Risk factors and consequences. *Clinical Psychology and Psychotherapy, 7*, 54–60.

Moritz, S., Pfuhl, G., Ludke, T., Menon, M., Balzan, R. P., & Andrew, C. (2017). A two-stage cognitive theory of the positive symptoms of psychosis: Highlighting the role of lowered delusional thresholds. *Journal of Behavioral Theory and Experimental Psychiatry, 56*, 12–20.

Mosak, H. H. (1987). *Ha ha and aha: The role of humor in psychotherapy.* Muncie, IN: Accelerated Development, Inc.

Muran, J. C., & Barber, J. P. (Eds.) (2010). *The therapeutic alliance: An evidence-based guide to practice.* New York: Guilford Press.

Murphy, R., & Hutton, P. (2018). Practitioner review: Therapist variability, patient-reported therapeutic alliance, and clinical outcomes in adolescents undergoing mental health treatment: A systematic review and meta-analysis. *Journal of Child Psychology and Psychiatry, 59*(1), 5–19.

National Association of Social Workers. (2017a). *Code of ethics.* Washington, DC: Author.

National Association of Social Workers. (2017b). *NASW, ASWB, CSWE, & CSWA standards for technology in social work practice.* Washington, DC: Author.

Norcross, J. C., & Wampold, B. E. (2011). Evidence-based therapy relationships: Research conclusions and clinical practices. *Psychotherapy, 48*(1), 98–102.

O'Connell, W. (1985). Natural high therapy: Fighting guilt by "letting go." *Journal of Integrative & Eclectic Psychotherapy, 4*(1–2), 32–41.

O'Neill, M. (2015). Applying critical consciousness and evidence-based practice decision making: A framework for clinical social work practice. *Journal of Social Work Education, 51*(4), 624–637.

Orbach, S. (2003). Part II: Touch. *British Journal of Psychotherapy, 20*(1), 17–26.

Ormhaug, S. M., Jensen, T. K., Wentzel-Larsen, T., & Shirk, S. R. (2014). The therapeutic alliance in treatment of traumatized youths: Relation to outcome in a randomized clinical trial. *Journal of Counseling and Clinical Psychology, 82*(1), 52–64.

Osenbach, J. E., O'Brien, K. M., Mishkind, M., & Smolenski, D. J. (2013). Synchronous telehealth technologies in psychotherapy for depression: A meta-analysis. *Depression and Anxiety, 30*, 1058–1067.

Pallisera, M., Fullana, J., Palaudarias, J.-M., & Badosa, M. (2013). Personal and professional development (or use of self) in social educator training: An experience based on reflective learning. *Social Work Education, 32*(5), 576–589.

Parth, K., Datz, F., Seidman, C., & Loffler-Stastka, H. (2017). Transference and countertransference: A review. *Bulletin of the Menninger Clinic, 81*(2), 167–211.

Perrin, P. B., Rybarczyk, B. D., Pierce, B. S., Jones, H. A., Shaffer, C., & Islam, L. (2020). Rapid telepsychology deployment during the COVID-19 pandemic: A special issue commentary and lessons from primary care psychology training. *Journal of Clinical Psychology, 76*, 1173–1185.

Piguet, C., Dayer, A., Kosel, M., Desseilles, M., Vuilleumier, P., & Bertschy, G. (2010). Phenomenology of racing and crowded thoughts in mood disorders: A theoretical appraisal. *Journal of Affective Disorders, 121*(3), 189–198.

Piper, H., Powell, J., & Smith, H. (2006). Parents, professionals, and paranoia: The touching of children in a culture of fear. *Journal of Social Work, 6*(2), 151–167.

Pugh, N, E. (2012). Increasing access to therapist-assisted cognitive behaviour therapy in Saskatchewan: A description of the online therapy unit for service, education, and research. *Psynopsis, Canada's Psychology Newspaper, 34*(4), 10–13.

Purswell, K., & Bratton, S. (2018). Children's experiences in the therapeutic relationship: Development and validation of a self-report measure. *Journal of Humanistic Counseling, 57*(2), 82–102.

Quirk, K., Miller, S., Duncan, B., & Owen, J. (2013). Group session rating scale: Preliminary psychometrics in substance abuse group interventions. *Counselling and Psychotherapy Research, 13*(3), 194–200.

Ramsdell, P. S., & Ramsdell, E. R. (1994). Counselor and client perceptions of the effect of social and physical contact on the therapeutic process. *Clinical Social Work Journal, 22*(1), 91–104.

Ramsey, A. T., & Montgomery, K. (2014). Technology-based interventions in social work practice: A systematic review of mental health interventions. *Social Work in Health Care, 53*(9), 883–899.

Reamer, F. G. (2018). Ethical standards for social workers' use of technology: Emerging consensus. *Journal of Social Work Values and Ethics, 15*(2), 71–80.

Reamer, F. G. (2014). *Risk management in social work practice: Preventing professional malpractice, liability, and disciplinary action.* New York: Columbia University Press.

Reimer, E. C. (2013). Relationship-based practice with families where child neglect is an issue: Putting relationship development under the microscope. *Australian Social Work, 66*(3), 455–470.

Reupert, A. (2007). Social worker's use of self. *Clinical Social Work Journal, 35*, 107–116.

Ribeiro, E., Ribeiro, A. P., Gonçalves, M. M., Horvath, A. O., & Stiles, W. B. (2013). How collaboration in therapy becomes therapeutic: The therapeutic collaboration coding system. *Psychology and Psychotherapy: Theory, Research, and Practice, 86*, 294–314.

Richert, A. J. (2003). Living stories, telling stories, changing stories: Experiential use of the relationship in narrative therapy. *Journal of Psychotherapy Integration, 13*(1), 188–210.

Richman, J. (2007). The role of psychotherapy and humor for death anxiety, death wishes, and aging. *Omega, 54*(1), 41–51.

Richman, J. (1996). Points of correspondence between humor and psychotherapy. *Psychotherapy, 33*(4), 560–566.

Roest, J. J., van der Helm, G. H. P., & Stans, G. J. J. M. (2016a). The relation between therapeutic alliance and treatment motivation in residential youth care: A cross-lagged panel analysis. *Child and Adolescent Social Work Journal, 33*, 455–468.

Roest, J. J., van der Helm, P., Strijbosch, E., van Brandenberg, M., & Stams, G. J. (2016b). Measuring therapeutic alliance with children in residential treatment and therapeutic day care: A validation study of the Children's Alliance Questionnaire. *Research on Social Work Practice, 26*(2), 212–218.

Rogers, C. R. (1986). A client-centered/person-directed approach to therapy. In I. Kutash & A. Wolf (Eds.), *Psychotherapist's casebook* (pp. 197–208). San Francisco: Jossey-Bass.

Ross, M. (2020). Harnessing technology for the social good: Empowering consumers with immediate feedback and self-directed means of care to address affordability, access, and stigma in mental health. *Social Work, 65*(2), 135–137.

Rossberg, J. I., Karterud, S., Pedersen, G., & Friis, S. (2010). Psychiatric symptoms and countertransference feelings: An empirical investigation. *Psychiatry Research, 178*, 191–195.

Ruch, G. (2010). Self in relation to others: Use of self in relationship-based practice. In G. Ruch, D. Turney, & A. Ward (Eds.), *Relationship-based social work: Getting to the heart of practice* (pp. 46–65). Philadelphia: Jessica Kingsley Publishers.

Ruch, G., Turney, D., & Ward, A. (Eds.) (2018). *Relationship-based social work: Getting to the heart of practice*. Philadelphia: Jessica Kingsley Publishers.

Rutherford, K. (1994). Humor in psychotherapy. *Individual Psychology, 50*(2), 207–222.

Safran, J., & Muran, C. (2000). Resolving therapeutic alliance ruptures: Diversity and integration. *In Session: Psychotherapy in Practice, 56*(2), 233–243.

Saper, B. (1987). Humor in psychotherapy: Is it good or bad for the client? *Professional Psychology: Research and Practice, 18*(4), 360–367.

Savaya, R., Bartov, Y., Melamed, S., & Altshuler, D. (2016). Predictors of perceived changes by service users: Working alliance, hope, and burnout. *Social Work Research, 20*(3), 183–191.

Schamess, G., & Shilkret, R. (2016). Ego psychology. In J. Berzoff, L. M. Flanagan, & P. Hertz (Eds.), *Inside out and outside in* (pp. 64–99). New York: Rowman & Littlefield.

Scherer, R. G., & Ng, K. (2017). Trait anxiety as predictor of child therapist's perceived working alliance. *Journal of Behavioral and Social Sciences, 4*, 76–86.

Schneider, D. A., & Grady, M. D. (2015). Conscious and unconscious use of self: The evolution of a process. *Psychoanalytic Social Work, 22*, 52–70.

Schulze, N., Reuter, S. C., Kuchler, I., Reinke, B., Hinkelmann, L., Stöckigt, S., Siemoneit, H., & Tonn, P. (2019). Differences in attitudes toward online interventions in psychiatry and psychotherapy between health care professionals and nonprofessionals: A survey. *Telemedicine and e-Health, 25*(10), 926–932.

Schwartz, R. C., Del Prete-Brown, T. D., Pacino, H., Ninsky, J., La Maroo, J., Rotundo, M., Kalnicki, C., & Rogers, J. R. (2016). Collaboration between managed care and mental health agency staff: Consumer satisfaction, medication compliance, psychosocial improvement, and cost outcomes. *Journal of Counseling Practice, 7*(2), 78–96.

Scott, C. V., Hyer, L. A., & McKenzie, L. C. (2015). The healing power of laughter: The applicability of humor as a psychotherapy technique with depressed and anxious older adults. *Social Work in Mental Health, 13*, 48–60.

Segal, E. (2013). Beyond the pale of psychoanalysis: Relational theory and generalist social work practice. *Clinical Social Work Journal, 41*, 376–386.

Semrad, E. V. (1955). Psychotherapy of psychoses: An attempt at a working formulation of some of the clinical psychopathological factors observed in schizophrenic patients. *Journal of Clinical & Experimental Psychopathology, 16*, 10–21.

Shaeffer, Z. G. (2014). Transference, countertransference, and mutuality in relational social work with college students. *Clinical Social Work Journal, 43*, 13–21.

Shattock, L., Berry, K., Degnan, A., & Edge, D. (2018). Therapeutic alliance in psychological therapy for people with schizophrenia and related psychoses: A systematic review. *Clinical Psychology and Psychotherapy, 25*, 60–85.

Shevellar, L., & Barringham, N. (2016). Work in complexity: Ethics and boundaries in community work and mental health. *Australian Social Work, 69*(2), 181–193.

Shilkret, R., & Shilkret, C. J. (2016). Attachment theory. In J. Berzoff, L. M. Flanagan, & P. Hertz (Eds.), *Inside out and outside in (4th ed.)* (pp. 196–219). New York: Rowman & Littlefield.

Siebold, C. (2011). What do patients want? Personal disclosure and the intersubjective perspective. *Clinical Social Work Journal, 39*, 151–160.

Siebold, C. (2007). Every time we say goodbye: Forced termination revisited: A commentary. *Clinical Social Work Journal, 35*, 91–95.

Simpson, J. E. (2017). Staying in touch in the digital era: New social work practice. *Journal of Technology in Human Services, 35*(1), 86–98.

Simpson, J. E. (2013). A divergence of opinion: How those involved in child and family social work are responding to the challenges of the Internet and social media. *Child and Family Social Work, 21*(1), 94–102.

Simpson, S. G., & Reid, C. L. (2014). Therapeutic alliance in videoconferencing psychotherapy: A review. *Australian Journal of Rural Health, 22*, 280–299.

Sinason, V. (2017). The breathing boundary. *British Journal of Psychotherapy, 33*(1), 6–16.

Siporin, M. (1993). The social worker's style. *Clinical Social Work Journal, 21*(3), 257–270.

Sizemore, T. (2012). *The clinician's guide to exposure therapy for anxiety spectrum disorders utilizing techniques and applications from CBT, DBT, and ACT*. Oakland, CA: New Harbinger Press.

Sonne, J. L., & Jochai, D. (2013). The "vicissitudes of love" between therapist and patient: A review of the research on romantic and sexual feelings, thoughts, and behaviors in psychotherapy. *Journal of Clinical Psychology, 70*, 182–195.

Spaulding, W., & Nolting, J. (2006). Psychotherapy for schizophrenia in the year 2030: Prognosis and prognostication. *Schizophrenia Bulletin, 32*(Suppl. 1), S94–S105.

Srivastava, U. R., & Maurya, V. (2014). Sense of humor and psychological health among health care professionals. *Indian Journal of Positive Psychology, 5*(4), 376–381.

Stadnick, N. A., Lau, A. S., Barnett, M., Regan, J., Aarons, G. A., & Brookman-Frazee, L. (2018). Comparing agency leader and therapist perspectives on evidence-based practices: Associations with individual and organizational factors in a mental health system-driven implementation effort. *Administration & Policy in Mental Health & Mental Health Services Research, 45*(3), 447–461.

Stanghellini, G., & Raballo, A. (2015). Differential typology of delusions in major depression and schizophrenia: A critique to the unitary concept of "psychosis." *Journal of Affective Disorders, 171*, 171–178.

Storolow, R. D. (2013). Intersubjective-systems theory: A phenomenological-contextualist psychoanalytic perspective. *Psychoanalytic Dialogues, 23*, 383–389.

Strean, H. (Ed.) (1994). *The use of humor in psychotherapy.* Northvale, NJ: Jason Aronson.

Strijbosch, E., Stams, G. J., Wissink, I., van der Helam, P., & Roest, J. (2018). The relation between children's perceived group climate and therapeutic alliance with their mentor in residential care: A prospective study. *Residential Treatment for Children & Youth, 35*(4), 297–316.

Strik, W., Stegmayer, K., Walther, S., & Dierks, T. (2018). Systems neuroscience of psychosis: Mapping schizophrenia systems onto brain systems. *Neurobiology, 75*(3), 100–116.

Stromm-Gottfried, K., Thomas, M. S., & Anderson, H. (2014). Social work and social media: Reconciling ethical standards and emerging technologies. *Journal of Social Work Values and Ethics, 11*(1), 54–65.

Strozier, A. L., Krizek, C., & Sale, K. (2003). Touch: Its use in psychotherapy. *Journal of Social Work Practice, 17*(1), 49–62.

Sue, D. W., Rasheed, M. N., & Rasheed, J. N. (2016). *Multicultural social work practice: A competency-based approach to diversity and social justice (2nd ed.).* New York: John Wiley and Sons.

Sullivan, E. (2013). Is work a laughing matter? *Careers, 26*(4), 294–295.

Sullivan, H. S. (1947). Therapeutic investigations in schizophrenia. *Journal for the Study of Interpersonal Processes, 10*, 121–125.

Sultanoff, S. M. (2013). Integrating humor into psychotherapy: Research, theory, and the necessary conditions for the presence of therapeutic humor in helping relationships. *Humanistic Psychologist, 41*, 388–399.

Swade, T., Bayne, R., & Horton, I. (2006). Touch me never? *Therapy Today, 17*(9), 1–4.

Swan, M., Holt, S., & Kirwan, G. (2018). "Who do I turn to if something really bad happens?" Key working and relationship-based practice in residential child care. *Journal of Social Work Practice, 32*(4), 447–461.

Swart, J. (2015). Conceptualizing mode deactivation therapy as a Moodle-based on-line program for adolescents and adults to relieve belief-oriented stress. *International Journal of Behavioral Consultation and Therapy, 9*(4), 32–41.

Thomas, J. T. (2010). *The ethics of supervision and consultation: Practical guidance for mental health professionals.* Washington, DC: American Psychological Association.

Thompson, E. H., & Hampton, J. A. (2011). The effect of relationship status on communicating emotion through touch. *Cognition and Emotion, 25*(2), 295–306.

Tishby, O., & Wiseman, H. (2014). Types of countertransference dynamics: An exploration of their impact on the client–therapist relationships. *Psychotherapy Research, 24*(3), 360–375.

Toronto, E. L. K. (2002). A clinician's response to physical touch in the psychoanalytic setting. *International Journal of Psychotherapy, 7*(1), 69–81.

Trevithick, P. (2014). Human managerialism: Reclaiming emotional reasoning, intuition, the relationship, and knowledge and skills in social work. *Journal of Social Work Practice, 28*(3), 287–311.

Trimberger, G., & Bugenhagen, M. J. (2015). A new look at an old issue: A constructive-development approach to professional boundaries. *Journal of Social Work Values and Ethics, 12*(1), 13–28.

Tschacher, W., Junghan, U. M., & Pfammater, M. (2014). Toward a taxonomy of common factors in psychotherapy: Results of an expert survey. *Clinical Psychology and Psychotherapy, 21*, 82–96.

Turner, D. (2016a). Social work and social media: Best friends or natural enemies. *Social Work Education, 35*(3), 241–244.

Turner, D. (2016b). "Only connect": Unifying the social in social work and social media. *Journal of Social Work Practice, 30*(3), 313–327.

Turner, F. J. (Ed.) (2011). *Social work treatment (5th ed.)*. New York: Free Press.

Turner, S. G., & Maschi, T. M. (2015). Feminist and empowerment theory and social work practice. *Journal of Social Work Practice, 29*(2), 151–162.

Turney, D. (2012). A relationship-based approach to engaging involuntary clients: The contribution of recognition theory. *Child and Family Social Work, 17*, 149–159.

Uhlhaas, P. J., & Mishara, A. L. (2007). Perceptual anomalies in schizophrenia: Integrating phenomenology and cognitive neuroscience. *Schizophrenia Bulletin, 33*(1), 142–156.

Van de Luitgaarden, G., & van der Tier, M. (2018). Establishing working relationships in online social work. *Journal of Social Work, 18*(3), 307–325.

Van der Vaart, R., Witting, M., Riper, H., Kooistra, L., Bohlmeijer, E. T., & van Gemert-Pijnen, L. (2014). Blending online therapy into regular face-to-face therapy for depression: Content ratio and preconditions according to patients and therapists using a Delphi study. *BMC Psychiatry, 14*, 355.

Van Rensburg, S. H., Klingensmith, K., McClaughline, P., Qayyum, X., & van Schalkwyk, G. I. (2015). Patient–provider with psychiatric illness. *Health Expectations, 19*, 112–120.

Voshel, E. H., & Wesala, A. (2015). Social media and social work ethics: Determining best practices in an ambiguous reality. *Journal of Social Work Values and Ethics, 12*(1), 67–76.

Vrticka, P., Black, J. M., & Reiss, A. L. (2013). The neural basis of humour processing. *Nature Reviews in Neuroscience, 14*, 860–867.

Walker, J. (2008). Communications and social work from an attachment perspective. *Journal of Social Work Practice, 22*(1), 5–13.

Walsh, J. (2016). Can relational theory be appropriate for clients who have schizophrenia? *Practice: Journal of the British Association of Social Workers, 28*(4), 267–280.

Walsh, J. (2015a). The psychological person: Cognition, emotion, and the self. In E. D. Hutchison (Ed.), *Dimensions of human behavior: Person in environment (5th ed.)* (pp. 115–143). Thousand Oaks, CA: Sage.

Walsh, J. (2015b). The psychosocial person: Relationships, stress, and coping. In E. D. Hutchison (Ed.), *Dimensions of human behavior: Person in environment (5th ed.)* (pp. 145–176). Thousand Oaks, CA: Sage.

Walsh, J. (2013). *The recovery philosophy and direct social work practice*. Chicago: Lyceum.

Walsh, J. (2011). Countertransference with clients who have schizophrenia: A social work perspective. *Families in Society, 92*(4), 377–382.

Walsh, J. (2010). *Psychoeducation in mental health*. Chicago: Lyceum.

Walsh, J. (2007). *Endings in clinical practice: Effective closure in diverse settings (2nd ed.)*. Chicago: Lyceum.

Wampold, B. E. (2015). How important are the common factors in psychotherapy? An update. *World Psychiatry, 14*(3), 270–277.

Wapner, J. H., Klein, J. G., Friedlander, M. L., & Andrasik, F. J. (1986). Transferring psychotherapy clients: State of the art. *Professional Psychology: Research and Practice, 17*, 492–496.

Waska, R. (2007). Projective identification as an inescapable aspect of the therapeutic relationship. *Psychoanalytic Social Work, 14*(2), 43–64.

Watson, K. (2011). Gallows humor in medicine. *Hastings Center Report, 41*(5), 37–45.

Weiden, P., & Havens, L. L. (1994). Psychotherapeutic management techniques in the treatment of outpatients with schizophrenia. *Hospital & Community Psychiatry, 45*(6), 549–555.

Weil, M. P., Katz, M., & Hilsenroth, M. J. (2017). Patient and therapist perspectives during the psychotherapy termination process: The role of participation and exploration. *Psychodynamic Psychiatry, 45*(1), 23–43.

Westmacott, R., & Hunsley, J. (2010). Reasons for termination psychotherapy: A general population study. *Journal of Clinical Psychology, 66*(9), 965–977.

Whincup, H. (2017). What do social workers and children do when they are together? A typology of direct work. *Child & Family Social Work, 22*, 972–980.

White, M. (2007). *Maps of narrative practice*. New York: Norton.

Whitehead, M., Jones, A., Bilms, J., Lavner, J., & Suveg, C. (2019). Child social and emotion functioning as predictors of therapeutic alliance in cognitive-behavioral therapy for anxiety. *Journal of Clinical Psychology, 75*, 7–20.

Williams, L., & Winter, H. (2009). Guidelines for an effective transfer of cases: The needs of the transfer triad. *American Journal of Family Therapy, 37*, 146–158.

Willison, B. G., & Masson, R. L. (1986). The role of touch in therapy: An adjunct to communication. *Journal of Counseling and Development, 64*, 497–500.

Winnicott, D. W. (1949). Hate in the countertransference. *International Journal of Psychoanalysis, 30*, 69–74.

Wodarski, J. S., & Bagarozzi, D. A. (1979). *Behavioral social work*. New York: Human Sciences Press.

Woody, D. J., & Hutchison, E. D. (2019). Infancy and toddlerhood. In E. D. Hutchison (Ed.), *Dimensions of human behavior (6th ed.)* (pp. 74–114). Thousand Oaks, CA: Sage.

Yerushalmi, H. (2015). Impasses in the relationship between the psychiatric rehabilitation practitioner and the consumer: A psychodynamic perspective. *Journal of Social Work Practice, 29*(3), 355–368.

Zerwas, S. C., Watson, H. J., Hofmeier, S. M., Levine, M. D., Hamer, R. M., Crosby, R. D., Runfola, C. C., Peat, C. M., Shapiro, J. R., Zimmer, B., Moessner, M., Kordy, H., Marcus, M. D., & Bulik, C. M. (2017). CBT4BN: A randomized controlled study of online chat and face-to-face group therapy for bulimia nervosa. *Psychotherapy and Psychosomatics, 86*, 47–53.

Zilberstein, K. (2008). Au revoir: An attachment and loss perspective on termination. *Clinical Social Work Journal, 36*, 301–311.

Zilcha-Mano, S., Eubanks, C. F., Muran, J. C., Safran, J., & Winston, A. (2018). When the estimation of the process of treatment can predict patients' ratings on outcome: The case of the working alliance. *Journal of Consulting and Clinical Psychology, 86*(4), 398–402.

Zorzella, K. P. M., Rependa, S. L., & Muller, R. T. (2017). Therapeutic alliance over the course of child trauma therapy from three different perspectives. *Child Abuse & Neglect, 67*, 147–156.

Index

For the benefit of digital users, indexed terms that span two pages (e.g., 52–53) may, on occasion, appear on only one of those pages.

ABA (Applied Behavioral Analysis Therapy), 220–21
abstract thinking
   adolescents, 129–30
   thought disorders and, 193
adolescents
   abstract thinking, 129–30
   building working alliance with, 139–43
   building working alliance with parents or caregivers of, 143–48
   case vignettes, 140–43, 145–47
   CBT for, 132–33
   decision-making skills, 130
   developmental process, 129–30
   emotional brain, 129–30
   identity formation, 130
   peer conflicts, 128
   with PTSD, 132
   puberty, 129–30
   social orientation, 130
affiliative humor, 232–33
aggressive humor, 232–33
Alice (client), 122–24
Althea (client), 265–67
Alyn, J. H., 216–17
Amber (social worker), 162–65, 173–76
Amy (client), 217–19
Anderson, P. A., 224–25
Angela (social worker), 70–71, 133–34
Angie (client), 220–21
Annie (client), 140–43
anxiety
   crisis theory and, 22
   disorganized attachment style and, 15–16
   relationship between therapeutic alliance and, 132–33
   technology-assisted interventions, 260
   use of self, 59
anxious-ambivalent attachment, 15
Applied Behavioral Analysis Therapy (ABA), 220–21
Ashley (social worker), 185–88
assessment value, humor, 233
attachment theory, 15–16
   anxious-ambivalent attachment, 15
   avoidant attachment, 15
   disorganized attachment, 15–16
   secure attachment, 15
attraction to clients
   case vignettes, 152–57, 162–68
   countertransference, 150, 151–52
   friendship, 150–51
   intersubjectivity and, 150–51
   love for client, 151
   managing, 161–69
   over-identifying with client, 151–52
   romantic and sexual attraction, 158–61
   sources of, 149–50
auditory hallucinations, 193–94
authenticity. *See* congruence
avoidant attachment, 15
avoidant behavior, 224

Barbara (client), 214–15
behavior therapy, 20–21
belief systems, use of self, 53, 57–58, 59
Bess, J. M., 58
bipolar disorder
   case vignettes, 194–95, 198–99
   disordered thinking, 194–95
   hypomania, 194
   mania, 194

bipolar disorder (*cont.*)
Blake (social worker), 222–24
blind spots, self-knowledge, 52–53
Bowen, Murray, 23–24
Brenda Talley (client), 145–47
Brianna (social worker), 94–98

Caitlin (social worker), 121–24
Calmes, S. A., 213–14
Carrie (client), 42–43
case managers, concept of social workers as, 9–10
case vignettes
   adolescents, relationship development with, 140–43, 145–47
   attraction to clients, 152–57, 162–68
   children, relationship development with, 134, 135, 137–39
   client transfers, 122–24, 125–26
   cross-cultural competence, 82–84
   humor, using in practice, 234, 236–39, 240, 241, 242–44, 245, 246, 247–48
   negative feelings toward clients, 173–75, 178–80, 185–87
   physical contact in relationships, 214–15, 217–19, 220–21, 222–23, 225–27, 228–29
   psychotic clients, 196–97, 198–99, 204–6, 207–9
   relationship boundaries, 31–33, 34–37, 38–40, 42–43, 45–47
   relationship ruptures, 87–90, 95–97, 98–104
   structure of, 2–3
   technology-assisted interventions, 254–56, 265–69, 270–71
   termination of relationship, 108–10, 112–15, 116–19
   use of self, 49–51, 54–56, 60–62, 63–65
   working alliances, 70–72, 73–75, 79–81
CBT (cognitive-behavioral therapy), 132–33
CCC. *See* cross-cultural competence
children
   building working alliance with parents or caregivers of, 143–48
   case vignettes, 134, 135, 137–39
   CBT for, 132–33
   concrete thinking, 128–29
   conscience, 129
   developmental process, 128–29
   peer conflicts, 128
   role of physical touch in development, 212
   self-concept, 129
   strategies for relationship development with, 133–39
   working alliances with, 130–33
Chris (social worker), 54–56
Chuck (social worker), 145–48
Claire (client), 207–9
client consent. *See also* ethical issues
   forming emotional bond and, 68
   physical contact in relationships, 222–24
   relationship boundaries, 44
client engagement, 1, 5, 8–9, 262–63
   child clients, 129, 131
   expectation management and, 264
   relationship ruptures and, 91
client rejection of social worker, 172–76
client transfers, 119–27
   case vignettes, 122–24, 125–26
   guidelines, 120–21
   success predictors, 120
client violation of social norms, 177–80
code of ethics. *See* ethical issues
cognitive-behavioral therapy (CBT), 132–33
cognitive empathy, 12
cognitive theory, 21–22
common factors model, 1
computer-assisted interventions, 267–69. *See also* technology-assisted interventions
concrete thinking, 128–29
congruence
   person-centered theory, 12
   psychodynamic theories, 13
   relational theory, 17
conscience, development of in children, 129
coping/defense mechanisms
   cultural factors, 111
   humor, 231, 232–33, 246–48, 249–51
   projective identification, 14

INDEX 293

termination of client-worker
    relationship, 115–16
Core Conflicted Relationship Theme
    method, 183–84
Corinna (client), 60–62
countertransference, 150, 151–52,
    181. *See also* transference and
    countertransference
COVID-19 pandemic, impact on therapy
    experience, 252–53, 269, 272
crisis theory, 22–23
    anxiety and, 22
    stages of crisis experience, 22
cross-cultural competence (CCC)
    attitudes, 77–78
    case vignettes, 79–81, 82–84
    empathy, 78
    intervention skills, 78
    knowledge and awareness, 78
    motivation and curiosity, 77
    relationship ruptures and, 101–4
    working alliance and, 75–85

Dan (client), 79–81
Daryl (client), 98–100
decision-making
    adolescents, 130
    use of self and, 48–49
defense mechanisms. *See* coping/defense
    mechanisms
delusions, 192, 193–94, 203. *See also*
    psychotic clients
depression, 194
    adolescents, 129–30, 132–33
    practitioner's negative reactance to
        clients with, 181–82
    technology-assisted interventions for,
        258, 259–60
Destiny (social worker), 265–67
development process
    adolescents, 129–30
    children, 128–29
Dewane, C. J., 58, 65–66
Diamond, G. M., 144–45
Diamond, G. S, 144–45
digital literacy, 252
digital professional, 252
Dilks, S., 202

disorganized attachment, 15–16
Donald (client), 135
Dorinda (social worker), 137–39
Dorros, S., 216–17
dual relationships, 37, 44
Duncan, B. L., 8

EBP (evidence-based
    practice), 1, 7, 8, 11
Edwards, J. K., 58
El-Masri family (clients), 82–84
email, interventions by, 254–56
Emma (social worker), 49–52
emotional brain, adolescents, 129–30
emotional dwelling (optimal empathic
    attunement), 17
empathy
    adolescents, 130
    cognitive empathy, 12
    communicating with physical
        contact, 212–13
    cross-cultural competence and, 78
    empathic attunement, 190–91
    humanizing client, 177–78
    humor and, 244
    optimal empathic attunement, 17
    person-centered theory, 12
    psychodynamic theories, 13
    reactance and, 176–77
    relational dynamics, 59
ending worker-client relationship
    client transfers, 119–27
    termination process, 107–19
    types of relationship endings, 106–7
environmental influences on
    relationship, 24
    client's personal factors, 24
    client's social network factors, 24
    worker's personal factors, 24
    worker's social network factors, 24
e-professionalism, 252
equality of use of physical contact, 227
Erica (social worker), 63–66
ethical issues. *See also* relationship
        boundaries
    physical contact in
        relationships, 228–30
    professional boundaries, 28–33, 44

ethical issues. (*cont.*)
  technology-assisted interventions, 269–72
evidence-based practice (EBP), 1, 7, 8, 11
existential issues, psychotic clients, 190–91
exposure therapy, 1
Eyckmans, S., 213–14, 216–17, 219, 224–25

family systems theories, 23–24
  family emotional systems theory, 23
  structural family theory, 23–24
FearLess program, 260
forced humor, 233
Frank, Jerome, 7–8
Fromm-Reichmann, Frieda, 191

gallows humor, 249–51
  defined, 249
  guidelines for distinguishing appropriate and inappropriate use of, 250
  sarcasm, 249
Garrett, P. M., 219
genuineness. *See* congruence
George (social worker), 267–69
Goodman, G., 181
Gwendolyn (social worker), 34–37

hallucinations, 192, 193–94, 203. *See also* psychotic clients
Harriet (social worker), 253–56
Harrison, C., 216–17, 219
Havens, L. L., 191–92
Heather (client), 70–71
Helena (client), 34–37
Hubble, M. A., 8
humor
  affiliative humor, 232–33
  aggressive humor, 232–33
  assessment value, 233
  as avoidance mechanism, 246–48
  benefits of, 235–44
  case vignettes, 234, 236–39, 240, 241, 242–44, 245, 246, 247–48
  client's misinterpretation of, 246
  client's resentment about social worker's use of, 245
  commendation and, 241
  as context for discovery, 236–37
  creating distance between client and problem with, 240–41
  defined, 231–32
  demystifying intervention process with, 239
  facilitating discussion of difficult problem with, 242–43
  forced, 233
  gallows humor, 249–51
  guidelines, 235
  humor appreciation, 232
  humor generation, 232
  incongruity resolution theory, 232
  indication of mastery of problem, 237
  introducing less threatening perspective on problem with, 240
  natural high therapy, 233
  play function, 232
  provocative therapy, 233
  relief function, 232
  risks of using, 244–48
  sarcasm, 244–45
  self-defeating humor, 232–33
  self-enhancing humor, 232–33
  superiority function, 232
  taking edge off of painful interpretation with, 243–44
  therapeutic humor, 233
  using to reduce client's tension, 237–39
  using to relax reluctant client, 240
Hunter, M., 216–17, 219
Hutton, P., 131
Huws, J. C., 216–17, 219
hypomania, 194

ICBT (internet cognitive-behavioral therapy), 259–60
identity formation
  adolescents, 130
  infants, 212
  professional identity, 63
  psychosis and, 195

Imani (social worker), 178–80
incongruity resolution theory, 232
infant attachment styles, 15–16
informed consent. *See* client consent; ethical issues
internet cognitive-behavioral therapy (ICBT), 259–60
intersubjectivity
  attraction to clients and, 150–51
  use of self and, 49
Iris (social worker), 196–98

Jack (client), 173–75
Jacob (social worker), 207–10
Janet (social worker), 108–10
Jason (client), 101–4
Javid (client), 45–47
Jeffrey (social worker), 26
John (client), 38–40
Jones, R. S. P., 216–17, 219
Jordon (social work), 165–69
Josie (client), 222–23

Kailyn (social worker), 152–55
Kat (social worker), 82–85, 217–19
Kate (client), 196–97
Kelly (supervisor), 45–47
Ken (social worker), 214–16
Kevin (social worker), 87–90
Krizek, C., 213

Larry (client), 54–56
Laux, J. M., 213–14
Lia (social worker), 59–62
Liddle, H. A., 144–45
Lisa (client), 165–68
Lizzie (social worker), 101–4
loose speech, 192
love for clients, 151
Lynch, R., 219

Madeline (social work), 155–57
Maggie (social worker), 204–7
major depression, 194
  adolescents, 129–30, 132–33
  practitioner's negative reactance to clients with, 181–82
  technology-assisted interventions for, 258, 259–60
mania, 194–95
Marci (client), 125–26
Maria and Mike (clients), 95–97
Masson, R. L., 213
Matt (social worker), 124–27
McDaniel, E., 224–25
McNeil-Haber, F. M., 219
Meaghan (social worker), 98–101
medical model of practice, 10
Meghan (client), 31–33
Michael (client), 137–39, 155–57
Michael (social worker), 134–35
microruptures, relationship, 101
Miller, S. D., 8
Minuchin, S., 23–24
Miranda (client), 73–75
mirror neurons, 12
Monique (client), 225–27
mood disorders, 194–95
Morgan (client), 162–65
Mr. James (client), 63–65
Mr. Mark (client), 112–15
Mrs. Smith (client), 49–51
Murphy, R., 131
Murphy family (client), 108–10
mutuality, 16–17, 23, 30

narrative theory, 19–20
  developing storylines, 19, 20
  personal narratives, 19
  refocusing, 19–20
  relationship development in, 20
NASW (National Association of Social Workers). *See also* ethical issues
  Code of Ethics, 270, 271–72
  physical contact in relationships, 211
natural high therapy, 233
negative feelings toward clients, 170–72
  case vignettes, 173–75, 178–80, 185–87
  client rejection of social worker, 172–76
  client violation of social norms, 177–80
  negative reactance, 171–72, 176–77, 181–82
  Recognition theory, 172–76

negative feelings toward clients, (cont.)
  unconscious practitioner reactions, 181–88
Nolting, J., 202

object relations theory, 14
online interventions. *See* technology-assisted interventions
optimal empathic attunement (emotional dwelling), 17
Orbach, M., 219
over-identifying with client, 151–52, 162–65

Patricia (social worker), 220–21
Patty (client), 254–56
peer consolation, 44
personal boundaries, 27–28. *See also* relationship boundaries
  bridging and access, 28
  crossing vs. violating, 28
  emergence and development of, 27
  entangled or fluid, 27
  flexible, 27
  rigid, 27
  social, 27
personal style. *See* use of self
person-centered theory, 11–13
  congruence, 12
  defined, 11
  empathy, 12
  unconditional positive regard, 12
phobias, 1
physical contact in relationships
  assessing interpersonal patterns of client, 224
  case vignettes, 214–15, 217–19, 220–21, 222–23, 225–27, 228–29
  client consent, 222–24
  client's symptom status and, 224
  contact authentic to client's need, 225–27
  differing views of nature of relationship, 221–24
  equality of use concept, 227
  establishing boundaries for, 219–21
  guidelines for, 219–30
  handshakes, 211
  potential benefits and dangers, 211
  power dynamics and, 228
  respecting code of ethics, 228–30
  role of physical touch in human development, 212
  social worker's self-awareness of attitude about touch, 224–25
  therapeutic potential, 212–19
  "touch taboo," 212–13
Piazza, N. J., 213–14
play function, humor, 232
post-traumatic stress disorder (PTSD), 132
power dynamics
  mutuality and, 30
  physical contact in relationships and, 216–17, 228
  professional boundaries and, 30
  relationship with parents or caregivers, 144
  technology-assisted interventions, 263
private self, 52–53
professional boundaries, 28–33, 44. *See also* relationship boundaries
  case vignettes, 31–33, 34–37
  contact time, 29
  emotional space, 29
  importance of clarity, 29–31
  managing boundary dilemmas, 31
  patriarchal model vs. mutuality, 30
  physical closeness when together, 29
  power differential, 30
  territoriality, 29
  types of information to be shared, 29
  variation in appropriate, 30–31
professional style, 57
projective identification, 14
provocative therapy, 233
psychodynamic theories, 13–24
  attachment theory, 15–16
  behavior therapy, 20–21
  cognitive theory, 21–22
  crisis theory, 22–23
  family systems theories, 23–24
  narrative theory, 19–20
  object relations theory, 14
  relational theory, 16–19

transference and
    countertransference, 13–14
psychotic clients
  bipolar disorder, 194–95, 198–99
  case vignettes, 196–97, 198–99,
    204–6, 207–9
  "common sense" visual context, 193
  delusions, 192
  empathic attunement, 190–91
  encouraging client's expression of
    thoughts and feelings, 203–4
  encouraging client to consider
    alternative meanings, 204
  existential issues, 190–91
  experience of psychosis, 195–200
  guidelines for, 200–10
  hallucinations, 192, 203
  loose speech, 192
  mood disorders, 194–95
  paranoia, 204
  Recovery perspective, 192
  schizoaffective disorder, 204
  schizophrenia, 193–94
  social isolation, 193–94
  sustainment-related interventions,
    200–2, 210
  theories of relationship development
    with, 191–92
  thought disorders, 193–94
  understanding psychosis, 192
PTSD (post-traumatic stress
  disorder), 132
puberty, 129–30
public self, 52–53

Rachel (social worker), 140–43
reactance, negative, 171–72,
  176–77, 181–82
Rebecca (social worker), 116–19
Recognition theory, 172–76
Recovery perspective, psychotic
  clients, 192
reflective learning model,
  self-development, 62–63
  attending to self in practice
    relationships, 62
  constructing personal life paths, 62
  exploring professional identity, 63

relational dynamics, 59. *See also* use of self
relational theory, 16–19
  attention to transferences, 18
  clear boundaries, 19
  congruence, 17
  mutuality, 16–17
  optimal empathic attunement, 17
  self-disclosure, 18
  spontaneity, 17–18
relationship-based practice, 6. *See also*
  social worker-client relationship
relationship boundaries
  boundary dilemma management for
    social workers, 43–44
  boundary dilemma management for
    supervisors, 44–47
  case vignettes, 31–33, 34–37, 38–40,
    42–43, 45–47
  clarifying over time, 44
  client consent, 44
  managing attraction to clients, 161–62
  personal boundaries, 27–28
  physical contact, 219–21
  professional boundaries, 28–33
  relational theory, 19
  setting clear, 44
  warning signs of boundary
    violation, 34–43
relationship ruptures
  avoiding assumptions about, 86
  case vignettes, 87–90, 95–97, 98–104
  confrontational mode, 90–91
  cross-cultural competence and, 101–4
  defined, 86
  dynamics of, 90–92
  impact of repair process on
    relationship, 86–87
  microruptures, 101
  repair process, 92–101
  withdrawal mode, 90–91
relief function, humor, 232
repair process, relationship
  ruptures, 92–101
  acknowledging rupture, 92
  alliance dimension, 93
  case vignettes, 95–97, 98–101
  exploring rupture process, 93
  identifying individual responsibility, 93

impact on relationship, 86–87
moving forward, 94
negotiating resolution, 94
reparative conversations and understanding, 94
responding empathically, 92
shared reflective process, 93–94
Richard (client), 116–19
Rita (client), 185–87
rituals, 108, 124, 126–27
Robyn (social work student), 31–33
Roger (social worker), 79–82
romantic attraction to client, 158–61. *See also* attraction to clients

Sale, K., 213
Sandy (social worker), 228–30
sarcasm, 244–45, 249
schizophrenia, 191–92, 193–94
secure attachment, 15
self, defining, 52–53. *See also* use of self
self-awareness. *See also* use of self
  of children, 129
  social worker's, 66, 224–25
self-defeating humor, 232–33
self-disclosure, 40, 53–54
  relational theory, 18
  use of self, 59
self-enhancing humor, 232–33
self-inventory, 58–59
Semrad, Elvin, 191
sexual attraction to client, 158–61. *See also* attraction to clients
Shayla (client), 152–55
social media, 37–38, 258–59
social orientation, adolescents, 130
social presence theory, 256–57
social worker-client relationship, 1–2, 5–7
  common features of positive outcomes, 7–9
  environmental influences on, 24
  extent of influence on processes and outcomes, 1–2, 6–7
  formal nature of, 6
  importance of, 7
  obstacles to relationship-based practice, 9–10

one-directionality of purpose, 6
reciprocal, mutual influencing quality of, 6
self-disclosure, 53–54
theoretical perspectives on, 10–24
Sonja (client), 204–6
Sonya (social worker), 112–15
Spaulding, W., 202
spontaneity, relational theory, 17–18
Stacey (social worker), 225–27
Strozier, A. L., 213–14, 219
Struve, J., 216–17, 219
style, social worker's
  personal, 56–57
  professional, 57
Sullivan, H. S., 191
superiority function, humor, 232
sustainment, of psychotic clients, 200–2, 210
Swade, T., 219

TalkSpace company, 260–61
Tamira (social worker), 38–40
Tasker, F., 202
Taylor (social worker), 73–75, 270–72
technology-assisted interventions
  benefits and limitations, 261–62
  case vignettes, 254–56, 265–69, 270–71
  computer-assisted interventions, 267–69
  COVID-19 crisis and, 252–53
  digital literacy, 252
  digital professional, 252
  email, 254–56
  e-professionalism, 252
  ethical issues, 269–72
  FearLess program, 260
  hybrid intervention for persons with depression, 258
  internet cognitive-behavioral therapy (ICBT), 259–60
  for persons experiencing anxiety, 260
  for persons with bulimia, 259
  resistance to, 252
  social media, 258–59
  social presence theory, 256–57

social worker-client relationship
development and, 262–69
TalkSpace company, 260–61
telephone interventions, 263, 265–67
types of communication, 253–56
telephone interventions, 263, 265–67
termination of relationship, 107–19
case vignettes, 108–10, 112–15, 116–19
quality of social worker-client relationship and, 110–19
rituals, 108, 124, 126–27
social worker's tasks during, 107–8
theoretical perspectives, 10–24
person-centered theory, 11–13
psychodynamic theories, 13–24
therapeutic alliance, 8–9
therapeutic humor, 233
therapeutic physical contact, 212–19
Thomas (client), 178–80
thought disorders, 193–94
Tishby, O., 183
transference and countertransference, 13–14
attention to, in relational theory, 18
attraction to clients, 150, 151–52
Trevor (client), 87–90
two-stage learning process, use of self, 57–58

unconditional positive regard, person-centered theory, 12
unconscious feelings, 13–14
unconscious practitioner reactions, 181–88
unconscious self, 52–53
use of self, 1
anxiety, 59
belief systems, 53, 57–58, 59
case vignettes, 49–51, 54–56, 60–62, 63–65
defined, 48–49
defining self, 52–53
developing, 57–66
humor, 231
intersubjectivity and, 49
personality traits, 59

personal style and, 56–57
in practice, 53–56
professional style and, 57
reflective learning model, 62–63
relational dynamics, 59
self-disclosure, 59
self-inventory, 58–59
two-stage learning process, 57–58
unconscious use of self, 57–58

Vicki (social worker), 26

Walsh, Joseph, 3–4
Wampold, B., 8–9
warning signs of boundary violation, 34–43
accepting or giving gifts, 41
case vignettes, 34–37, 38–40, 42–43
contextual factors, 41–43
dual relationships, 37
exceptional behavior, 34
intrusion into client's physical or technological territory, 37–38
investigating certain details of clients' personal lives, 41
loaning, trading, or selling items to clients, 41
out-of-office in-person contact with clients, 41
referring to clients as friends, 41
self-disclosure, 40
strong positive or negative feelings about client, 34
touching or physically comforting clients, 41
Weiden, P., 191–92
Willison, B. G., 213
Wiseman, H., 183
working alliance
with adolescents, 139–43
case vignettes, 70–72, 73–75, 79–81, 82–84
with children, 130–33
cross-cultural competence and, 75–85
defined, 67–69
forming emotional bond, 68
with parents or caregivers, 143–48

working alliance (*cont.*)
    practitioner characteristics and, 69–75
    short-term versus long-term
        interventions, 69–70
    social worker-client goal consensus, 68
    task collaboration, 68
    working alliance model, 1
Wren, B, 202

Zeke (client), 134